Financial Advertising
and Marketing Law

Financial Advertising and Marketing Law

First Edition

Dennis Rosenthal

Partner, Forsyte Saunders Kerman

LAW & TAX

© Pearson Professional Ltd 1997

Dennis Rosenthal has asserted his
right under the Copyright, Designs and
Patents Act 1988 to be identified as
the author of this work

ISBN 0752 003313

Published by
FT Law and Tax
21–27 Lamb's Conduit Street
London WC1N 3NJ

http://www.ftlawandtax.com

A Division of Pearson Professional Limited

Associated offices
Australia, Belgium, Canada, Hong Kong, India, Japan, Luxembourg,
Singapore, Spain, USA

First edition 1997

A CIP catalogue record for this book is available from the British Library.

Printed in Great Britain by Biddles
Typeset by Servis Filmsetting Ltd, Manchester

Contents

Preface

Anyone involved in financial advertising and marketing law is aware of the conflicting interests and concerns of persons engaged in marketing and advertising activities on the one hand and lawyers on the other. Financial advertising and marketing law is so diverse and the sources so widely dispersed that it was thought that a work of this kind would assist both categories of practitioners. It is hoped that the text will prove to be a compact and easy work of reference and a useful and informative guide to those seeking answers to day-to-day problems.

For their patience and forbearance during the course of the production of this work, I wish to thank my dear wife and children. I owe a special debt of gratitude to my publisher, Nick Bliss and all those at FT Law and Tax who assisted me with its publication. Nick Bliss's involvement began by showing interest in the work and ended with his becoming a pillar of support to the writer. My gratitude is also extended to Susan Ross for typing the manuscript so ably and efficiently and acting as critic and judge of the first instance. Finally, many thanks to Ruth Cornes, librarian at Forsyte Saunders Kerman, for her unfailing assistance in finding sources however esoteric and remote.

The law is stated as at August 1997 save for reference to the new Directive on comparative advertising in Chapter 2 at 2.6.

London
August 1997.

Table of Cases

(All references are to paragraph number)

Table of Statutes

(All references are to paragraph number)

Table of Statutory Instruments

(All references are to paragraph number)

Table of European Legislation

(All references are to paragraph number)

Chapter 1

Introduction

1.1 Background

Advertising and marketing activities are at the frontier of the fields to which they relate. In the same way, advertising and marketing law are at the leading edge of evolving law, endeavouring to hold back the tidal wave of promotional activity and to soften the abrasiveness of the advertising message.

Law concerns itself with the balancing of different and often conflicting interests. In the case of advertising and marketing law the conflicting interests are those of freedom of expression and approach for the advertiser and marketing promoter on the one hand and the protection of the potential customer or target on the other. Inevitably the result is to muzzle the messenger and muffle the message. Within the parameters of fair play and truthfulness both messenger and message are allowed a considerable degree of latitude and scope for initiative.

The parameters are those imposed variously by law, regulation and self-regulation in the form of codes. Codes are themselves divisible into binding and voluntary codes, general codes applying across several sectors and specific codes applying possibly only to one industry. Although this plethora of controls creates a complex web of law, regulation and restriction, the fact that it is imposed at different levels provides the opportunity to distinguish between degrees of seriousness of infringement.

To quote from a guide to self-regulation:

> It is now generally accepted that self-regulation works best within a framework of statute law, to define broad principles and to act as a last resort in cases where all else has failed. In handling the detail of advertising content, particularly those 'important trivia' which matter very much to consumers,

self-regulation has advantages of speed, flexibility and cheapness which detailed legislation cannot equal.

The law and self-regulation complement each other, rather like the frame and strings of a tennis racquet, to reproduce a result which neither could fully achieve alone[1].

1.2   The role of the criminal law

Perhaps the role of the criminal law in the policing of advertising and marketing activities is the one most open to question. First, criminal consequences of advertising infringements often appear inappropriate; indeed, at times this may well be an impediment to their rigorous enforcement. Secondly, the burden of proof in relation to an alleged breach of the criminal law may result in an acquittal when a corresponding civil breach, involving the same act or omission, might have been capable of proof[2]. Thirdly, the defence of due diligence which is available in relation to most offences involving advertising or marketing law, emasculates the regulatory régime. Fourthly, as an offence is committed each time an offending publication is made, if the law were strictly enforced there would be the unnatural consequences of an offender being criminally liable in respect of each advertisement distributed and advertising message disseminated[3]. It is submitted that the criminal law should be reserved for persistent offences and offenders.

1.3   The scope for change

The International Code of Advertising Practice[4] has set standards of ethical conduct in advertising since 1937, whilst recognising the fundamental principle of freedom of communication as embodied in art 19 of the United Nations International Covenant of Civil and Political Rights. It espouses amongst its basic principles that all advertising should be legal, decent, honest and truthful.

The new global village calls for a new international treaty on advertising and marketing controls possibly along the lines of recent European

---

1   The European Advertising Standards Alliance (EASA) Guide to Self-Regulation 1997 pp 8–9.
2   *SCF Finance Co Ltd v Masri (No 2)* [1987] 1 All ER 175; *National Westminster Bank v Devon County Council and Devon County Council v Abbey National plc* (1993) *The Times* 16 July.
3   *R v Thomson Holidays Ltd* [1974] 1 All ER 823 at 828 and 829.
4   Published by the International Chamber of Commerce (ICC) No 432B.

Directives which contain general provisions applying across Europe but preserve individual member's régimes, differentiating between 'home states' and 'host states'; a 'European passport' enables financial services providers to market their products in different Member states. With newspapers and periodicals carrying advertising and marketing messages across the world; radio and television transmitting such messages to all corners; and now the Internet bringing the marketplace into the living room of the PC user, national laws and régimes must interlock into an international régime or a system of controls. Distance and speed of communication together with the accessibility of the advertisement or promotional message create the need for some international supervisory régime.

In the United Kingdom there are sufficient common threads running through statutes, regulations, codes and rule books to provide an opportunity for a general statute along the lines of the Interpretation Act 1978 in relation to advertising and marketing law. This would identify general fundamental requirements such as truthfulness and the basis for comparative advertisements; define and harmonise such terms as 'advertisement', 'advertise', 'false or misleading' and 'publication'. It would also circumscribe criminal offences and the defence of due diligence and possibly create a civil infringement in respect of advertising and marketing law.

As regards marketing law, one can again perceive common threads which have developed over time and appear in various marketing statutes, codes and rulebooks, especially in relation to disclosure, canvassing, cancellation rights, and the production of Key Features documents.

The UK government recently embarked on a wholesale restructuring of the supervisory jigsaw as it affects the financial, banking and investment services market. This will result in the supervisory powers of the Bank of England, the Securities and Investments Board (SIB) the self-regulating organisations (SROs), the Building Societies Commission and the Recognised Investment Exchanges, including the London Stock Exchange being embodied in an enhanced SIB and in the demise of the SROs. It is premature to speculate on the ultimate form and content of the regulatory régime but it would be iconoclastic and unhelpful if, in the process, current advertising and marketing law, which has evolved over time, were simply wiped off the slate. On the other hand, there is considerable scope for harmonisation and consolidation of various existing statutory and self-regulatory controls.

The rulebooks of the SROs have so much in common, at least in so far as advertising and marketing is concerned, that they ought to be capable of being consolidated into one uniform set of rules, with limited variants to cater for the differences. Indeed, it seems ironical that the SROs each with its own set of rules, spawned by the SIB, should now face absorption into and consolidation with their source. The regulatory regime will have moved full circle in just two decades.

Chapter 2

Advertising in General

2.1 Meaning of 'advertisement'

In ordinary parlance an advertisement is any public notice, printed display in a newspaper, short film on television, or announcement on radio, designed to sell goods or publicise an event[1] or a public announcement[1bis]. Various attempts at a definition can be reduced to 'a publication or broadcast to announce or promote its subject matter'.

As will be observed, the expression 'advertisement' is differently defined in various statutes. Statutes and regulations usually define an advertisement by reference to its form or representation rather than its function or purpose. Exceptionally an advertisement is defined by reference to its function. An example is the definition of advertisement as meaning any form of representation which is made in connection with a trade, business, craft or profession in order to promote the supply or transfer of goods or services, immovable property, rights or obligations[2]. Another attempt at such definition, which becomes bogged down in the representational form of an advertisement, is the following:

> 'Advertisement' means any word, letter, model, sign, placard, board, notice, awning, blind, device or representation, whether illuminated or not, in the nature of, and employed wholly or partly for the purposes of, advertisement, announcement or direction, and (without prejudice to the previous provisions of this definition), includes any hoarding or similar structure used or designed or adapted for use, for the display of advertisements[3].

---

1 Collins: *Dictionary of the English Language* 2nd edn 1990.
1bis *Concise Oxford Dictionary* 7th edn.
2 Control of Misleading Advertisements Regulations 1988 (SI 1988 No 915), reg 2(1).
3 Town and Country Planning Act 1990, s 336(1).

2.2   Definitions

Most definitions of advertisement are even less meaningful from a substantive point of view. They list all forms of representation and presentation and, lest any be omitted, include references to every other form of
presentation or are stated to be non-exhaustive of different forms of
presentation, by use of the expression 'include'. Thus, the Trade
Descriptions Act defines 'advertisement' as including a catalogue, a circular and a price list[4]. Another example is the definition of advertisement as
including any notice, circular, label, wrapper, invoice or other document,
and any public announcement made orally or by any means of producing
or transmitting light or sound[5].

The Sex Discrimination Act defines 'advertisement' as including every
form of advertisement, whether to the public or not, and whether in a
newspaper or other publication, by television or radio, by display of
notices, signs, labels, showcards or goods, by distribution of samples, circulars, catalogues, price lists or other material, by exhibition of pictures,
models, films or in any other way[6]. Perhaps it is not surprising, therefore,
that even when we turn to financial statutes and regulations, the expression
'advertisement' is still couched in a similar uninformative manner by reference to the representation of the advertisement rather than its substantive
meaning. In the Consumer Credit Act 'advertisement' includes every form
of advertising, whether in a publication, by television or radio, by display
notices, signs, labels, showcards or goods, by distribution of samples, circulars, catalogues, price lists or other material, by exhibition of pictures,
models, or films, or in any other way[7].

It is somewhat unsatisfactory that all the foregoing definitions, as well
as those which follow, attempt to achieve the same objective, yet there is no
comprehensive definition, let alone uniformity of expression.

The Insurance Companies Act defines 'advertisement' as including every
form of advertising, whether in a publication, by the display of notices, by
means of circulars or other documents, by an exhibition of photographs or
cinematograph films, by way of sound broadcasting or television or by inclusion in any programme service (within the meaning of the Broadcasting Act
1990) other than a sound or television broadcasting service[8].

---

4   Trade Descriptions Act 1968, s 39(1) and (2).
5   Food Safety Act 1990, s 53(1).
6   Sex Discrimination Act 1975, s 82(1); a similar definition with the addition of
reference to 'advertisement or notice' appears in the Race Relations Act 1976, s 78(1).
7   Consumer Credit Act 1974, s 189(1).
8   Insurance Companies Act 1982, s 72(6).

The Financial Services Act expands the definition so as to include every form of advertising whether in a publication, by the display of notices, signs, labels or showcards, by means of circulars, catalogues, price lists or other documents, by an exhibition of pictures or photographic or cinematographic films, by way of sound broadcasting or television or by inclusion in any programme services (within the meaning of the Broadcasting Act 1990) other than a sound or television broadcasting service, by the distribution of recordings, or in any other manner[9].

Finally, in our set of examples, the Building Societies Act adopts a more novel approach, at least in its layout. There, 'advertisement' includes every form of advertisement, whether:

(1) documentary;
(2) by way of sound broadcasting or television or by inclusion in any programme service (within the meaning of the Broadcasting Act 1990) other than a sound or television broadcasting service; or
(3) by any pictorial means not falling within paragraphs (1) or (2) above[10].

Although there has been an evolution in the production of advertisements the differences in definition owe more to the draftsman of the particular enactment than to any developments that have taken place in advertising.

It would be helpful if enactments were to adopt a common definition of advertisement, possibly by reference to a definition in an Interpretation Act or a statute setting out provisions common to all advertising. This would produce fairer, clearer and more accessible law.

2.3 Form of the advertisement

There is no limit to the form which an advertisement might take. From a legal perspective this apparently trite statement is relevant to the care which must be exercised over what a business might regard as simply a confidential letter to an addressee but which the law construes as an advertisement. Furthermore, the content and presentation of what the law deems to be an advertisement will be subject to controls. Thus, in *R v Delmayne*[11] the Court of Appeal considered a printed circular which invited people to whom it was addressed to deposit money with the society to be an advertisement.

---

9   Financial Services Act 1986, s 207(2).
10   Building Societies Act 1986, s 50(10).
11   [1969] 2 All ER 980.

The form in which an advertisement might appear is virtually limitless and includes a newspaper or journal, representation in a poster, leaflet, brochure and circular, presentation in a film, video, sound broadcast, teletext, on the Internet or in the form of a hologram.

2.4 Balancing of legal interests

In the arena of advertising the law seeks to achieve a balance between freedom of expression, of commercial communication and industrial freedom to compete on the one hand and the necessary safeguards and protections of the advertiser's target and the advertiser's competitors on the other hand. In broad terms the various safeguards and controls can be summarised in the statement that the advertisement should not convey any information which is false or misleading. All advertisements should be legal, decent, honest and truthful, should be prepared with a sense of responsibility to consumers and to society, should respect the principles of fair competition generally accepted in business and should not bring advertising into disrepute[12].

On a narrower and more specific plane, the protections commonly accorded to the advertiser's audience by statute, regulation, rules, codes of practice and the like, include the following:

(1) clarity of expression;
(2) legibility;
(3) prescribed minimum or maximum information, depending on the nature and type of the advertisement;
(4) a reasonable belief on the advertiser's behalf in the content of the advertisement and that it will continue to be true throughout its period of publication;
(5) controls on comparative advertising; and
(6) restrictions on references to guarantees and on comparisons with past performance, especially in the case of investment advertisements.

2.5 Responsibility for an advertisement

Legislation and Codes covering advertisements generally bind persons who issue advertisements or cause advertisements to be issued. This will usually include the person named in the advertisement who would ordinarily assume primary responsibility for observing the legislation and Codes

---

12   Advertising Code of The British Codes of Advertising and Sales Promotion: Principles.

applicable to it, advertising agencies, the publishers and other service suppliers.

Before submitting an advertisement for publication advertisers are required to hold documentary evidence to prove all claims whether direct or implied that are capable of objective substantiation. The Advertising Standards Authority (ASA) requires evidence to be submitted to it to enable it to judge whether it supports the detailed claims and the overall impression created by the advertisement. If there is a significant division of informed opinion about claims made in an advertisement they should not be portrayed as universally agreed[13].

Breach of the governing statutory regulations ordinarily constitutes an offence and might in addition give rise to civil remedies either by statute or at common law. Depending upon the particular legal regime applying to the advertisement, civil remedies might include an injunction, a claim for damages and the setting aside of a transaction entered into pursuant to the advertisement.

It is usually a defence to a criminal charge to prove that the defendant acted in reliance on information supplied by another person or that his act was due to a mistake of another person and that he himself took all reasonable precautions and acted with all due diligence to avoid any breach on his part.

2.6   Comparative advertising

Comparative advertising is relatively new in the United Kingdom. In certain Member States of the European Union including Germany, Belgium, France and the Netherlands, it is currently outlawed. However, after years of debate, a Directive on comparative advertising was finally adopted by the Council and the European Parliament on 15/16 September 1997, to be adopted by Member States within 30 months of coming into force[14].

The Advertising Code[15] prescribes that advertisements should respect the principles of fair competition generally accepted in business and that comparisons are permitted and may be explicit or implied and can relate to advertisers' own products or to those of their competitors. Comparisons should be clear and fair and the elements of any comparison should not be

---

13   *Ibid*: Substantiation.
14   The Directive, 97/55/EC, extends the scope of Directive 84/450/EEC on Misleading Advertising.
15   Advertising Code of the British Codes of Advertising and Sales Promotion: Principles and Comparisons.

selected in a way that gives the advertiser an artificial advantage. It is further provided that advertisers should not unfairly attack or discredit other businesses or their products.

Similar provision is contained in the ITC Code of Advertising Standards and Practice which relates to TV and radio advertisements. Under the foregoing Code it is expressly provided that comparative advertisements are permissible in the interests of vigorous competition and public information. All comparative advertisements must respect the principles of fair competition, must be so designed that there is no likelihood of the consumer being misled, the subject matter must not be chosen so as to confer an artificial advantage upon the advertiser and points of comparison must be based on facts which can be substantiated and must not be unfairly selected. In particular the basis of comparison must be the same for all products or services being compared and generalised superiority claims must not be made on the basis of selective comparisons. Advertisements must not unfairly attack or discredit other products or services[16].

Comparative advertising has been facilitated by the increasing sophistication of the advertising market and of the underlying advertised products and services. Thus the crystallisation of criteria and formulae on which products are based enables comparisons to be made. An example is the annual percentage rate of charge (APR) based on statutory formulae and tables. This creates an opportunity for credit grantors to compare their rates of interest with those charged by other advertisers. Comparative credit advertising is regulated in that a credit advertisement may not include an indication, whether express or implied, that any of the terms of the credit agreement impose on customers a lesser expense or obligation than is imposed by other persons except in a full credit advertisement where the advertisement states, in close proximity to that indication and with no less particularity and prominence, the other persons concerned and their comparable terms[17].

The British Code of Advertising prohibits an advertiser from making unfair use of the goodwill attached to the trade mark, name, brand or advertising campaign of any other business. It also lays down that no advertisement should so closely resemble any other that it misleads or causes confusion[18].

Section 10(6) of the Trade Marks Act 1994 has also had a liberating influence on comparative advertising in the use of another advertiser's trade

---

16   See Code's provisions on 'Comparisons' and 'Denigration'.
17   Consumer Credit (Advertisements) Regulations 1989, reg 7(b).
18   *Loc cit* paras 21.1 and 22.1.

mark. Under the previous Trade Marks Act of 1938 a registered trade mark could be infringed by a party who used it in comparative advertising for promoting his own products[19]. However in *Barclays Bank plc v RBS Advanta*[20] the court held that s 10(6) of the Trade Marks Act 1994 permits advertisers to use the trade mark of another person for the purposes of identifying the goods or services of that person and hence allows the utilisation of trade marks in comparative advertising. It is subject to the limitation that any such use otherwise than in accordance with honest practices in industrial or commercial matters will be treated as infringing the registered trade mark if the use, without due cause, takes unfair advantage of or is detrimental to the distinctive character or repute of the trade mark[21].

Comparative advertising is permitted by the various rules relating to investment advertising. The Conduct of Business Rules of the Securities and Investments Board prohibits comparative or contrasting advertisements unless the comparisons and contrasts are fair in relation to what is promoted having regard to what is stated as well as to what is not stated. The Securities and Investments Board considers that it would be a breach of this rule to omit a feature of possible comparison or contrast so as to exaggerate the significance of what is included or to misrepresent or unfairly criticise the alternative or the person who offers it. The advertisement of units in a regulated collective scheme may only adopt comparisons or contrasts with the performance of investments in units of other regulated collective investment schemes[22]. Other self-regulating organisations contain similar rules[23].

2.7 Probity of advertising

The ultimate purpose of the complex web of mandatory and voluntary controls on advertising is to protect the advertiser's target against false or misleading promotions. At the same time, regulation is aimed at creating a springboard for the promotion of the advertiser's products and services which is fair as between the advertiser and his audience on the one hand and the advertiser and his competitors on the other.

---

19 See *Bismag Ltd v Amblins (Chemists) Ltd* (1940) 57 RPC 209; *Chanel Ltd v l'Arome (UK) Ltd* (1993) RPC 32.
20 (1996) *The Times*, 8 February.
21 Section 10(b).
22 Part 7, para 7.16.
23 Eg Rules of Personal Investment Authority, s 7.16.

Chapter 3

The Legal Characterisation of an Advertisement

Advertisements fall into four categories:

(1) Notices and announcements
(2) Inducements
(3) Advertisements of bilateral contracts
(4) Advertisements of unilateral contracts

3.1 Notices and announcements

Advertisements in this category take the form of a formal notice or publication. They are purely informative and are not intended to promote the sale of any goods or services although they may invite a response or action on the part of the reader.

Examples of advertisements in this class are notices by an administrator in the *Gazette* and newspapers following the making of an administration order so as to ensure that the order comes to the notice of the company's creditors[1]; an advertisement of the appointment of an administrative receiver[2]; and of a winding-up petition[3].

Other instances in this category are advertisements by trustees or personal representatives to draw the attention of interested persons to their

---

1 Insolvency Act 1986, s 21(1)(a) and Insolvency Rules 1986 (SI 1986 No 1925), r 2.10(2).
2 Insolvency Rules 1986, r 3.2.
3 Insolvency Rules 1986, r 4.11(1).

intention to make a conveyance or distribution[4] and publication by lenders of changes in interest rates for borrowers[5].

It is worth pointing out that certain enactments specifically refer to the foregoing publications as advertisements whereas others describe them as notices. In each case the objective is the same and it is merely a question of terminology.

3.2 Inducements

An inducement may take the form of a mere 'puff' or of a representation. In the former case it is self-evident that the statement is a hyperbole or exaggeration for effect which is not intended to legally bind its maker and which will therefore not form part of any subsequent contract.

A representation on the other hand which is intended to and has the effect of inducing a person to enter into a contract would be legally binding on the representor. A statement relating to the marketed product may be more than a puff and less than a warranty: it may be so important that it may induce a contract, may not amount to a negligent misrepresentation, and may nearly amount to a warranty[5bis]. It may entitle the representee to rescission or to enforce it as a term of the contract in which event the representee's contractual remedies for damages for breach of contract would apply. Under the Misrepresentation Act 1967 the representee is entitled to a statutory claim for damages where another party made a false representation, unless the latter can show that he had reasonable grounds to believe and did believe that the facts represented were true[6]. The claim may be one based in tort for damages for fraudulent misrepresentation, negligent misrepresentation or even for innocent misrepresentation[6bis].

In practice the distinction between a mere puff and a representation will lie in the fact that the former does not lend itself to any verification, eg the greatest car on the road, whereas a representation does, eg the fastest and most economical car on the road. A recent example where an advertiser was

---

4   Trustee Act 1925, s 27; Insolvency Act 1986, s 98 and Insolvency Rules 1986, r 4.106(1).
5   Consumer Credit (Notice of Variation of Agreements) Regulations 1977 (SI 1977 No 328).
5bis   *Howard Marine and Bridging Co Ltd v Ogden & Sons (Excavations) Ltd* [1978] QB 574 cited in *Lambert v Lewis* [1982] AC 225 at 262; [1980] 1 All ER 978 at 1002.
6   Misrepresentation Act 1967, s 2.
6bis   In *Royscot Trust Ltd v Rogerson* [1991] 2 QB 297 the Court of Appeal held that under s 2(1) of the Misrepresentation Act 1967 damages in respect of an honest but careless representation are to be calculated as if the representation had been made fraudulently.

held bound by its 'representation', involved the Norwich and Peterborough Building Society. Marketing literature of the Society promised that its TESSA account would pay 'a very competitive rate of interest'. However, it was alleged before the Norwich County Court that over four years the Society had failed to fulfil this claim by maintaining an interest rate near the bottom of the recognised league tables. The court found in favour of the plaintiff holding that the words 'very competitive' in the advertising section in the brochure had become a term of the contract and meant 'very competitive with our competitors', which in turn meant 'as good as, if not better than, those of its competitors from time to time.' It awarded him a sum equal to the extra interest he would have earned had his money been in an account paying an average rate[6ter]. The Society subsequently compensated all relevant investors of its own accord.

A significant opportunity for the admission of apparently non-contractual information into the contract itself has been created by The Unfair Terms in Consumer Contracts Regulations 1994. The Office of Fair Trading has struck down 'entire agreement clauses', namely those which state that the agreement contains all the terms and conditions agreed between the customer and the company, as being *prima facie* unfair under para 1(n) of Sched 3 of those Regulations. That paragraph deems unfair a term which has the object or effect of limiting the seller's or supplier's obligation to respect commitments undertaken by his agents or making his commitments subject to compliance with a particular formality. It follows that potentially any representation in marketing material may be deemed to be incorporated into the contract notwithstanding the fact that the contract states that it contains all the terms and conditions agreed between the parties.

A third type of inducement which lies somewhere between a puff and a representation is a statement of opinion which, in certain circumstances, may give rise to the same liability as a representation[7].

3.3   Advertisements of bilateral contracts

In this and the following subsection we are adopting the distinction drawn by *Chitty on Contracts*[8]. A unilateral contract is one in which only one party is bound whereas a bilateral contract is one in which both parties exchange promises, eg 'I will do X if you will do Y'.

6ter   *Robert Anthony v Norwich and Peterborough Building Society* (1997) *The Times*, 24 January.
7   See *Chitty on Contracts* (27th edn 1994) Vol 2: Specific Contracts para 41–039.
8   *Chitty on Contracts* loc cit Vol 1: General Principles paras 2–009 and 2–010.

Traditionally advertisements falling under the head of bilateral contracts have been construed as invitations to treat rather than offers open for acceptance by those responding to the advertisement. It has been said that 'it is indisputable that the mere advertisement of an auction, without further qualification, is an invitation to treat and not an offer. The auction need not be held and prospective purchasers have no legal complaint if they have wasted their time and money in coming to the sale rooms'[9].

In *Partridge v Crittenden*[10] the appellant had inserted an advertisement in a periodical *Cage and Aviary Birds* containing the words 'quality British ABCR . . . bramble finch cocks, bramble finch hens, 25s each'. In no place was there any direct use of the words 'offer for sale'. An information was preferred by the respondent, Crittenden, on behalf of the RSPCA against the appellant charging that the appellant had unlawfully offered for sale a wild bird contrary to the Protection of Birds Act 1954. He was convicted but on appeal his conviction was quashed as the court found that there had been no offer for sale and that the insertion of an advertisement in the form adopted under the title 'Classified Advertisements' was simply an invitation to treat. Lord Parker stated rather stridently: 'I think that when one is dealing with advertisements and circulars, unless they indeed come from manufacturers, there is business sense in their being construed as invitations to treat and not offers for sale'[11]. He further cited with approval a statement by Lord Herschell that the transmission of a price-list does not amount to an offer to supply an unlimited quantity of the wine described at the price named so that as soon as an order is given there is a binding contract to supply that quantity. If it were otherwise, the merchant might find himself involved in any number of contractual obligations to supply wine of a particular description which he would be quite unable to carry out, his stock of wine of that description being necessarily limited.

Partridge v Crittenden was approved in *British Car Auctions Ltd v Wright*[12]. Like the earlier case, this also involved the issue of criminal liability.

It is submitted that in the context of commercial contractual obligations the position may be less certain because of a growing trade usage in which certain advertisements for the sale of goods or the supply of services are expressly or implicitly acknowledged to be offers. For example, the Direct

---

9   Cheshire, Fifoot & Furmston's *Law of Contract* (12th edn 1991) p 32 citing *Harris v Nickerson* (1873) LR QB 286.
10   [1968] 2 All ER 421.
11   *Ibid* at p 424.
12   [1972] 3 All ER 462.

Marketing Association Code of Practice defines the term 'offer' as meaning any presentation or solicitation of goods or services and as including an invitation to treat. Whilst this does not affect the meaning of 'offer', the Code treats offers and invitations to treat identically. This would also explain the presence of the qualification 'subject to availability' in relation to goods and of the words 'subject to status' in an advertisement for credit. Ultimately it is a question of the intention of the parties, which might be evident from the presentation of the availability of the product or service and the context of the advertisement.

3.4   Advertisements of unilateral contracts

Whilst it may be debatable whether advertisements of bilateral contracts can lead directly to the creation of a contract on acceptance, advertisements of unilateral contracts are commonly held to be offers[13]. In the famous case of *Carlill v Carbolic Smoke Ball Co*[14] the defendant advertised a preparation and offered to pay £100 to any purchaser who used it and caught influenza within a given period. This was held to be an offer made to the world at large, the defendant's intention to be bound being made clear by the statement that it had deposited £1,000 with its bankers. The court distinguished the offer from invitations to treat stating: 'It is not like cases in which you offer to negotiate, or you issue advertisements that you have got a stock of books to sell, or houses to let, in which case there is no offer to be bound by any contract. Such advertisements are offers to negotiate – offers to receive offers – offers to chaffer'.

In a commercial context courts are reluctant to hold advertised promotions to be mere puffs, not intended to create legal relations. It follows that advertising, the purpose of which is the promotion of business, is likely to be construed by the courts as giving rise to legal rights and obligations[15].

Some advertisements might constitute advertisements of a unilateral promise, though not of a unilateral contract eg an advertisement by an auctioneer that the sale would be without reserve[16]. An analogous situation in relation to tenders has been recognised by the House of Lords[17].

---

13   *Chitty loc cit* at para 2–010.
14   [1893] 1 QB 256.
15   *Esso Petroleum Ltd v Commissioner of Customs and Excise* [1976] 1 All ER 117 HL at 121.
16   *Obiter dicta* in *Warlow v Harrison* (1859) 1 E & E 309 and *Rainbow v Howkins* [1904] 2 QB 322.
17   *Harvela Investments Ltd v Royal Trust Co of Canada (CI) Ltd* [1985] 2 All ER 966.

Chapter 4

The Regulatory Framework

In this chapter we consider the background tapestry to the broad range of advertisements by focusing on the law and voluntary codes which impact on advertisements generally.

4.1 Historical background

The earliest form of regulation was self-regulation in relation to consumer protection within the medieval guild[1]. However, this century has seen a growing paternalistic attitude towards advertising as evidenced by the increasing number of Acts, regulations and codes.

The common law always afforded a certain degree of protection against those who were misled by fraudulent misrepresentations in advertisements as evidenced by the leading case of *Derry v Peek*[2]. Until the later landmark decision of *Hedley Byrne & Co Ltd v Heller & Partners Ltd*[3] it was assumed that no action would lie for negligent misrepresentation which produced purely financial loss. This case held that in certain circumstances an action would lie in tort for negligent misstatements. At about the same time the Law Reform Committee's recommendation was adopted in the form of the Misrepresentation Act 1967. This extended the remedies of rescission and damages for innocent, negligent and fraudulent misrepresentation.

The case of *Caparo Industries plc v Dickman*[3bis] might be applied to advertisements so as to give rise to liability for negligent misstatements in advertisements. The House of Lords stated that

---

1 *Financial Advertising Law:* Circus, Lawson, Newell & Russell (October 1992) at A 2.0020.
2 (1899) 14 App Cas 337.
3 [1963] 2 All ER 575.
3bis [1990] 1 All ER 568 HL at 573–574 *per* Lord Bridge.

what emerges is that, in addition to the foreseeability of damage, necessary ingredients in any situation giving rise to a duty of care are that there should exist between the party owing the duty and the party to whom it is owed a relationship characterised by the law as one of 'proximity' or 'neighbourhood' and that the situation should be one in which the court considers it fair, just and reasonable that the law should impose a duty of a given scope on the one party for the benefit of the other[3ter].

An advertisement is *ipso facto* addressed to the public at large and it follows that there is a duty of care owed by the advertiser to the public to whom the advertisement is presented.

In *Hedley Byrne* the plaintiffs failed because of the defendant's disclaimer of liability. The Unfair Contract Terms Act 1977 restricts *inter alia* the extent to which persons can exclude liability by notice given to persons generally or to particular persons. Thus a person cannot by such notice exclude or restrict liability for death or personal injury resulting from his or her own negligence or, in the case of other loss or damage, liability for any negligence whatsoever except in so far as the notice satisfies the requirement of reasonableness[4].

An instructive recent case in which reliance was placed on *Hedley Byrne* and the Unfair Contract Terms Act is that of *McCullagh v Lane Fox & Partners Ltd*[4bis]. The plaintiff sued the estate agent for damages arising out of an erroneous description of the property and the Court of Appeal held that because of a disclaimer there was no assumption of responsibility by the estate agent. The court held the disclaimer to be fair and reasonable and therefore enforceable.

It is an offence to publish a statement in an advertisement which is intended to induce persons to enter into consumer transactions containing a statement purporting to exclude or restrict liability for breach of obligations in relation to sale or hire purchase and which exclusion is prohibited by the Unfair Contract Terms Act 1977[4ter].

More recently The Unfair Terms in Consumer Contracts Regulations 1994[4quat] contain provisions which indirectly impact on advertisements. The regulations implement Council Directive 93/13/EEC on Unfair Terms in Consumer Contracts and apply, with certain exceptions, to standard contracts entered into with consumers. The regulations deem certain contract terms to be unfair and, as such, unenforceable.

3ter   *Ibid* pp 573–574.
4   Section 2(1) and (2).
4bis   (1995) *The Times*, 22 December CA.
4ter   SI 1976 no 1813.
4quat   SI 1994 no 3159.

4.2 Self-regulation and codes of practice

An informal procedure of self-regulation by the Newspaper Society can be traced back to 1840 and a system of self-regulation in respect of poster advertising to the 1880s. The International Chamber of Commerce (ICC) founded in 1919 established the International Code of Standards of Advertising Practice in 1937.

The various voluntary codes which evolved in Britain were finally brought together in a single uniform code, the British Code of Advertising Practice in 1961, through the efforts of the Committee of Advertising Practice. This was followed by the setting up of the Advertising Standards Authority (ASA) in 1962 as an independent body responsible for ensuring that all non-broadcast advertisements adhered to the Code and were legal, decent, honest and truthful. The ASA is a limited company and is independent of both government and the advertising business. It investigates complaints and, when found justified, the ASA Council requests advertisers to withdraw or amend their advertisements or promotions. The adjudications of the ASA are subject to judicial review[5]. Examples of rulings by the ASA are to be found in Appendix 3.

The Committee of Advertising Practice constantly reviews its Advertising Code which is now in its ninth edition and its Sales Promotion Code (which first appeared in 1974) which is now in its sixth edition. The reviews take place in the light of changes in advertising and marketing practice, the mores of society, legislative changes and complaints received by the Committee.

Various trade associations have their own codes of practice which will often contain rules relating to advertising and marketing by their members. These might refer to or incorporate provisions of the British Codes of Advertising and Sales Promotion in addition to their own measures and safeguards. Examples include the Codes of Practice of the Finance and Leasing Association and the Consumer Credit Trade Association, the Good Banking Code of Practice and the Code of Practice of the Direct Marketing Association.

4.3 Control of radio and television advertising

The Broadcasting Act 1990 makes it the statutory duty of the Radio Authority and the Independent Television Commission (ITC) to draw up,

---

5   See, for example, the unreported case of *R v Advertising Standards Authority, ex parte City Trading Ltd* (High Court 1 November 1996).

after appropriate consultation, and to periodically review and enforce, a code governing standards and practice in radio and television advertising and programme sponsorship.

The Radio Authority has produced the Radio Authority Code of Advertising Standards and Practice and Programme Sponsorship[5bis]. Radio Authority licensees are responsible for ensuring that any advertising and sponsorship they broadcast comply with the Code and the Authority monitors compliance by investigating complaints. Radio Authority Programme Code 1 governs news programmes and coverage of matters of political or industrial controversy or relating to current public policy[6]. Radio Authority Programme Code 2 governs issues of violence, sex, taste and decency, children and young people, appeals for donations, religion and other matters[7].

The ITC Code of Advertising Standards and Practice[8] was made pursuant to the Broadcasting Act 1990 and also gives effect to provisions relating to television advertising in the EC Directive on Television Broacasting[9] ('television without frontiers') and the 1989 Council of Europe European Convention on Transfrontier Television. The Code applies to all television services regulated by the ITC and to all holders of relevant ITC licences. The ITC does not make rulings on the acceptability of particular advertisements in advance of their broadcast but these are required to be referred to the relevant television company or, if appropriate, to the Broadcast Advertising Clearance Centre.

The ITC Code of Programme Sponsorship[10] provides, as its name suggests, a code setting standards for the sponsorship of programmes. The ITC rules on advertising breaks[11] and regulates the amount, distribution and presentation of advertising.

4.4   Control of misleading advertisements

Originally the European Community wished to adopt measures to govern misleading, unfair and comparative advertising, restricting the former and

---

5bis   December 1994 adopted pursuant to s 92(1)(a), Broadcasting Act 1990.
6   January 1994 based on the requirements of ss 90 and 107 *ibid.*
7   May 1995 based on the requirements of ss 90 and 91 *ibid.*
8   Published Autumn 1995.
9   89/552/EEC. And see *Konsvmentombudsmannen (KO) v De Agostini (Svenska) Förlag AB* (Joined Cases C-34/95–C-36/95. Judgment of 9 July 1997 on the duty of a Member State to protect consumers against misleading TV advertising broadcast from another Member State.)
10   January 1994.
11   January 1991.

legalising the latter. The final version of the Council's Directive[12], however, did not extend to unfair or comparative advertising but was limited to misleading advertising as no common ground could be found to regulate the other heads. The EC Directive relating to misleading advertising was implemented in the UK in the form of the Control of Misleading Advertisements Regulations 1988[13]. An advertisement is misleading if, in any way, including presentation, it deceives or is likely to deceive the persons to whom it is addressed or whom it reaches and, if by reason of its deceptive nature, it is likely to affect their economic behaviour or, for those reasons, injures or is likely to injure a competitor of the person whose interests the advertisement seeks to promote[14].

The regulations do not apply to investment advertisements which are governed by the Financial Services Act 1986 and rules made by the Securities and Investments Board and self-regulating organisations.

The regulations do not reproduce the non-exhaustive list set out in the Directive of examples of material to be taken into account in deciding whether advertisements are misleading.

The administrative authorities for enforcing the provisions of the regulations are the Director General of Fair Trading, the Radio Authority and the ITC. The Director General is empowered to seek an injunction against any person concerned or likely to be concerned with the publication of a misleading advertisement[15]. In practice, however, advertisements are monitored by two channels, as follows:—

(1) Trading Standards (or Consumer Protection) Departments to be found in the London Boroughs, Metropolitan Boroughs, County Councils and Scottish Regional and Island Councils. In Northern Ireland, the Trading Standards branch is part of the Department of Economic Development;

(2) the Advertising Standards Authority which administers the British Codes of Advertising and Sales Promotions.

The Director General can act only when a complaint has been received. He cannot clear advertisements in advance of publication but can start proceedings to prevent their publication. For the purposes of controlling misleading advertisements he can refer any complaint and pass any information he receives to any other appropriate person or organisation.

---

12 84/450/EEC.
13 SI 1988 no 915.
14 Regulation 2(2) *ibid.*
15 Regulation 5.

There are few reported cases relating to the intervention of the Director General of Fair Trading in relation to misleading advertisements. One such case is *Director General of Fair Trading v Tobyward Ltd*[15bis]. This case involved alleged misleading statements relating to slimming aids. The Advertising Standards Authority received complaints about the advertisements and referred the breaches of the British Code of Advertising Practice to the Director General of Fair Trading who applied under the Control of Misleading Advertisements Regulations for an interlocutory injunction to restrain the advertisers from publishing misleading advertisements. An injunction was granted restraining the particular advertisements and advertisements which were in similar terms or likely to convey a similar impression. Hoffmann J (as he then was) opined that it is desirable and in accordance with the public interest that the courts should support the principle of self-regulation. He added that advertisers would be more inclined to accept the rulings of their self-regulatory bodies if it were generally known that in cases in which their procedures had been exhausted and the advertiser was still publishing an advertisement which appeared to the court to be *prima facie* misleading, an injunction would ordinarily be granted.

4.5   Statutes and subordinate legislation of general application

In this section reference is made to legislation which is of broad general application to different types of advertisements.

4.5.1   Trade Descriptions Act 1968

This Act makes it an offence for a person in the course of his trade or business to make a statement which he knows to be false or recklessly to make a statement which is false as to any of several identified matters, including:

(1) the provision in the course of any trade or business of any services, accommodation or facilities;
(2) the nature of any services, accommodation or facilities provided in the course of any trade or business;
(3) the time at which, or persons by whom, any services, accommodation or facilities are provided;

15bis   [1989] 2 All ER 266.

(4) the examination, approval or evaluation by any person of any services, accommodation or facilities so provided; or

(5) the location or amenities of any accommodation so provided[16].

'False' means false to a material degree. False statements in a brochure are made when communicated to readers and can therefore give rise to more than one prosecution[17].

It is interesting to note that the relevant section of the Act is entitled 'False or Misleading Statements as to Services etc', whilst the corresponding section which relates to goods is entitled merely 'False Trade Descriptions'. The latter makes express reference to misleading trade descriptions whilst the former does not. However, by deduction from an interpretation of the two sections[17bis] a description which is not 'false' but is misleading, is deemed to be a false statement.

If a body corporate commits an offence under the Act, any officer of the body who consented to or connived at or acted negligently in relation to the offence is guilty of the offence[17ter]. It is a legitimate defence to prove that the commission of the offence was due to the act or default of some other person. It is also cogent to prove that the offence was due to a mistake or reliance on information supplied by another or on an accident or cause beyond the alleged defendant's control provided that all reasonable precautions were taken and all due diligence exercised[17quat].

The leading illustrative cases are *Tesco Supermarkets Ltd v Nattrass*[17quin] and *MFI Warehouses v Nattrass*[17sext]. In *Tesco* the House of Lords stated that in the case of a large-scale business the owner could not personally supervise the activities of all its servants so that it would be consistent with the taking of reasonable precautions and the exercise of due diligence to have instituted an effective system to avoid the commission of offences. In *MFI* the Court of Appeal held that 'recklessly' in the context of the Trade Descriptions Act did not involve dishonesty. It was sufficient to found a valid conviction on a charge of recklessly making a statement which is false or misleading that the chairman of the company had considered the

---

16   Section 14(1).

17   *R v Thompson Holidays Ltd* [1974] 1 All ER 823 CA and see *Wings Ltd v Ellis* [1984] 3 All ER 577 HL.

17bis   Compare ss 3 and 14, Trade Descriptions Act 1968.

17ter   Section 20 *ibid.*

17quat   Sections 23 and 24.

17quin   [1971] 2 All ER 127 HL; compare *Warwickshire County Council v Johnson* [1993] 1 All ER 299 HL.

17sext   [1973] 1 All ER 762 CA.

advertisement for several minutes before approving it without having regard to its truth or falsity.

In *Wings Ltd v Ellis*[17sept] the court held that an offence under s 14, Trade Descriptions Act (making a statement which the maker knows to be false or recklessly making a statement which is false) is avoided by taking such available opportunity as would be reasonable to prevent the result. Thus, where a quarter of a million brochures containing a false statement had already been printed and distributed and their total recall or correction was impossible it was a valid defence for the appellant on discovering the error to have sent a memorandum to its staff instructing them to amend the brochures and to send letters of correction to clients and sales agents.

The Secretary of State for Trade and Industry is authorised to make orders including in relation to information which is to appear in advertisements. However, the bulk of the Act and orders made under it apply to the supply of goods and not of services.

4.5.2   Consumer Protection Act 1987

Part III controls the method of pricing goods, services, accommodation or facilities available to consumers and makes it an offence for a person in the course of his business to give an indication to consumers that is misleading as to price[18]. Amongst the items which might give rise to a misleading indication as to price is a statement of facts or circumstances by reference to which consumers might reasonably be expected to judge the validity of any relevant comparison made or implied by the indication not being what in fact they are represented to be. 'Services or facilities' are expressly stated to include the provision of credit, banking or insurance services and facilities incidental to them[18bis].

By way of an improvement on the drafting of the Trade Descriptions Act[19] this Act expressly defines services or facilities to which it applies and includes the following:

(1) the provision of credit or of banking or insurance services and the provision of facilities incidental to the provision of such services;
(2) the purchase or sale of foreign currency.

17sept   [1984] 1 All ER 1046 CA.
18   Section 20 and for meaning of 'misleading' see s 21.
18bis   Section 22.
19   Section 22(1)(a) and (b).

It also expressly provides for the exclusion of services or facilities provided by an authorised person or appointed representative in the course of the carrying on of an investment business[20].

The Act makes provision for the establishment of codes of practice approved by the Secretary of State after consultation with the Director General of Fair Trading and the making of regulations by the Secretary of State after consultation with the Director General of Fair Trading. Orders made include the Consumer Protection (Code of Practice for Traders on Price Indications) Approval Order 1988[21] approving the Code of Practice for Traders on Price Indications 1988. Also relevant in our context is the Price Indications (Bureaux de Change) (No 2) Regulations 1992[22], and the Price Indications (Method of Payment) Regulations 1991[23]. The latter regulations apply when consumers are given an indication of a price in an advertisement containing an invitation, whether express or implied, to place orders by post or by means of a telecommunications system, but do not apply to advertisements covered by the Consumer Credit Act 1974[24]. The regulations address situations where the price does not apply to each method of payment or there is a difference in the price payable between different methods of payment. The Council of Ministers of the European Union has adopted a common position on a proposed Parliament and Council Directive on consumer protection in respect of indications of price on products offered to consumers. In due course this should be incorporated into UK law.

The Code of Practice for Traders on Price Indications[25] covers amongst other matters price comparisons including comparisons with the trader's own previous price; comparisons with prices related to different circumstances; comparisons with another trader's prices; what the price indication should include eg value added tax; and the position relating to price indications which become misleading after they have been given. The Code provides that if the advertisement does not state otherwise the price indication should apply for a reasonable period (as a general guide, for at least seven days or until the next issue of the newspaper or magazine in which the advertisement was published, whichever is longer). If the price indication becomes misleading within this period customers should be given the correct information before they are committed to buying the product. This applies also to mail order advertisements, catalogues and leaflets.

---

20 Section 22(3).
21 SI 1988 no 2078.
22 SI 1992 no 737.
23 SI 1991 no 199.
24 Regulation 6.
25 November 1988 issued by the DTI.

4.5.3 Companies Act 1985

An advertisement might appear in a company's business letter in which case the requirements of the Companies Act 1985 must be complied with. The following must appear in legible characters:

(1) the company's name[26];
(2) the company's place of registration, its registration number, the address of its registered office, in the case of an investment company the fact that it is such a company and in the case of a limited company exempt from the obligation to use the word 'limited' as part of its name, the fact that it is a limited company[27];
(3) where the name of any of its directors appears, the name of every director of the company[28].

4.5.4 Business Names Act 1985 and the Companies and Business Names Regulations 1981[29]

The Business Names Act regulates the use of certain business names and the foregoing regulations specify words and expressions whose use requires the prior approval of the Secretary of State. The Business Names Act also requires the disclosure in legible characters in documents and business letters issued in the course of a business, in the case of a partnership of the name of each partner, in the case of an individual of his name and in the case of a company its corporate name. It is also necessary in relation to each person so named to provide an address in Great Britain at which service of any document relating to the business will be effective. The foregoing does not apply to a document issued by a partnership of more than 20 persons which maintains at its principal place of business a list of the names of the partners and the document states that the list is open to inspection at the partnership's principal place of business[30].

4.5.5 Consumer Transactions (Restrictions on Statements) Order 1976[30bis]

These regulations prohibit the publication in the course of a business of an advertisement (including a catalogue or circular) which is intended to

---

26 Section 349(1).
27 Section 351(1).
28 Section 305(1).
29 SI 1981 no 1685.
30 Section 4.
30bis SI 1976 no 1813.

induce persons to enter into consumer transactions and which contains certain statements. These statements relate to implied terms in sale and hire purchase contracts which, by virtue of ss 6 and 20, Unfair Contract Terms Act 1977, cannot be excluded or which are inconsistent with a warranty implied by the Trading Standards Act 1964 or the Trading Standards Act (Northern Ireland) 1965.

4.6 Intellectual property considerations

4.6.1 Passing off

A person may not pass off his goods as those of another. If he does so he commits the tort of passing off. This tort is wide-ranging as described by Lord Scarman in his oft-quoted *dictum*:

> The tort is no longer anchored, as in its 19th century formulation, to the name or trade mark of a product or business. It is wide enough to encompass other descriptive material, such as slogans or racial images, which radio, television or newspaper advertising campaigns can lead the market to associate with a plaintiff's product, provided always that such descriptive material had become part of the goodwill of the product, and the test is whether the product has derived from the advertising a distinctive character which the market recognises[31].

The plaintiff must prove three elements in order to succeed with his passing-off action. First he must establish a goodwill or reputation attached to the goods or services which he supplies and which is established with the purchasing public by association with the identifying 'get-up', and that such 'get-up' is recognised by the public as distinctive, specifically of the plaintiff's goods or services. Secondly, he must prove a misrepresentation by the defendant to the public whether or not intentional, leading or likely to lead the public to believe that the goods or services offered by the defendant are those of the plaintiff. Thirdly, he must demonstrate that he suffers or is likely to suffer damage or injury to his business or goodwill[32].

The passing off must be distinguished from an action for slander of goods where the plaintiff must prove that the defendant falsely and maliciously made a representation about the plaintiff's business or goods as a result of which the plaintiff suffered damage. The courts will be astute to

---

31 *Cadbury-Schweppes Pty Ltd v the Pub Squash Co Ltd* [1981] RPC 429 at 440 PC.
32 *Reckitt & Colman v Borden ('Jif')* [1990] RPC 341 HL at 406, and see the *Parma Ham Case* [1991] RPC 351.

distinguish between a mere puff and a comparison of products based upon alleged but incorrect facts[33].

4.6.2   Trade marks and copyright

The Trade Marks Act 1994 protects the right of the owner of a registered trade mark. A trade mark is the only sign capable of being represented graphically which can distinguish the goods or services of one undertaking from those of other undertakings. A person infringes a registered trade mark if he uses in the course of trade a sign which is identical with or similar to the trade mark in relation to goods or services for which the sign has been registered.

A limited exception is made permitting the use of another's registered trade mark for comparative advertising. In *Barclays Bank plc v RBS Advanta*[35] RBS Advanta issued a mailshot listing 15 ways in which its card was said to be a better card and one page of which included a comparative table listing six competitors' cards including Barclaycard, Standard Visa and RBS' card. Barclays Bank argued that the result of the advertising was that RBS' card would have an unfair advantage in the market. In refusing an application for interlocutory relief the court rejected the submission that the comparative advertising would not be considered honest by members of a reasonable audience, honesty being gauged against what was reasonably to be expected by the relevant public of advertisements for that kind of goods or services.

A trade mark is also infringed if the sign is used in relation to similar goods or services and gives rise to a likelihood of confusion on the part of the parties, which includes the likelihood of association[35bis].

The Copyright, Designs and Patents Act 1988 protects the author or owner of a copyright against its infringement. Copyrights exist in the following descriptions of work:

(1) original literary, dramatic, musical or artistic works;
(2) sound recordings, films, broadcasts, or cable programmes; and
(3) the typographical arrangement of published editions[36].

The general principle that copyright is vested in the author is capable of

---

33   David Young: *Passing Off* (FT Law & Tax 3rd edn p 18 and Cases cited).
34   Section 10(6).
35   *Barclays Bank plc v RBS Advanta*, (1996) *The Times*, 8 February.
35bis   Section 10(1) and 2 of the Trade Marks Act 1994 and see the *British Sugar Case* [1996] RPC 281.
36   Section 1(1).

being proven otherwise, for example that the commissioning company of an advertisement is its copyright owner[37].

The owner of the copyright has the exclusive right to copy the work, to issue copies of the work to the public, to perform, show or play the work in public, to broadcast the work when included in a cable programme service and to make an adaptation of the work. The copyright in a work is infringed by any person who, without the copyright owner's licence, does or authorises another to do any of the foregoing acts[38]. One notable exception in our context is that it is not an infringement of copyright in an artistic work to copy it or to issue copies to the public for the purpose of advertising the sale of the work[39]. The Copyright, Designs and Patents Act also governs the proprietorship in designs. The designer is the first owner of any design right in a design which is not created pursuant to a commission or in the course of employment; in the latter case the person commissioning the design is its first owner[40]. A design right is infringed by a person who, without the licence of its owner, does or authorises another to do anything which infringes the owner's rights.[41]

There is no provision for registration of copyright and there is no need to register a design or printed matter of a literary or artistic character including in respect of a trade advertisement.

4.7 Discrimination issues

It is unlawful to publish or cause to be published an advertisement which indicates or might reasonably be understood to indicate an intention to discriminate against a person on racial grounds[42] or on sexual grounds[43]. An advertisement will constitute such an offence if it indicates or might reasonably be understood to indicate an intention by a person to discriminate.

For the purposes of determining whether an advertisement contravenes the sexual discrimination barriers, any sexual connotation, such as 'waiter', 'salesgirl', 'postman', or 'stewardess' is taken to indicate an intention to discriminate unless the advertisement contains an indication to the contrary. The test is what a normal reasonable person would understand by the words[44].

---

37 *Harold Drabble Ltd v Hycolite Manufacturing Co* (1928) 44 TLR 264.
38 Section 16 *loc cit.*
39 Section 63(1) *ibid.*
40 Section 215 *ibid.*
41 The Registered Designs Rules 1995, r 26.
42 Race Relations Act 1976, s 29.
43 Sex Discrimination Act 1975, s 38.
44 *Race Relations Board v Associated Newspapers Group Ltd* [1978] 3 All ER 419 CA on s 6(1) of the Race Relations Act 1968.

Chapter 5

Advertising Modes and Media

This chapter addresses certain aspects and principles relating to specific advertising modes and media.

5.1 Advertisements *in situ*

There are numerous controls on advertisements which are positioned on property, particularly in urban areas and on public roads. The relevant legislation is the Town and Country Planning Act 1990 and regulations[1] made under it, the Local Government Act 1992 and the Highways Act 1980.

Restrictions include regulation as to the dimensions, appearance and position of advertisements, sites on which they may be displayed and the manner in which they may be affixed to land. The legislation also deals with advertisements on tethered balloons, vehicles, flags and hoardings.

5.2 Advertisements in newspapers and journals

5.2.1 Principles

The Advertising Code of the British Codes of Advertising and Sales Promotion[2] contains the rules agreed for all advertisements, sales promotions and direct marketing in the United Kingdom non-broadcast media. *Inter alia* the codes apply to advertisements in newspapers, magazines and other printed publications.

---

1 Town and Country Planning (Control of Advertisements) Regulations 1992 (SI 1992 No 666).
2 9th Edition.

The code obliges advertisers, publishers and owners of media to ensure that advertisements are designed and presented in such a way that they can be easily distinguished from editorial matter. Mail order and direct response advertisements must contain the name and address of the advertiser.

The code's provisions are in addition to requirements applying to specific categories of advertisement.

As investment advertising may be connected with investment advice, which is investment business under the Financial Services Act 1986[3], it is relevant to point out that there is a specific exemption for investment advice published in a newspaper, journal, magazine or other periodical publication if the principal purpose of the publication, taken as a whole and including any advertisements contained in it, is not to lead persons to invest in any particular investment[4]. The Secretary of State, on application, may certify that a publication is of the nature so described and such certificate shall be conclusive. The Securities and Investment Board (SIB) has issued a useful guidance note on the Financial Services Act and the press[5].

5.2.2 Applicable law and jurisdiction

The Brussels Convention on Jurisdiction and the Enforcement of Judgments in Civil and Commercial Matters 1968 governs the issue of the jurisdiction where a person may be sued if the parties belonged to relevant states, namely those that were parties to the Convention. Article 5(3) provides that a person domiciled in a contracting state may in another contracting state be sued in matters relating to tort, delict or quasi-delict in the courts for the place where the harmful event occurred.

In *Shevill and others v Presse Alliance SA*[6] the French domiciled defendants published a daily newspaper, *France Soir*, which had a circulation of 200,000 in France, and 15,000 outside France, including 230 in England and Wales. It was alleged that the article was defamatory of various persons including the first plaintiff who was domiciled and resident in and a national of England and worked in the Paris *Bureau de Change* through which it was alleged that money had been laundered. The benefit of suing in an English court was that, certainly prior to the Defamation Act 1996, the plaintiff did not have to show that he or she had suffered any actual

---

3   Financial Services Act 1986, Sched 1, Pt II, para 15.
4   *Ibid* Sched I, Pt III, para 25.
5   Guidance Release No 4/89.
6   [1992] 1 All ER 409 CA.

damage for once publication was proved damage was presumed. The Court of Appeal stated that once it is established that there is an arguable case upon which the plaintiffs can rely to establish a publication carrying with it the presumption of damage, then jurisdiction under art 5(3) may be assumed by the court.

The House of Lords referred to the European Court the question as to whether there was more than one harmful event, one for each of the contracting States in which a newspaper was published, in circumstances where a newspaper containing a libellous article was published and distributed in several countries. The European Court answered the question in the affirmative and rejected the argument raised in the Court of Appeal that the correct jurisdiction was that of the country with the most significant connection with the tort[7]. In the opinion of the European Court the victim of a libel in a newspaper distributed in States which were parties to the Convention could sue the publisher either in the contracting State where the publisher was established or in any other contracting State where the publication was distributed and the victim claimed to have suffered injury to his reputation. The courts of the State where the publisher was established had jurisdiction to award damages for all the harm caused by the defamation but the courts of other States could only rule in respect of the harm caused in that State. The substantive and evidential criteria to be applied by the national court in deciding whether and to what extent harm had occurred were governed not by the Convention but by the national conflict of laws rules, providing that it did not impair the effectiveness of the Convention. The court also stated that the object of the Convention was not to unify the rules of substantive law and procedure of the different contracting States but to determine which court had jurisdiction and to facilitate the enforcement of judgments.

The significance of the judgment in the *Shevill* case is that advertisements circulating in newspapers or journals in different contracting States within the European Union can give rise to civil claims against advertisers, publishers and others in any of those States.

In general it is the substantive law and the evidentiary law of the country in which the advertisement is published which would apply to the advertisement. This would include the common law, primary and subordinate legislation, rules and codes of practice. Within the European Union the European Court of Justice has always ruled that the need to protect the recipient of a service may justify limitations on the cross-

---

7   Case 68/93 [1995] All ER (EC) 289; (1995) *The Times,* 6 April.

border provision of services. In other words, the consumer's home state law will take precedence over the law of the supplier provided that it respects the 'general good' criteria laid down by the Court of Justice, namely proportionality, necessity, non-discrimination and non-duplication. This gives rise to enormous practical problems where the rules and regulations of different states differ, as they are bound to. The ultimate harmonisation of European Union, if not international law, on advertising would prove a tremendous boost to trade.

Legislation does sometimes come to the assistance of a plaintiff in the context of responsibility for the issue of an advertisement. The Financial Services Act 1986 provides that for the purposes of that Act an advertisement or other information issued outside the United Kingdom shall be treated as issued in the UK if it is directed to persons in the UK or is made available to them otherwise than in a newspaper, journal, magazine or other periodical publication published and circulating principally outside the UK or in sound or television broadcast transmitted principally for reception outside the UK[7bis].

As regards potential defamatory matter the Defamation Act 1996 comes to the rescue of anyone other than the author, editor or publisher of a statement if he was only involved in printing, producing, distributing or selling printed material containing the statement or in processing, making copies of, distributing or selling a film or sound recording containing the statement or any electronic medium in which the statement is recorded or as the broadcaster of a live programme or operator of or provider of access to a communications system containing or transmitting the statement and has no effective control over the maker of the statement[7ter]. This defence will be of inestimable value to persons involved in the distribution of publications containing defamatory advertisements, for example in the form of comparative advertisements.

5.3 Radio and television advertising

5.3.1 Principles

The British Codes of Advertising and Sales Promotion do not apply to broadcast commercials: these are the responsibility of the Radio Authority or the Independent Television Commission. The Radio Authority's code is the Radio Authority Code of Advertising Standards and Practice and

---

7bis   Section 207(3).
7ter   Section 1(3)(a), (b), (c), (d) and (e).

Programme Sponsorship[8]. The code applying to television advertising is the ITC Code of Advertising Standards and Practice[9]. Obligations under these codes are in addition to those which apply in any event to the category of advertisement in question. The requirements of the codes are fundamentally the same in relation to radio and television advertising and are set out below[10].

5.3.1.1   Legal responsibility

It is the responsibility of the advertiser to ensure that advertisements comply with all relevant legal and regulatory requirements.

5.3.1.2   Misleadingness

Each code provides that advertisements must present the financial offer or service in terms which do not mislead whether by exaggeration, omission or in any other way.

The codes stipulate particular requirements relating to statements of tax benefits, interest on saving and insurance premiums and cover. As regards tax benefits, these must be properly explained and qualified to make clear what they mean and whether full advantage may only be received by those paying income tax at the standard rate. A statement of interest on savings must meet the following requirements:

(1)   they must be stated clearly and be factually correct at the time of the transmission or broacast;
(2)   calculations of interest must not be based on unstated factors which might affect the sum received by individuals or be capable of misunderstanding in any other way;
(3)   interest must be stated as gross or net of tax;
(4)   interest rates which are variable must be so described. Where insurance premiums and cover are referred to in an advertisement, references to rates and conditions must be accurate and not misleading and in specifying rates of premium cover, there must be no misleading omission of conditions. In life assurance advertising reference to specific sums assured must be accompanied by all relevant qualifying conditions.

5.3.1.3   Investment Advertisements and approval

The following are permitted categories of advertising:

---

8   December 1994 edition.
9   Autumn 1995 edition.
10   See Radio Code Appendix 1; ITC Code Appendix 2.

(1) investment advertisements issued by an authorised person or the contents of which have been approved by an authorised person;

(2) advertisements issued in respect of the investment business of an authorised person, which are not themselves investment advertisements;

(3) investment advertisements which by virtue of the Financial Services Act 1986 do not require to be issued or approved by an authorised person.

As regards approval, each of the codes provides as follows:

(1) the compliance officer or equivalent officer of the advertiser or authorised person issuing or approving the proposed advertisement must have confirmed that the final recorded version of the advertisement is in accordance with the rules of the Securities and Investments Board (SIB) or the relevant recognised Self-Regulating Organisation (SRO) or Recognised Professional Body (RPB);

(2) where the investment advertisement is proposed by an appointed representative, it must have been approved by the authorised person to whom the appointed representative is responsible.

5.3.1.4   Unacceptable categories of advertising

The following are unacceptable categories of advertising although, in the case of television advertising, they may be approved in given circumstances:

(1) advertisements for investments in metals, commodities, futures and options, securities which are not readily realisable, volatile or complex investments such as swaps and currency or interest rate instruments, contracts based on market indices, and such other categories which the Radio Authority or the Independent Television Commission may from time to time consider inappropriate for advertising;

(2) advertisements for the issue of shares or debentures other than advertisements announcing the publication of listing particulars or a prospectus in connection with an offer to the public of shares or debentures to be listed on the Stock Exchange or to be dealt in on the Unlisted Securities Market;

(3) advertisements recommending the acquisition or disposal of an investment in any specific company other than an Investment Trust Company Ltd on the Stock Exchange; and

(4) advertisements which appear to have the effect of publicising indirectly any investment.

The ITC Code states that approval for advertising in the foregoing categories, where the circumstances are approved by the Commission, will normally only be considered in respect of special interest financial channels.

5.3.1.5   *Advertisements for deposit and savings facilities*

The following deposit and savings facilities may be advertised:

(1) local government savings and deposit facilities in the UK, the Isle of Man and the Channel Islands;

(2) such facilities provided by building societies in accordance with the Building Societies Act 1986;

(3) such facilities provided by the National Savings Bank and authorised institutions (ie banks) under the Banking Act 1987;

(4) such facilities provided by registered credit unions regulated by the Credit Unions Act 1979;

(5) such facilities, guaranteed by the national government of an EU country, in currencies other than sterling, provided that a warning statement is included as to the effect of exchange rate fluctuations on the value of savings; and

(6) building society and authorised institutions' 'appropriate personal pension schemes' as established in accordance with the Social Security Act 1986.

5.3.1.6   *Insurance advertisements*

(1) Life assurance, sickness and disability insurance advertising is acceptable with the prior approval of the Radio Authority or Independent Television Commission, as the case may be. Such policies may only be advertised by companies authorised to carry on long-term business under the Insurance Companies Act 1982 or companies which have complied with Sched 2F to that Act in respect of carrying out insurance business or providing insurance in the UK or registered friendly societies which are authorised under the Friendly Societies (Long Term Insurance Business) Regulations 1987.

(2) Except with prior approval, general insurance (eg motor, household, fire and personal injury) may only be advertised by insurance companies which carry on business under the Insurance Companies Act 1982 or have complied with Sched 2F referred to above or if they are Lloyd's Underwriting Syndicates.

(3) Except with the prior approval, as above, insurance brokerage services in respect of general insurance, sickness insurance and other

forms of long-term assurance which are not covered by the Financial Services Act 1986 may only be advertised by brokers registered under the Insurance Brokers (Registration) Act 1977 or companies enrolled under that Act, intermediaries who have undertaken to abide by the provisions of the Association of British Insurers Code for the Selling of General Insurance or building societies empowered to offer such services.

5.3.1.7 *Lending and credit advertisements*

The advertising of mortgages, other lending facilities and credit services is acceptable from government and local government agencies, building societies, authorised or permitted insurance companies, registered friendly societies, authorised institutions under the Banking Act 1987, registered credit unions regulated by the Credit Unions Act 1987 and persons and bodies granted a licence under the Consumer Credit Act 1974.

No additional requirements are stipulated over and above those required under the Consumer Credit (Advertisements) Regulations 1989.

5.3.1.8 *Direct remittance*

The code relating to radio advertising renders advertisements unacceptable if they directly or indirectly invite the remittance of money direct to the advertiser or any other person without offering an opportunity to receive further details. The code on television advertising permits direct remittance advertisements in the case of permitted categories of investment advertisements on regulated additional services such as public teletext. Apart from such advertising it prohibits invitations for the remittance of money direct to the advertiser or any other person without further formality.

5.3.1.9 *Financial publications*

Advertisements for publications on investments and other financial matters must make no recommendations on any specific investment offer. Advertisements for subscription services must be in general terms and make no reference to any specific investment offer.

5.3.2 Applicable law and jurisdiction

The principles discussed above in the section on applicable law and jurisdiction in relation to newspaper and journal advertising[10bis], generally speaking, apply equally to radio and television advertising. Specific

---

10bis Para 5.2.2. *supra.*

provision for television, sound and teletext advertising is made in the Financial Services Act which provides that advice does not constitute investment advice if it is given in any programme included or made for inclusion in any television broadcasting service or other television programme service, any sound broadcasting service or licensable sound programme service or any teletext service. For this purpose 'programme' includes an advertisement[11].

We have already noted that for the purposes of the Financial Services Act an advertisement or other information issued outside the UK is treated as issued in the UK if it is directed to persons in the UK or is made available to them otherwise than in a newspaper, journal, magazine or other periodical publication published and circulating principally outside the UK or in a sound or television broadcast transmitted principally for reception outside the UK[12].

With regard to potentially defamatory advertisements or other material, a person will not be considered the author, editor or publisher of a statement if he is only involved as the broadcaster of a live programme containing the statement in circumstances in which he has no effective control over the making of this statement, or as the operator of or provider of access to a communications system by means of which the statement is transmitted or made available, by a person over whom he has no effective control[13].

5.3.3   European Union and conflict of law issues

Some of these issues have been alluded to above. The reader is referred to Chapter 18 for a fuller discussion.

---

11   Sched 1, Pt III, para 25(A).
12   Section 207(3).
13   Defamation Act 1996, s 1(3)(d),(e).

Chapter 6

Advertising on the Internet

6.1 Introduction

The Internet is a mechanism or system which, by virtue of its sophistication, magnifies and multiplies the problems which already exist in the mundane world of financial advertising and marketing. Whilst the Internet's starting point is that it is merely another medium, ultimately the sophistication of the system results in issues appearing to be different in kind to those outside the Internet's sphere. It is generally recognised that the legal approach to the Internet must be based upon established legal principles although these will undoubtedly require a degree of adaptation.

6.2 Meaning of the Internet

The Internet has been defined as a global network of computers all speaking the same language[1]. Data is transferred through various telephone systems and access is often provided by means of personal computers (PCs) which connect to the Internet through a modem linking the PC to the telephone network. Internet Access Providers control ports of call to the Internet and their computers are called servers. A service provider sells an access code to the PC user enabling him to log on to and be recognised by the server.

The Internet application that has had the most widespread ramifications is the World Wide Web. The Web is a hypertext Internet application which allows the user, during the course of one telephone connection and using

---

1 Clive Gringras: *The Laws of the Internet* (Butterworths 1997) p 1.

familiar graphical software interfaces, to point, click and jump across the Internet, leaping from one seductively designed Web site to the next[2].

6.3   Advertising and marketing law on the Internet: the law in general

As already mentioned, the general principles of advertising and marketing law apply equally to advertising and marketing on the Internet. Some of the legal issues arising on the Internet are exacerbated and take a modified form by virtue of the medium. We shall focus on some of these.

The Copyright, Designs and Patents Act 1988 makes provision for the first time for electronic media and for reproducing an artistic work by means of storing it in any medium by electronic means[3]. Any Internet host or access provider who uses or knowingly permits others to use his Internet service to disseminate unauthorised copies of advertisements may be liable for infringement, possibly even where the host or access provider does this unknowingly[4].

As regards defamation, the Defamation Act 1996[5] introduced new defences available to persons utilising the Internet for advertising materials so as to focus responsibility for publication on those responsible for the publication. It is a defence in defamation proceedings to show that the person was not the author, editor or publisher of the statement complained of, that he took reasonable care in relation to his publication and that he did not know, and had no reason to believe, that what he did caused or contributed to the publication of a defamatory statement.

A person is not considered to be the author, editor or publisher of a statement if he is only involved in processing, making copies of, distributing or selling any electronic medium in or on which the statement is recorded, or in operating or providing any equipment, system or service by means of which the statement is retrieved, copied, distributed or made available in an electronic form. Likewise, he is not considered the author, editor or publisher of a statement if he is only involved as the operator of or provider of access to a communications system by means of which the statement is transmitted, or made available, by a person over whom he has no effective control[6]. The latter is intended to cover computer network service operators and providers.

---

2   *Internet Law and Regulation* edited by Graham J H Smith (Bird and Bird) (FT Law and Tax 1996) p 5.
3   Sections 17 and 178, Copyright, Designs and Patents Act 1988.
4   Internet Law and Regulation *loc cit* pp 17–18.
5   Defamation Act 1996, s 1(3)(c).
6   *Ibid* s 1(3)(e).

Where there is a risk of defamation, Internet service providers and others should immediately remedy the alleged defamation by circulating an appropriate apology and corrective statement.

The Internet gives rise to the separate question of claims made in respect of acts committed in and outside the jurisdiction of the courts. The Supreme Court has jurisdiction in respect of a tort committed within its jurisdiction or in respect of an act committed outside its jurisdiction if damage was suffered within its jurisdiction[7]. If the tort has in substance been committed in a foreign country the court will only have jurisdiction if the act complained of is one which, if done in England, would constitute a tort and is also actionable according to the law of the foreign country where it has been committed[8]. The court is obliged to look at the tort alleged in a commonsense way and to ask whether damage has resulted from substantial and efficacious acts committed within the jurisdiction, regardless of whether or not such acts have been committed elsewhere[9].

As regards the choice of law applicable to the particular tort, the position in relation to the Internet is largely resolved by the Private International Law (Miscellaneous Provisions) Act 1995. This states that the general rule is that the applicable law is the law of the country in which the events constituting the tort in question occurred. Where elements of those events occur in different countries, the applicable law under the general rule is to be taken as being:

(1) for a cause of action in respect of damage to property, the law of the country where the property was when it was damaged; and

(2) in any other case, the law of the country in which the most significant element or elements of those events occurred[10].

There is one respect in which the Internet does not create any legal issues. The authors or publishers of Web sites used for advertising a product or service are readily identifiable as publishers or promoters of the advertised wares. There may be a line to be drawn between those who are and those who are not legally responsible for the publication but the determination of such an issue should not be different in principle to that involved in the case of a hard copy advertisement.

---

7   RSC Ord 11, r 1(1)(f).
8   *Boys v Chaplin* [1969] 2 All ER 1085 HL.
9   See commentary on 7 above in *The Supreme Court Practice 1997* ('*The White Book*') citing *Metal und Rohstoff AG v Donaldson Lufkin & Jenrette Inc* [1990] 1 QB 391 CA.
10   Section 11(2)(b) and (c).

6.4   Advertising and marketing on the Internet: specific regulated areas

In this section we turn to specific areas of advertising and marketing law where controls have either been implemented or are understood to extend, in their present form, to the Internet.

The Distance Selling Directive[11] applies to contracts concluded by 'means of communication at a distance' and refers, *inter alia*, to contracts concluded by electronic mail and television (teleshopping). As the list is not exhaustive it would include sales by means of the Internet. The Directive imposes obligations on the supplier in relation to the provision of written information and a cooling-off period[11bis]. Undoubtedly, the most attention attracted by the Internet is in relation to the advertising and marketing of investments within the meaning of the Financial Services Act 1986. The Securities and Investments Board (SIB) has consistently taken the view that the Internet is essentially no different from other media and that the provisions of the foregoing Act apply in the usual way[12].

The following observations may be made:

(1) As advertisers on the Internet cannot control the persons who have access to the Web site they cannot rely upon relevant exemptions eg for advertisements directed only at professional or business investors. It is also submitted that a disclaimer or warning in the advertisement to the effect that it is only intended for such persons would not avail the advertiser.

(2) An advertisement issued outside the United Kingdom and which is intended to be directed only at persons outside the United Kingdom, will, it is submitted, also be deemed to be directed at persons in the United Kingdom if they have access to it.

(3) Though it appears unlikely that an Access or Web site provider will be conducting investment business by merely acting as a conduit through which persons or companies gain access to or a presence on the Net where it has no knowledge of or control over the information or service being provided, the position may be otherwise if it is involved commercially with an investment firm to which it is providing access or a site. In the view of the Securities and Investments

---

11   97/7/EC (OJ 1997 L1 44/19).

11bis   See the useful article on Financial Services on the Internet: Can the Present Regulatory System Cope? Daniel Tunkal Butterworth, *Journal of International Banking and Financial Law*, April 1996 and also para 17.4.3 *post*.

12   See *post* paras 11.2 and 16.5.4.

Board there is a possibility that such persons would be conducting investment business if they were to:

(a) provide access or an off-the-shelf Net site over which they had control as regards what was placed on the Net or over the nature of information about investments or investment services provided on the site;

(b) have a joint venture arrangement with someone carrying on investment business (such as a firm providing share dealing services) for whom they have provided access or a site;

(c) promote an investment service under their own name; or

(d) promote another person's investment service or put investment material on the Net[13].

6.5 The Internet raises interesting questions, such as those set out below

(1) If overseas persons operate an on-line dealing service that may be accessed through access providers in the UK, any or all of the servers operated by those access providers become a permanent place of business in the UK with the result that the business requires authorisation from the Financial Services Act.

(2) If an overseas person were to offer on-line investment dealing services, would this amount to engaging in investment business in the UK which would then require authorisation, unless the activities are exempt or excluded?[13bis]

(3) Does advertising on the Internet amount to 'cold-calling' so that it is caught by the prohibition on unsolicited calls, being a personal visit or oral communication made without express invitation[14]? It would appear that it does not.

(4) The SIB has expressed concern at, and would appear impotent to stop, what is known as 'share-plugging', and the promotion to British investors of unwanted or bogus share tips by unauthorised companies over the Internet. These activities often involve fraudsters who solicit cheques or other payments. Access is gained to the Net user's personal computer addresses without the advertiser using

13   Standard letter issued by SIB in December 1995.
13bis   See Financial Services Act 1986, s 1(3). The writer's view is that it would. However, the Securities and Futures Authority (SFA) for one has not to date authorised any such person.
14   Section 56, Financial Services Act 1986.

his own Web site so that he evades identification. There have been similar solicitations for bank deposits, sums of currencies and the like.

6.6   Use of the Internet

Providers of financial services are pre-eminent in their utilisation of the Internet for the advertising and marketing of financial services and products. These range from banking services on the one hand to Internet share dealing and trading on the other. In addition, various regulatory bodies such as the Securities and Investments Board (SIB) has used its Internet site to issue alerts to Internet users. The Personal Investment Authority (PIA) and the Investment Management Regulatory Organisation (IMRO) have established their own sites on the Internet.

6.7   The future

There seems little doubt that at a time when some 50 million people have access to the Internet, and this number is expected to reach 200 million within two years, the world has shrunk rapidly by virtue of the ability to communicate cheaply and instantly over the Internet, there is a serious and urgent need to regulate the situation internationally by means of a treaty or convention.

A survey conducted by Ernst & Young discloses that about 13 per cent of 130 financial services companies surveyed in seven countries use the Internet for transactions with customers and that by 1999 this is expected to leap to 60 per cent, and to 87 per cent for US businesses[15].

---

15   (1997) *The Times,* 6 June.

Chapter 7

Credit Advertisements

7.1 Meaning of credit advertisement

'Credit' includes a cash loan and any other form of financial accommodation[1]. It is very widely defined so as to include every form of deferment of payment permitted by the creditor.

Credit advertisements are governed by the Consumer Credit Act 1974 and the Consumer Credit (Advertisements) Regulations 1989[2] (in this chapter referred to as 'regulated credit advertisements') if they fall within the parameters set out below. Otherwise they are unregulated save for provisions which apply generally to all advertising.

An advertisement is regulated if it is published for the purposes of a business carried on by the advertiser indicating that he is willing to provide credit[3]. The business referred to must be one of consumer credit or consumer hire or a business in the course of which the advertiser provides credit to individuals secured on land or a business which comprises or relates to unregulated credit agreements or unregulated hire agreements where the law applicable to those agreements is that of a country outside the United Kingdom and if they were governed by United Kingdom law, they would be regulated agreements[4].

A credit advertisement is not regulated if it indicates that the credit must exceed the limit of a consumer credit agreement (ie £15,000 or such higher

---

1   Section 9(1), Consumer Credit Act 1974.
2   Section 189 *ibid* for definition of 'advertisement' and SI 1985 No 1125 generally; 'credit advertisement' is defined in r 1(2) *ibid*. The Regulations are set out in Appendix 1.
3   Section 43(1) *ibid*.
4   Section 43(2) *ibid*.

sum as may be prescribed by regulation from time to time) and that no security is required or that the security required is to consist of property other than land, or that the credit advertised is available only to a body corporate[5]. In other words, a credit advertisement for credit to an individual in any sum secured on property will always be a regulated credit advertisement. Advertisements for mortgages are therefore always regulated credit advertisements.

7.2 Credit advertisements exempt from regulation[5bis]

In this section we shall briefly identify credit agreements which, but for the exemptions referred to below, would be regulated credit advertisements. They are the following:

(1) advertisements relating to consumer credit agreements referred to in art 3(1)(a), (c), and (d) of the Consumer Credit (Exempt Agreements) Order 1989[6]. These are credit agreements under which the number of payments to be made by the debtor does not exceed a specified number, generally four;

(2) advertisements relating to consumer credit agreements to which art 4(1)(b) of the said Order applies. This relates to consumer credit agreements where the rate of the total charge for credit does not exceed a specified rate;

(3) advertisements relating to consumer credit agreements to which art 5 of the said Order applies. This relates to certain consumer credit agreements having a connection with a country outside the United Kingdom;

(4) advertisements for business purposes where the advertiser expressly or by implication indicates that he is willing to provide credit for the purposes of a person's business and does not indicate, expressly or by implication, that he is willing to do so otherwise than for the purposes of such a business[7]. 'Business' does not include the business of a credit-broker.

---

5   Consumer Credit (Exempt Advertisements) Order 1985 (SI 1985 No 621).
5bis   Section 43(3) *loc cit.*
6   Consumer Credit (Exempt Agreements) Order 1989 (SI 1989 No 869) *loc cit.* This is essentially a consolidation of previous orders.
7   Consumer Credit (Advertisements) Regulations 1989 (SI 1989 No 1125), reg 9.

7.3 Carrying on a business

'Business' is defined as including a profession or trade[8]. A person is not to be treated as carrying on a particular type of business merely because occasionally he enters into transactions belonging to a business of that type[9]. In practice it is usually not difficult to distinguish between the operation of a business and the conduct of an activity which is not a business. Once it is established that the advertiser is carrying on a business, the nature of that business, be it a finance company, a retailer, a car dealer, dentist or any other business, is irrelevant.

7.4 Publication

The Consumer Credit Act applies to an advertisement published for the purposes of a business carried on by the advertiser. 'Publication' is not restricted in any way and is therefore to be construed in its widest sense. Thus, publication would include dissemination of information by a poster, a circular letter, a notice in a newspaper or other publication, a card or price tag placed in a store or on an article for sale. Publication may also be on film, by sound, laser or in any other visible or audible form.

There is no requirement that publication should be to the public at large or to a section of the public.

7.5 Indication of willingness to provide credit

The consumer credit regime applies to advertisements indicating a willingness to provide credit. This expression is also found in the parameters applying to intermediate credit advertisements[10].

An indication of willingness to provide credit has a wider connotation than a statement of willingness to do so. The meaning of an indication of willingness to provide credit was the subject matter of the leading case of *Jenkins v Lombard North Central plc*[11]. In that case Lombard North Central which provided a wide range of financial services to the public on a nation-wide scale supplied a car dealer with stickers to be placed on cars offered for sale. The stickers displayed the price of the car and the company's name and logo. It was argued for the prosecution that each sticker constituted an advertisement

---

8   Section 189(1) *ibid.*
9   Section 189(2) *ibid* and see *Hare v Schwek* [1993] CCLR 47 CA, *R v Marshall* (1989) 90 Cr App Rep 73 CA.
10   Advertisements Regulations *loc cit* Sched 1, Part II, para 10.
11   [1984] 1 All ER 828.

indicating that the company was willing to provide credit facilities for the purchase of cars. On appeal from the dismissal of the prosecution's case, the court held that a suggestion of credit is not enough, particularly where the suggestion is derived in part from the knowledge of the advertiser's business, obtained not from the advertisement itself. An advertiser indicates that he is willing to provide credit only if he states in some way as a fact, rather than merely suggests, that he is willing to provide credit. It is submitted that a sticker stating the cash price and bearing the name of a company which was clearly a credit or finance company eg 'A1 Finance plc' would likewise not constitute an indication of willingness to provide credit as the sticker itself does not state as a fact that the company is willing to provide credit.

In contrast to the *Jenkins* decision is *Jessop v First National Securities Ltd*[12]. This is a decision of the Sheriff's Court in Scotland where it was held that a picture of credit cards accompanied by the expression 'lower rate of interest' and followed by the word 'no' was an indication that the advertiser was offering better terms than any of the other advertised credit companies. The decision was correctly held to be within the purview of reg 7(b) of the Consumer Credit (Advertisements) Regulations[13] which requires a comparative credit advertisement to take the form of a full credit advertisement together with an indication of the comparable terms of the other advertisers.

The *Jenkins* case is authority too for the proposition that the courts will not refer to the regulations under the Consumer Credit Act in order to assist them to construe the provisions of that Act[14].

7.6   General requirements of regulated credit advertisements

7.6.1   Misleading information

An advertisement may not convey information which is in a material respect false or misleading or information stating or implying an intention on the advertiser's part which he has not got. In each case the advertiser commits an offence[15].

In *Metsoja v H Norman Pitt & Co Ltd*[16] the Divisional Court held that a credit advertisement advertising 0 per cent APR where the credit pur-

---

12   [1993] CCLR 33.
13   SI 1989 No 1125.
14   *Ibid* at p 833.
15   Section 46 *loc cit*.
16   [1990] CCLR 12.

chaser was in fact given a less favourable part-exchange allowance than a comparable cash purchaser was a misleading advertisement. The court stated that whilst it is true that the legislation does not prohibit lenders and purchasers from negotiating such terms as they choose, it does prevent prospective purchasers from being misled by an advertisement into thinking superficially attractive credit terms involve no greater financial outlay on their part than a cash transaction, if that is not the case. Likewise, in *Roller Group Ltd and Roller Finance Ltd v Sumner*[17] an advertisement was held misleading where the price quoted for a new car was stated exclusive of the cost of delivery, road fund tax and number plates. A contravention of s 46 of the Act does not require that the false or misleading information relates to the terms of credit. On the other hand, advertisements containing false or misleading information could equally be the subject of a prosecution under the Consumer Protection Act 1987 or the Trade Descriptions Act 1968.

In *Currys Ltd v Alexander Smethurst Jessop*[18] an advertisement featuring the statement 'nothing to pay for three months' was held to be misleading where payments only commenced after three months but interest in fact began to accrue immediately from the date of purchase. It is submitted that if the advertisement had clearly stated that interest ran immediately the statement would not have been found to be wanting.

7.6.2 Prohibition of advertisement where goods not sold for cash

If an advertisement indicates that the advertiser is willing to provide credit under a restricted-use credit agreement and at the time when the advertisement is published the advertiser is not holding himself as prepared to sell the goods or provide the services for cash, the advertiser commits an offence[19].

7.7 Form and content of regulated credit advertisements

7.7.1 Regulations

The Act[20] makes provision for the Secretary of State to make regulations governing the form and content of advertisements. The governing regulations are the Consumer Credit (Advertisements) Regulations 1989[21].

---

17 [1995] CCLR 1.
18 [1988] CCLR 25.
19 Section 45 *loc cit.*
20 Section 44 *loc cit.*
21 SI 1989 No 1125.

A credit advertisement must fit into one of three categories of advertisement: a simple credit advertisement, an intermediate credit advertisement or a full credit advertisement[22]. The specified information which these advertisements must contain must be clearly and easily legible (and in the case of sound advertisements this is generally interpreted as meaning 'audible'). Save for the name and address or telephone number of the advertiser, the specified information must be shown together as a whole. However, the Advertisements Regulations are not as strict as the regulations relating to regulated agreements which require the specified information to be shown not only together as a whole, but also not interspersed with other information. Information in any book, catalogue, leaflet or other document which is likely to vary from time to time is deemed to be shown together as a whole if it is set out together as a whole in a separate document issued with the book, catalogue, leaflet or other document and the other information in the credit advertisement is shown together as a whole[22bis]. Typical examples are rate cards and other loose-leaf information specifying the rate of charge for credit which is correct at the time of publication but may well vary subsequently when it will be replaced by a rate card showing the new rate of charge.

7.7.2 Representative terms

As information may vary from one type of transaction to another the Advertisements Regulations make provision for the inclusion of representative terms or typical examples[23]. In a credit advertisement where the advertisement refers to transactions of a particular class and the APR in the advertisement or the cash price and the frequency, number or amount of any payment or charge or any repayment of credit for the total amount payable by the debtor may vary from one transaction to another in the same class, the advertisement may contain representative information. This is information shown as a typical example which the advertiser may reasonably expect at the date the information is published to be representative of transactions of the class in question, being transactions which he might then reasonably contemplate that he would enter into on or after that date[23bis]. There will not be compliance with this requirement if an advertiser who is a dealer in furniture is willing to provide credit in respect of

---

22   Regulation 2 *ibid.*
22bis   Regulation 2(6) *ibid.*
23   Regulation 3 *ibid.*
23bis   Regulation 3(3) *ibid.*

furniture with a cash price exceeding £1,000 but the advertisement contains a typical example with a cash price of £100. Similarly, where the advertiser is willing to provide interest-free credit only on purchases for a sum in excess of £3,000, the typical example in the advertisement may not relate to purchases of less than that sum. Indeed, not only would these advertisements not comply with the relevant regulations but they would be misleading.

7.8   Special provisions applying to credit advertisements

7.8.1   Credit advertisements in dealers' publications

The Advertisements Regulations contain provisions relating to dealers' publications covering a calendar or seasonal period. These advertisements need not comply with the requirements of a simple, intermediate or full credit advertisement provided that they contain certain minimal information. The information required is the name of the creditor, credit-broker or dealer and a postal address of his, with or without his occupation or a statement of the general nature of his occupation and an indication that individuals may obtain on request a quotation in writing about the terms on which the advertiser is prepared to do business[24].

7.8.2   Full credit advertisements in dealers' publications

Owing to the difficulty of stating all credit information in relation to a full credit advertisement wherever the cash price is stated in a dealer's catalogue, the regulations permit the splitting of information. Either the catalogue may show the cash price with all the remaining particulars set out together elsewhere or it may show the cash price and specified financial particulars, with the remaining information set out elsewhere. There must also be an indication as to the goods or services to which the information relates[25].

7.8.3   Credit advertisements on dealers' premises[26]

So as to enable dealers to advertise the credit price of goods without having to state the credit particulars whenever the cash price is stated, the Advertise-

---

24   Regulation 4 *ibid.*
25   Regulation 5 *ibid.*
26   Regulation 6 *ibid.*

ments Regulations permit the advertiser to separate off the bulk of the credit information into a separate advertisement, which might be contained in a poster, placard or other form of display. The credit information so tagged off must, in the case of goods, be clearly marked on or displayed in close proximity to the goods and in the case of services, displayed at any place on the premises at which customers may enquire about them. In addition, the information must contain an indication that other information relating to the supply of goods or services on credit is displayed on the premises. The information contained in the two parts of the split advertisement will together constitute an intermediate credit or a full credit advertisement. The information detached from the main advertisement is limited to the following:

(1) the cash price (eg a price tag on goods); or
(2) the cash price and details of the APR (in the case of an intermediate credit advertisement) or total amount payable (in the case of a full credit advertisement).

The 'split credit' advertisement rules only apply to a situation where the advertisement is conspicuously displayed on the dealer's premises and specifies goods or services the acquisition of which from the dealer may be financed by credit and may be acquired from that part of the premises. The expression 'specifies' means more than 'indicates'. It means that there can be no doubt but that the advertisement refers to the goods or services in question.

7.8.4   Restrictions on certain expressions in credit advertisements

(a)   The expression 'overdraft'[26bis]

An advertisement may not contain the expression 'overdraft' or any similar expression describing any agreement for running-account credit except if it refers to an agreement enabling the debtor to overdraw on a current account. The term 'current account' is defined as an account under which the customer may, by means of cheques or similar orders payable to himself or to any other person or by any means, obtain or have the use of money held or made available by the person with whom the account is kept and which records alterations in the financial relationship between the person and the customer[27]. A current account with an overdraft facility in any event enjoys privileged status under the Consumer Credit Act[28].

26bis   Regulation 7(a) *ibid.*
27   Regulation 1(2) *ibid.*
28   See s 74(1)(b).

(b) Expressions indicative of comparative advertisements[29]

A credit advertisement may not include an indication, whether express or implied, that any of the terms of a credit agreement impose on customers a lesser expense or obligation than is being imposed by other persons except:

(1) in the case of a full credit advertisement
(2) which states in close proximity to that indication, with no less particularity and prominence, the other persons concerned and their comparable terms.

This provision is important in practice as it is sufficiently extensive to include advertisements which impliedly indicate a comparison of terms with other credit grantors. It is restricted to comparisons which suggest that the advertiser is imposing a lesser expense or obligation than is being imposed by other persons.

In *Carrington Carr Ltd v Leicestershire County Council*[30] an advertisement for a low-start mortgage scheme contained words stating that borrowers would be 'paying a lot less the next month' and 'maybe even less in the future'. The Divisional Court ruled that the advertisements held out a promise that anyone who took advantage of the scheme was likely to be better off than under his or her previous arrangements and that therefore the advertisement constituted a breach of the relevant regulation. Likewise in *Jessop v First National Securities Ltd*[31] an advertisement featuring credit cards with the word 'no' alongside the statement 'lower rate of interest' was held to indicate that the advertiser was offering better terms than any other person.

There is no restriction on a bland statement of fact which does not constitute a comparative advertisement eg 'low interest rate', 'easy repayment terms'; nor does the provision apply to a comparison by the advertiser of its current terms compared to previous terms eg 'our best ever offer', 'our lowest ever rate'.

It is submitted that reference to 'our competitive rates' is not necessarily a comparative statement as it may amount to no more than a statement that 'our rates are comparable with those of our competitors'[32].

(c) The expression 'interest free'[33]

An advertiser may not use the expression 'interest free' or any expression to the like effect eg 0 per cent APR, indicating that a customer is liable to pay

---

29 Regulation 7(b), Advertisements Regulations *loc cit*.
30 [1994] CCLR 14.
31 [1993] CCLR 33.
32 See definition in the *Concise Oxford Dictionary*
33 Regulation 7(c), Advertisements Regulations.

no greater amount in respect of a transaction financed by credit than he would be liable to pay as a cash purchaser, except where the total amount payable by the debtor does not exceed the cash price. In other words, the expression 'interest free' must genuinely mean what it says.

The Advertisements Regulations define 'cash price'[33bis] as meaning the price or charge at which goods, services, land or other things may be purchased by, or supplied to, persons for cash, account being taken of any discount generally available from the dealer or supplier in question. Likewise 'cash purchaser' is defined in the regulations as a person who, for a money consideration, acquires goods, land or other things or is provided with services under the transaction which is not financed by credit[34]. It follows that if a dealer generally offers goods at a discount for cash, the discounted price is the cash price not only in cash transactions but also for the purposes of credit transactions. Therefore any 'interest free' promotion must be based upon the discounted cash price. The position would be otherwise where the discount off the cash price is a one-off discount given to a particular customer, for whatever reason, in which event it would not be a 'discount generally available from the dealer or supplier in question'.

In *Metsoja v H Norman Pitt & Co Ltd*[35] the Divisional Court held that an advertisement offering 0 per cent APR where the credit purchaser was given a less favourable part-exchange allowance than a cash purchaser was a misleading advertisement which infringed the regulations. It is of no avail for the advertiser to promote credit as allegedly interest free when it is not accompanied by an explanation as to its meaning. Thus, in *Ford Credit plc v Procurator Fiscal*[36] the High Court of Justiciary found the words '0 per cent finance or 10 per cent discount' offensive, holding that the first words were the equivalent of interest free and that the suggestion of an alternative did not ameliorate the mischief created. It rejected the argument that as the position was clear from the wording there was nothing misleading about the advertisement. The restriction is literally construed and as the credit customer had to pay more than he would as a cash customer, a breach of the regulations was established. There have been many unreported convictions of traders who have contravened this prohibition by failing to take into account discounts generally offered by them when advertising 0 per cent interest or interest-free credit.

33bis   Regulation 1(2) *ibid.*
34   Regulation 1(2), Advertisements Regulations *loc cit.*
35   [1990] CCLR 12.
36   [1993] CCLR 83.

(d)   The expression 'no deposit'[37]

An advertisement may not feature the statement 'no deposit' or any expression to the like effect except where the customer is not required to make any advance payment. The expression 'advance payment' includes any deposit but does not include a repayment of credit or any insurance premium or any amount entering into the total charge for credit[38].

7.9   Analysis of content of credit advertisements

7.9.1   Credit advertisements

Credit advertisements fall into three categories: a simple credit advertisement, an intermediate credit advertisement and a full credit advertisement[39]. It is important to note that the advertisement must fit into one or other of such categories and comply with the requirements of such category in order not to contravene the Consumer Credit Act and the Advertisements Regulations made under it.

7.9.2   Information in credit advertisements

Any credit advertisement, be it a simple, intermediate or full credit advertisement, may contain any information whatsoever except that information relating to credit is strictly controlled either by reference to the maximum information that the advertisement may contain or the minimum information that it must contain. If the information exceeds that permitted in a simple credit advertisement the advertisement must be drafted as an intermediate credit advertisement: if the information exceeds that permitted by an intermediate credit advertisement it must be drafted as a full credit advertisement.

7.9.3   Simple credit advertisements[40]

A simple credit advertisement is very restricted in the information it may contain. The following is the maximum information allowed:

(1) the name of the advertiser. In the Advertisements Regulations references to the name of any person is, in the case of a person covered

37   Regulation 7(d), Advertisements Regulations.
38   Regulation 1(2) *ibid.*
39   Regulation 2(1) *ibid.*
40   Advertisements Regulations, Sched 1, Part I.

by a standard licence under the Consumer Credit Act, a reference
to any name of his specified in the licence. Thus, it would suffice to
refer to the advertiser's name as 'Barclaycard' without having to refer
to Barclays Bank plc. In the case of a person not covered by a standard licence, the name is that under which he carries on business, ie
his trade name;

(2) a logo of the advertiser, of his associate and of his trade association;
(3) a postal address of the advertiser;
(4) a telephone number of the advertiser; and
(5) an occupation of the advertiser or a statement of the general nature
of his occupation.

As already indicated, the advertisement may contain any other information except for information that a person is willing to provide credit or the
cash price, or other price, of any goods, services, land or other things.

Examples of simple credit advertisements are:

(1) Busy Bee Mortgages Ltd
(2) Pedigree Credit, telephone 073549, for car finance.

7.9.4   Intermediate credit advertisements[41]

The Advertisements Regulations stipulate compulsory information which
each intermediate credit advertisement must contain and certain optional
information which it may contain. The compulsory information together
with the optional information constitute the maximum information which
an intermediate credit advertisement may contain. If the credit advertisement is to exceed such information it must be converted into a full credit
advertisement and comply with the requirements of a full credit advertisement. If it does not, it contravenes the Advertisements Regulations.

(a)   Compulsory information

An intermediate credit advertisement must contain the following
minimum information:

(1) The name and address or telephone number (or a freephone
number) of the advertiser. Strictly speaking, the postal address or
telephone number (or freephone number) are alternatives and
cannot both be contained in the advertisement.

The foregoing information is not required in the case of

---

41   *Ibid* Sched 1, Part II.

advertisements in any form on the premises of a dealer or creditor unless the advertisement is in writing which customers are intended to take away; in the case of advertisements which include the name and address of a dealer; and in the case of advertisements which include the name of a credit-broker and a postal address or telephone number (or freephone number) of the creditbroker.

(2) Security: a statement that any security is or may be required and where the security comprises or may comprise a mortgage or charge on the debtor's home a statement in the following form:

YOUR HOME IS AT RISK IF YOU DO NOT KEEP UP REPAYMENTS ON A MORTGAGE OR OTHER LOAN SECURED ON IT.

(3) Insurance: a statement of any contract of insurance required, not being a contract of insurance against the risk of loss of damage to goods or land or any use relating to the use of goods or land.

(4) Deposit of money in an account: a statement of any requirement to place on deposit any sum of money in any account with any person.

(5) Credit-broker's fee: this need only be stated in an advertisement published for the purposes of a business of credit brokerage.

(6) Information about terms of business: a statement that individuals may obtain on request in writing the terms on which the advertiser is prepared to do business, eg 'a written quotation is available on request'; or a statement that individuals may obtain on request a document containing no less information than a full credit advertisement. The latter provision is rarely resorted to; indeed the original Consumer Credit (Quotations) Regulations 1989 were revoked in March 1997.

(7) APR: this need only be stated in any of the following circumstances:

(a) where a cash price is given in the advertisement relating to any specified goods, services, land or other things having a particular cash price, the acquisition of which from an identified dealer may be financed by credit, eg 'new Renault Clio' (unless the total cash price does not exceed the credit price when it suffices to set out a statement to this effect). Because of this requirement intermediate credit advertisements which do not state the APR should not be placed near goods displaying a cash price;

(b) where the advertisement specifies the rate of interest on the credit; or

(c) where the advertisement specifies whether an advance payment is required.

Where the amount of any item included in the total price for credit will or may be varied, the advertisement must include a statement to such effect. There is no need to state that the APR itself is variable although in practice this is usually included.

(8) Cash price: in the case of an advertisement relating to a debtor-creditor-supplier agreement, where the advertisement specifies goods, services, land or other things having a particular cash price, the acquisition of which from an identified dealer may be financed by credit, the advertisement must state such cash price. 'Specifies' means that the goods etc are sufficiently described so that they have an identifiable price.

(9) Foreign currency mortgages: where the advertisement is for a mortgage or loan secured on property and repayments are to be made in a currency other than sterling, the advertisement must contain a statement in the following form:

THE STERLING EQUIVALENT OF YOUR LIABILITY UNDER A FOREIGN CURRENCY MORTGAGE MAY BE INCREASED BY EXCHANGE RATE MOVEMENTS

(b) Optional information

An intermediate credit advertisement may contain any information whatsoever except that additional information relating to credit is restricted to the following:

(1) A logo of the advertiser, of his associate and of his trade association.

(2) An occupation of the advertiser or a statement of the general nature of his occupation. Under this head one might be permitted to state eg 'providers of mortgage facilities', 'credit-brokers', 'home and general financiers'.

(3) Credit facilities: a statement that credit facilities are or that a specified category of credit facility is available, and where applicable a statement indicating the period or the maximum period of availability.

This head of additional information permits the obvious type of description of credit facilities eg 'all types of vehicle finance available, including leasing, rental, contract hire and general credit facilities'. The period of availability refers to the period during which the facility is available eg 'special contract hire facilities available during the promotional period until 18 August'. However, 'category of credit facility' is not defined in the

Consumer Credit Act or the regulations made under it and accordingly, in the writer's view, it can be used to refer to any category of credit facility recognised in law or established in commercial or business practice eg hire purchase, conditional sale, discounted mortgage, cashback mortgage, credit card facility with Air Miles.

(4) In the case of credit which is available only to, or on terms which are applicable only to persons who fall within any class or group, a statement of that fact identifying that class or group. Examples include promotions available only to holders of store cards, discounted mortgages available only to first-time buyers, credit offers available only to employees.

(5) Where the APR is not required to be stated (as to which see above), it may be stated by way of optional information.

(6) Where the APR is specified in the advertisement, the rate of any interest on the credit.

(7) The amount of credit which may be provided under the credit agreement or an indication of one or both of the maximum and minimum amounts of credit which may be provided.

(8) The nature of any security required where this does not comprise a mortgage or charge on the debtor's home (the latter information, of course, being compulsory).

(9) Where the APR is specified in the advertisement, a statement as to whether an advance payment is required and if so the amount or minimum amount of the payment expressed as a sum of money or as a percentage.

(10) A statement indicating any respect in which cash purchasers are treated differently from credit purchasers. In certain circumstances, a failure to include this information can in fact amount to an offence. Section 45, Consumer Credit Act provides that if an advertisement indicates that the advertiser is willing to provide credit under a restricted-use credit agreement but at the time when the advertisement is published he does not hold himself as being prepared to sell the goods or provide the services for cash, he commits an offence. Furthermore, s 46 provides that if an advertisement conveys information which is in a material respect false and misleading, the advertiser commits an offence. Information stating or implying an intention on the advertiser's part which he has not got is false. Accordingly, in the context of certain advertisements, the so-called 'optional information' under this head would be peremptory. An example would be where cash purchasers are given a cashback when they buy goods but credit purchasers are not.

This head of optional information opens a window of opportunity for the draftsman of intermediate credit advertisements as it can be used to permit information which is indicative of willingness to provide credit which would not otherwise fall under any other head of permitted information. It allows a credit grantor to advertise incentives, bonus points, loyalty points and the like to users of credit if the same benefits are not made available to cash purchasers.

(11) In the case of an advertisement which includes the name of a credit-broker and his postal address or telephone number (or his freephone number) the advertisement may also contain the name of the creditor and the corresponding details.

7.9.5   Full credit advertisements[42]

Needless to say, full credit advertisements require minimum information which exceeds the compulsory information in intermediate credit advertisements. The requirements are the initial compulsory information of intermediate credit advertisements plus certain additional information. The compulsory (or minimum) information required in full credit advertisements is as follows:

(1) The name and a postal address of the advertiser. Unlike the position under intermediate credit advertisements, a telephone number or freephone telephone number cannot be supplied as an alternative to the advertiser's postal address.

The same exceptions to the requirement of stating the name and address of the advertiser apply as in intermediate credit advertisements, as to which see above.

(2) Security: where the security required is a mortgage or charge on the debtor's home, the same provision applies as set out above in relation to intermediate credit advertisements.

(3) Insurance: the same requirements apply as with intermediate credit advertisements, as to which see above.

(4) Deposit of money in an account: the same requirements apply as with intermediate credit advertisements, as to which see above.

(5) Credit-broker's fee: the requirements are the same as for intermediate credit advertisements, as to which see above.

(6) A statement that individuals may obtain on request a quotation in

---

42   Advertisements Regulations, Sched 1, Part III.

writing about the terms on which the advertiser is prepared to do business. Usually this takes the form of a statement that a written quotation is available upon request. There is no compliance with this requirement if it does not include reference to 'writing' eg if the advertisement states 'please ask for details'.

(7) APR: the APR must be stated unless the advertisement relates to credit under which (and indicates that) the total amount payable by the debtor does not exceed the total cash price of the goods, services, or other things to be financed by the credit agreement.

Where an item entering into the calculation of the APR is variable the advertisement must contain a statement indicating that fact. In practice it is expressed by referring to the APR as variable. Although strictly speaking this is incorrect and does not meet the requirements of the regulations it is submitted that it achieves the same objective and, indeed, in a way which is more comprehensible to the public.

(8) Restricted offers of credit to a class or group of persons: in the case of any credit which is available only to, or on terms which are applicable only to, persons who fall within any class or group, a statement of that fact identifying that class or group, eg first-time buyers, existing credit card holders, current account holders. This requirement is the same as the equivalent head under optional information in intermediate credit advertisements (as to which see above).

(9) The nature of any security required where this does not comprise a mortgage or charge on the debtor's home.

(10) A statement of the frequency and number of any advance payments required and of the amount or minimum amount expressed as a sum of money or as a percentage or a statement indicating the manner in which the amount will be determined.

(11) A statement indicating any respect in which cash purchasers are treated differently from those requiring goods, land, services or other things, under a transaction financed by credit. This head corresponds to the equivalent head under optional information in intermediate credit advertisements (as to which see above).

(12) The frequency, number and amount of repayments of credit: a distinction is drawn between the information required to be stated for running-account credit and fixed-sum credit. In the case of running-account credit, reference must be made to the frequency of the repayments of credit and of the amount of each payment stating whether it is a fixed or minimum amount or indicating the

manner in which the amount will be determined. In practice stating whether it is a fixed or minimum amount can be confusing. For example, in the case of an option account a statement that the monthly payments are fixed might suggest, contrary to the truth, that the debtor cannot increase his monthly payment at will. On the other hand, to describe it as a minimum payment defeats the objective of portraying such accounts as being generally payable by equal monthly payments. Presumably the legal requirement is intended to reflect the fixed monthly payment in budget accounts (where the credit limit is expressed as a multiple of the monthly payment) and the minimum monthly payment in option accounts (where the debtor can pay the monthly outstanding indebtedness in full). However, it is an illustration of where the statement of legal requirements and product characteristics conflict.

In the case of fixed-sum credit advertisements the advertisement must contain a statement of the frequency, number and amount of repayments of credit.

The advertisement may not refer to a repayment by reference to the 'weekly equivalent' or any expression to the like effect unless weekly payments or other periodical payments are provided for under the agreement.

(13) Other payments and charges: the advertisement must contain a statement indicating the description and amount of any other payments and charges which may be payable under the transaction. Where the liability cannot be ascertained at the date the advertisement is published it must contain a statement indicating the description of the payment and the circumstances in which it may arise.

There is no requirement to include reference to default charges or other payments which become due in the event of the debtor not fulfilling his obligations.

(14) Total amount payable by the debtor: the advertisement must state the total amount payable by the debtor and by reference to a typical example where necessary.

This requirement does not apply where the total amount payable by the debtor does not exceed the cash price or in the case of running-account credit where the advertisement does not specify goods, services, land or other things having a particular cash price, the acquisition of which may be financed by credit.

(15) Cash price: this requirement is the same as that relating to intermediate credit advertisements, as to which see above.

(16) Foreign currency mortgage: this requirement is the same as that relating to intermediate credit advertisements as to which see above.

7.9.6 Prominence requirements of the Credit Advertisements Regulations[43]

(a) *APR*

The regulations require the statement of the APR to be afforded greater prominence than a statement relating to any other rate of charge and no less prominence than a statement relating to any period, the amount of any advance payment or any indication that no such payment is required or the amount, number or frequency of any other payment or charges or any repayment of credit. The APR need not be as prominent as the cash price.

The APR must be denoted as 'APR' or 'annual percentage rate' or 'annual percentage rate of the total charge for credit'.

The European Commission has adopted a proposal modifying the rules relating to the comparison of the cost of consumer credit by amending Council Directive 90/88/EEC. In addition to approving the term APR it will permit a percentage sign surrounded by 12 stars. The logo will be identical in all Member States.

(b) *Prominence of statutory notices*

Where the schedules to the Advertisements Regulations show prescribed wording in capital letters, this wording must be reproduced in the credit advertisement with no less prominence than any other information relating to credit.[43bis] Prominence does not necessarily require the statutory notices to be stated in capital letters; printing in bold, underlining, italics or a different colour might well suffice in the circumstances. Prominence is a relative issue and depends on the context of each advertisement.

7.10 A note on APR

The APR is the annual percentage rate of charge for credit determined in accordance with the Total Charge for Credit Regulations[44] and reflected as

---

43   Regulation 8 *ibid.*
43bis   Eg the statements set out in para 7.9.4(a)(2) and (9) *supra.*
44   Consumer Credit (Total Charge for Credit) Regulations 1980 (SI 1980 No 51) (as amended).

provided by Sched 3 to the Advertisements Regulations. The former sets out formulae for the calculation of the APR but there are in addition 15 parts of the Consumer Credit Tables setting out APRs and where the tables provide for an APR they prevail over any other calculation[45]. The tables are published by Her Majesty's Stationery Office.

Schedule 3 to the Advertisements Regulations provides *inter alia* permissible tolerances in the disclosure of the APR. There is sufficient compliance with the requirement to state the APR if the rate stated in the advertisement exceeds the APR by not more than one or falls short of the APR but not more than 0.1.

The statement of the APR assumes somewhat of a nonsense in circumstances of an initial fixed-rate loan or mortgage where, when advertised, the rate was either unusually high or low. The landmark cases on the subject were *National Westminster Bank v Devon County Council* and *Devon County Council v Abbey National plc*[46]. Interpreting reg 2(1)(d) of the Regulations, where the rate may vary during the period of the loan, the Divisional Court held that there was due compliance with the Regulations where the advertiser calculated the rate applying throughout the period of the loan on the basis of the original rate. This approach became the accepted practice and was certainly not disadvantageous to credit grantors at a time when rates were generally low although it would be unattractive when rates are high. As was pointed out in the judgment, the interpretation can lend itself to abuse where a disreputable lender secures an advantage by offering a very low rate of interest for a short fixed-interest period and calculates the APR on that basis. So as to avoid the advertisement constituting a misleading advertisement, although apparently complying with the Regulations, prudent advertisers might state that there is no certainty that the advertised APR rate will in fact apply throughout the period of the loan. Such a statement was in fact carried by the advertisers in the foregoing case.

In *Scarborough Building Society v Humberside Trading Standards Department*[47] the Divisional Court distinguished the facts of the case from those in the *Devon County Council* case. In the latter the advertised fixed-interest rate was 13.85 and 14.85. In the *Scarborough Building Society* case the Society advertised discount mortgages as from only 1 per cent, 1.1 per cent variable APR. In fact for the first six months the borrower was required to pay only 1 per cent interest (a discount of 7.5 per cent to the Society's variable rate of 8.45 per cent). Subsequently the borrower paid interest in

---

45   Regulation 10 *ibid.*
46   (1993) *The Times*, 16 July.
47   Unreported Case Co/3332/96 dated 14 November 1996.

different stages at varying discounted rates from the Society's prevailing variable base rate. After two years the borrower would pay the Society's standard variable base rate. The Divisional Court was again faced with the question of interpreting the meaning of reg 2(1)(d) of the Total Charge for Credit Regulations which utilises the expression 'variation of the rate . . . in consequence of the occurrence . . . of any event . . .; 'event' . . . does not include an event which is certain to occur'. The court rejected the metaphysical question as to whether an event was 'certain' to happen and instead substituted the pragmatic test of whether, for all practical purposes, a change of interest rate from 1 per cent was bound to occur. Whilst there was a possibility that the rate would not change from the initial 1 per cent, the court held such a possibility to be so remote that it could be ignored. After all, opined the court, judges and magistrates are supposed to exercise common sense from time to time and are not expected to be entirely ignorant of everything that happens in the world.

The encouraging feature of the *Scarborough Building Society*'s decision is the realistic and commonsense interpretative approach of the courts to the Total Charge for Credit Regulations. However, the facts in the *Devon County Council* case and the *Scarborough Building Society* case are at opposite ends of the interest rate spectrum so as to justify diametrically opposed conclusions. This is wholly unsatisfactory in practice as the credit grantor is required to guess which principles will apply in given circumstances and will be left floundering in borderline situations. It is all the more disquieting as the APR is calculated on the basis of mathematical formulae with quantitative constituents.

The following principles can be derived from the *Devon* and *Scarborough* cases:

(1) the same test is to be applied to a fixed-rate mortgage as is applied to a discounted rate mortgage;

(2) a commonsense approach is to be applied to the test of 'certainty' in reg 2(1)(d) of the Total Charge for Credit Regulations;

(3) the test in determining the issue of 'certainty' involves a degree of subjectivity;

(4) the relative uncertainty arising from the decisions renders the possibility of making comparisons between different APRs less effective;

(5) promotional literature citing the APR should further amplify or explain it so that it is not misleading;

(6) as a misstatement of the APR in an advertisement constitutes a criminal offence the courts will construe the language of the regulations strictly and literally.

LACOTS (the local authorities co-ordinating body on food and trading standards) has issued its own guidelines on the application of the *Devon* and *Scarborough* cases. It distinguishes between what it describes as a 'heavily discounted' product and a 'lightly discounted' product. A heavily discounted product is one where a rate change upwards at the end of the fixed or discounted period is for all practical purposes bound to happen. The APR should not therefore, in its view, be calculated on the assumption that the initial low interest rate will continue for the lifetime of the agreement. A lightly discounted product is one where there is a real possibility, albeit remote, that the rate will not change. In the latter circumstances the principle established in *Devon* would apply and the APR should be calculated on the basis that no rate change will take place.

The practical difficulty is to establish where to draw the dividing line between a 'heavily discounted' loan product and a 'lightly discounted' loan product.

7.11   The Banking Code and the Mortgage Code

The Banking Code, now in its third edition, and the new Mortgage Code, are voluntary codes adopted by banks, building societies and other lenders in their relations with personal customers in the UK.

The Codes have almost identical provisions in relation to the common ground covered by them and require all advertising and promotional material to be clear, fair, reasonable and not misleading.

7.12   Enforcement

The enforcement of the provisions of the Consumer Credit Act relating to false or misleading advertisements and compliance with the Advertisements Regulations is provided for in s 46, 47 and 167(2) of the Act. Not only does the advertiser commit an offence but the like offence is committed by the publisher of the advertisement; any person, who in the course of a business carried on by him, devised the advertisement or part of it relevant to the offence and any person who procured the publication of the advertisement[48].

Defences are contained in the Act. It is a defence for the publisher of the advertisement to prove that the advertisement was published in the course of a business carried on by him, that he received the advertisement in the course of that business and did not know and had no reason to suspect that

---

48   Section 47(1) *loc cit.*

its publication would be an offence[49]. It is also a defence for any person charged to prove that his act or omission was due to a mistake, to reliance on information supplied to him, to any act or omission by another person, or to an accident or some other cause beyond his control and that he took all reasonable precautions and exercised all due diligence to avoid such an act or omission[50]. In *Coventry City Council v Lazarus* the Divisional Court held that once a precaution had been identified by the court as reasonable, and that precaution was not taken, that was the end of the due diligence defence[51].

7.13 Reflections on the Credit Advertisements Regulations

The Credit Advertisements Regulations are extremely complex and some-what artificial in their requirements and application. One would be justified in asking whether the objective of the Advertisements Regulations, and at times an even fairer representation of the position, could not be achieved by a less rigid and formalistic regime.

Checklist

Information in Credit Advertisements

Key

C=Compulsory
O=Optional
S=Same as Intermediate
P=Prohibited

Information	*Simple*	*Intermediate*	*Full*
Name of advertiser	O	C (subject to certain exceptions)	S
Logo of advertiser (or of his associate or trade association)	O	O	O
Postal address of advertiser	O	C (or telephone or freephone number subject to certain exceptions)	C

---

49 Section 47(2) *loc cit.*
50 Section 168(1) and (2) *loc cit.*
51 [1996] CCLR 5.

Telephone number of advertiser	O	C (or address) (subject to certain exceptions)	O
Occupation of advertiser	O No other information relating to willingness to provide credit or the cash or other price	O	O
Security	P	C (together with notice YOUR HOME IS AT RISK etc if applicable)	S
Insurance	P	C (except reference to insurance relating to risk of loss or damage to or use of goods or land)	S
Requirement of deposit money in an account	P	C	S
Credit-broker's fee	P	C	S
Information about terms of business/ quotation	P	C must refer to availability of written information	S
APR	P	C if cash price, interest rate or reference to advance payment (deposit) is stated; unless total amount payable equals cash price, when that must be indicated; otherwise O	C or statement indicating total amount payable equals cash price
Cash price	P	C if relating to debtor-creditor-supplier agreement and specifies goods etc having a particular cash price	S
Foreign currency, mortgages	P	C notice stating THE STERLING EQUIVALENT etc	S

Statement of available credit facilities and period of availability	P	O	O
Restricted offer to class or group	P	O	C
Interest	P	O provided APR shown	O
Credit amount (or maximum and/or minimum amount of credit)	P	O	O
Security not affecting debtor's home	P	O	C
Advance payment	P	O provided APR stated	C (including frequency, number and amount)
Different treatment of cash and credit purchasers	P	O	C
Name and address or telephone (or free-phone number) of creditor	P	O (where similar information stated about credit-broker)	O
Frequency, number and amount of repayments of credit	P	P	C
Other payments and charges	P	P	C
Total amount payable	P	P	C (unless equal to cash price or, in running-account credit, if advertisement does not specify goods etc having a particular cash price)

Chapter 8

Hire Advertisements

8.1 Meaning of hire advertisement

An advertisement relating to hire, lease or rental facilities is unregulated, except for provisions which apply to advertisements generally, unless it relates to regulated hire agreements. In the latter event it is governed by the Consumer Credit Act and the Advertisements Regulations made under it[1].

A consumer hire agreement is a regulated agreement if it is made by a person with an individual, the hirer for the bailment or in Scotland, the hiring, of goods; is capable of subsisting for more than three months, and does not require the hirer to make payments exceeding £15,000[1bis]. A consumer hire agreement is a regulated agreement if it is not an exempt agreement[1]. The only exempt consumer hire agreements are those where the owner is a body corporate which supplies gas, electricity or water and the subject of the agreement is metering equipment used in connection with the supply[2].

The Consumer Credit Act governs an advertisement published for the purposes of a business carried on by the advertiser indicating that he is willing to enter into an agreement for the bailment or in Scotland, the hiring, of goods by him unless the advertiser does not carry on a consumer credit business or consumer hire business or a business in the course of

---

1 Section 189, Consumer Credit Act 1974 and Consumer Credit (Advertisements) Regulations 1989 (SI 1989 No 1125), r 1(2). The Regulations are set out in Appendix 1.
1bis Section 15 *ibid*.
2 Section 16(6) *ibid* read with Consumer Credit (Exempt Agreements) Order 1989 (SI 1989 No 869), art 6 and the Consumer Credit (Exempt Advertisements) Order 1985 (SI 1985 No 62).

which he provides credit to individuals secured on land or a business which comprises or relates to unregulated agreements where, if the agreement was entered into in the UK, it would be a regulated agreement[3]. Unlike credit agreements, if a hire agreement is secured on land and the hirer is required to make payments exceeding £15,000 the advertisement does not become a regulated hire advertisement.

'Individuals' includes partnerships. However, an advertisement for hire facilities directed exclusively at incorporated companies or which indicates that the advertiser is not willing to enter into consumer hire agreements is exempt from regulation under the Consumer Credit Act[3bis].

The reader is referred to Chapter 7 in relation to the meaning of 'carrying on a business' and 'publication'.

8.2 General requirements of regulated hire advertisements

Advertisements for hire facilities must not convey information which is false or misleading in a material respect as otherwise the advertiser commits an offence. Information stating or implying an intention on the advertiser's part which he has not got is false[4].

The general offence created by the Act is separate and independent of offences created by virtue of breaches of the Advertisements Regulations. Thus, even though the advertisement might comply with the Advertisements Regulations the advertiser would be committing an offence if he advertised attractive terms of hire for vehicles when he was not in fact prepared to hire the vehicle on those terms or if he advertised his willingness to hire equipment for business purposes only when in fact he was also willing to hire equipment for non-business use.

8.3 Comparison of credit and hire advertisements

The general observation should be made that hire advertisements are subject to less stringent provisions than credit advertisements due to the fact that concepts of 'cash price' and the annual percentage rate of charge are alien to hire agreements.

---

3   Section 43(1) and (2) *ibid.*
3bis   Section 43(4) *ibid.*
4   Section 46(1) and (2).

8.4   Form and content of regulated hire agreements

(1) The provisions relating to regulated hire agreements are a mirror image of those relating to regulated credit agreements, discussed in Chapter 7[5]. The relevant regulations are the Consumer Credit (Advertisements) Regulations 1989[6]. They divide hire advertisements into three categories of advertisement and the publisher of an advertisement must ensure that the advertisement does indeed meet the requirements of one or other category[7]. The categories are as follows: a simple hire advertisement, an intermediate hire advertisement and a full hire advertisement. The information which these advertisements must contain is set out in Sched 2 to the Advertisements Regulations. It must be clear and easily legible and, subject to the latitude allowed in respect of information in any book, catalogue, leaflet or other document which is likely to vary from time to time, must be shown together as a whole, save for the name and address or telephone number which can be shown separately[8].

(2) Representative terms: as in the case of a credit advertisement where information contained in an advertisement may vary from one transaction of a particular class to another transaction of the same class, the advertisement may contain representative information ie information by way of a typical example of that class[9].

8.5   Information in hire advertisements[10]

As in the case of credit advertisements the regulations provide minimum and/or maximum information in hire advertisements which, as already observed, largely reflects the same criteria and information that apply to credit advertisements.

8.6   Simple hire advertisements[11]

Very limited information is permitted in these advertisements so that they are inevitably very rudimentary hire advertisements. The following is the maximum information permitted:

---

5   Chapter 7, para 7.7.
6   SI 1989 No 1125.
7   Regulation 2(2) *ibid.*
8   Regulation 2(6) and (7) *ibid.*
9   Regulation 3.
10   Sched 2 *ibid.*
11   Sched 2, *ibid*, Part I. See also the narrative to this under Simple Credit Advertisements, Chapter 7, para 7.9.3.

(1) the name of the advertiser;

(2) a logo of the advertiser, his associate and of his trade association;

(3) a postal address of the advertiser;

(4) a telephone number of the advertiser;

(5) an occupation of the advertiser or statement of the general nature of his occupation.

The advertisement may contain any other information except information that a person is willing to enter into a hire agreement and the cash price or other price of any goods.

8.7 Intermediate hire advertisements[12]

As with intermediate credit advertisements the regulations require minimum or compulsory information to be set out and permit certain additional optional information to be included in the advertisement.

8.7.1 Compulsory information

The following is the minimum information required in an intermediate hire advertisement:

(1) the name of the advertiser and his postal address or telephone number (or a freephone number) except that such information is not required if the advertisement is to remain on the premises of a dealer or owner, or if the advertisement already contains the name and address of the dealer or the name and postal address or telephone number (or freephone number) of a credit-broker;

(2) a statement indicating that the transaction advertised is the bailment of goods. Any equivalent expression is acceptable such as hiring, leasing, rental or contract hire. There is no equivalent requirement in the case of an intermediate credit advertisement;

(3) security: a statement that any security is, or may be, required and where it comprises a mortgage or charge on the hirer's home a statement in the following form:

YOUR HOME IS AT RISK IF YOU DO NOT KEEP UP PAYMENTS ON A HIRE AGREEMENT SECURED BY A MORTGAGE OR OTHER SECURITY ON YOUR HOME;

---

12   Sched 2 *ibid*, Part II.

(4) insurance: a statement of any contract of insurance required not being a contract of insurance against the risk of loss or damage to goods or any other risk relating to the use of the goods;

(5) deposit of money in an account: a statement of any requirement to place on deposit any sum of money in any account with any person. This does not refer to an advance payment or deposit under the hire agreement but to a deposit of money into an account in order to secure the hire agreement;

(6) credit-broker's fee: in the case of a credit brokerage advertisement the amount of any fee payable by the hirer or an associate of his to a credit-broker or statement of the method of its calculation must be set out in the advertisement;

(7) information about terms of business: the advertisement must contain a statement that individuals may obtain on request a quotation in writing or document containing no less information than in a full hire advertisement setting out the terms on which the advertiser is prepared to do business.

8.7.2   Optional information

The following optional information is permitted to be contained, but not required, in intermediate hire advertisements:

(1) a logo of the advertiser, of his associate and of his trade association;

(2) an occupation of the advertiser or statement of the general nature of his occupation. Eg ABC for long-term contract-hire and short-term rental facility; Worldwide TV and video rental equipment specialists;

(3) restricted offers of hire facilities to a class or group of persons: where hire facilities are only available to, or on terms which are applicable only to, persons who fall within any class or group a statement of that fact identifying that class or group. This head sometimes creates the opportunity to insert information which might otherwise exceed the maximum permitted information;

(4) nature of security not affecting the hirer's home;

(5) advance payment: a statement as to whether an advance payment or deposit is required and if so the amount or minimum amount of the payment expressed as a sum of money or as a percentage;

(6) duration of hire: the maximum or minimum period of the hire agreement may be stated. Regrettably there is no corresponding permission in intermediate credit advertisements to state the period of the loan;

(7) name and address or telephone number of the owner where the advertisement is that of a credit-broker.

8.8 Full hire advertisements[13]

Once again the requirements virtually mirror those of full credit advertisements and are as follows:

(1) the name and a postal address of the advertiser. It is not sufficient to state the telephone number or a freephone number of the advertiser as is permitted in an intermediate hire advertisement. The foregoing information is not required where the advertisement is on the premises of a dealer or owner and is not intended to be taken away by customers, or in the case of advertisements which include the name and address of a dealer or the name and the postal address of a credit broker;

(2) nature of transaction: this is the same requirement as in an intermediate hire advertisement;

(3) security: this is the same requirement as in an intermediate hire advertisement;

(4) insurance: this is the same requirement as in an intermediate hire advertisement;

(5) deposit: this is the same requirement as in an intermediate hire advertisement;

(6) credit-broker's fee: this is the same requirement as in an intermediate hire advertisement;

(7) quotation: a statement that individuals may obtain on request a quotation in writing about the terms on which the advertiser is prepared to do business;

(8) restricted offers of hire facilities to a class or group of persons: a statement of the fact indicating the class or group;

(9) nature of security not affecting the hirer's home: a statement of any security where this does not comprise a mortgage or charge on the hirer's home;

(10) frequency, number and amount of advance payments: the amount of any advance payment can be expressed as a sum of money, as a percentage or by way of a statement indicating the manner in which it is to be determined;

(11) duration of hire: where goods are to be bailed or hired for a fixed

---

13   Sched 2 *ibid*, Part III.

period a maximum or minimum period, a statement indicating this fact and the duration of that period;

(12) frequency and amount of hire payments: the frequency and amount of each hire payment stating if it is a minimum amount and where it may be varied, indicating that the amount will or may be varied and the circumstances in which it would happen. The expression 'weekly equivalent' or any expression of any other periodical equivalent may not be used unless this is the method of payment under the hire agreement;

(13) other payments and charges: a description and amount of any other payments and charges and where these cannot be ascertained when the advertisement is published a statement indicating a description of the payment in question and the circumstances in which the liability to make it will arise. There is no need to set out any payment payable in event of the hirer's default;

(14) variable payments and charges: where any payment or charge may be varied otherwise than in respect of a change in value added tax a statement indicating the same.

It is interesting to note that there is no requirement to state the total amount payable during a minimum or fixed hire period under the hire agreement, unlike the situation in a full credit advertisement where the advertisement must state the total amount payable by the debtor. Indeed, it is true to say that hire advertisements, including full hire advertisements, are much less informative than the corresponding credit advertisements. This is a failure in the advertising regime rather than a necessary consequence of the distinction between credit and hire.

8.9   Prominence requirements of advertisements regulations[14]

Once again the prominence requirements equate to those relating to credit advertisements save for the APR which is irrelevant to hire advertisements. Where words are shown in capital letters in any prescribed form of statement[15] they must be shown with no less prominence than any other information relating to hire.

---

14   Regulation 8 *ibid.*
15   Eg the statement set out in para 8.7.1(3) *supra.*

8.10 Enforcement

The provisions relating to the enforcement of the law in relation to hire facilities are identical to those applying to credit facilities, as to which see Chapter 7, para 7.12.

Checklist

Information in Hire Advertisements

Key

C=Compulsory
O=Optional
S=Same as Intermediate
P=Prohibited

Information	*Simple*	*Intermediate*	*Full*
Name of advertiser	O	C (subject to certain exceptions)	S
Logo of advertiser (or of his associate or trade association)	O	O	O
Postal address of advertiser	O	C (or telephone or freephone number subject to certain exceptions)	C
Telephone number of advertiser	O	C (or address) (subject to certain exceptions)	O
Occupation of advertiser	O	O	O
	No other information relating to willingness to enter into an agreement for the hire of goods or the cash or other price of goods		
Statement that transaction is for hire of goods	P (except as statement of advertiser's occupation)	C	S

Security	P	C (together with notice YOUR HOME IS AT RISK etc if applicable)	S
Insurance	P	C (except reference to insurance relating to risk of loss or damage to or use of goods or land)	S
Requirement of deposit money in an account	P	C	S
Credit-broker's fee	P	C	S
Information about terms of business/ quotation	P	C (must refer to availability of written information)	S
Restricted offer to class or group	P	O	C
Security not affecting hirer's home.	P	O	C
Advance payment	P	O	C (including frequency, number and amount)
Duration of hire	P	O	C (indicating whether fixed, maximum or minimum period)
Name and address or telephone (or free-phone number) of owner	P	O (where similar information stated about credit-broker)	O
Frequency and amount of hire payments	P	P	C (including, where variable, a statement to that effect and circumstances in which variable)
Other payments and charges	P	P	C
Variable payments and charges	P	P	C

Flowchart relating to regulated credit and hire advertisements (see Chapters 7 and 8)

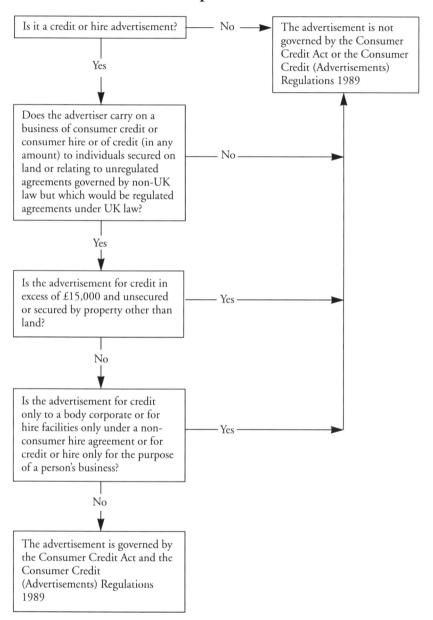

Is it a credit or hire advertisement? — No → The advertisement is not governed by the Consumer Credit Act or the Consumer Credit (Advertisements) Regulations 1989

Yes ↓

Does the advertiser carry on a business of consumer credit or consumer hire or of credit (in any amount) to individuals secured on land or relating to unregulated agreements governed by non-UK law but which would be regulated agreements under UK law? — No →

Yes ↓

Is the advertisement for credit in excess of £15,000 and unsecured or secured by property other than land? — Yes →

No ↓

Is the advertisement for credit only to a body corporate or for hire facilities only under a non-consumer hire agreement or for credit or hire only for the purpose of a person's business? — Yes →

No ↓

The advertisement is governed by the Consumer Credit Act and the Consumer Credit (Advertisements) Regulations 1989

Chapter 9

Advertisements for Current Accounts and Deposit Accounts

9.1 Overview

Advertisements for deposit accounts and current accounts are much less rigorously regulated than advertisements for credit facilities or hire facilities. This is largely due to the nature of the product, namely the fact that there are no provisions relating to repayment. The main concerns of the depositor are the rate of interest, the period of notice required to be given for repayment of the deposit and the security of the deposit or the creditworthiness of the deposit-taker. The latter is governed by other rules.

9.2 Code of conduct for the advertising of interest bearing accounts[1]

This code was drawn up by the British Bankers' Association, the Building Societies Association and the Finance Houses' Association (now the Finance and Leasing Association) and carries the approval of the Bank of England. The code applies to the advertising of all interest-bearing accounts maintained in the United Kingdom.

The following is a summary of the code's provisions:

---

1   December 1990; produced by the British Bankers' Association in conjunction with the Building Societies' Association and the Finance and Leasing Association (formerly the Finance Houses' Association).

(1) for the purposes of the code the term 'advertisement' includes press and broadcast advertisements, direct marketing, window displays, posters, brochures, leaflets and automated teller machine displays;

(2) advertisements must comply with the spirit and letter of the code, the British Code of Advertising Practice, the Independent Broadcasting Authority Code and with any relevant legislation;

(3) advertisers of interest-bearing accounts must take special care to ensure that members of the general public are fully aware of the nature of any commitment into which they may enter as a result of responding to an advertisement;

(4) the registered or business name (and in the case of press advertisements, direct marketing, brochures and leaflets, the address) of the deposit-taking institution must be clearly stated;

(5) where an agent advertises a deposit-taking facility on behalf of a principal or a principal indicates that it will accept deposits through an agent it must be made clear which body is agent and which is principal;

(6) interest rates may not be advertised unless they are appropriately described and in accordance with prescribed terms, namely '. . . per cent gross', '. . . per cent net', '. . . per cent tax free', '. . . per cent compounded annual rate' and where each of those descriptions conforms to the requirements specified for them respectively in the code. In the case of each of the foregoing descriptions of interest rates the statement of the rate must be followed by an explanatory phrase qualifying the rate, eg . . . per cent gross, not taking account of the deduction of income tax at the basic rate. The acronym 'CAR' following a percentage rate is acceptable as the abbreviation of 'compounded annual rate'.

   All advertisements in which the rate is quoted must include the contractual rate. No rate may be given greater prominence in size of type or otherwise than the contractual rate provided interest is due at least annually. Where interest is paid less frequently than annually eg after five years, the contractual rate may be given no greater prominence than the compounded annual rate. Where rates are quoted on the basis of other than a 12-month period, this must be clearly stated;

(7) advertisements quoting a rate of interest must contain a specific statement indicating:

   (a) the term, if any, of the deposit,
   (b) the frequency of payments of interest and either that
   (c) the rate quoted is fixed for any term specified or
   (d) interest rates are subject to variation;

(8) advertisements, quoting a rate of interest or yield, which are intended for media or direct mail with long copy dates must contain a suitable qualification eg 'rates correct at time of going to press' and may state that time;

(9) the explanatory phrases and statements required by the code must be clearly audible or legible;

(10) the code prescribes notice to customers of changes in rates, or a simple list of the range of accounts and their rates displayed in offices on a rate board, primarily to fulfil contractual obligations. In the case of such notices or lists, the words 'gross', 'net', 'tax free' and 'CAR', as appropriate, need not appear after each rate provided it is made clear which term applies to which rate;

(11) the advertisement must set out the terms and conditions applying to the deposit by reference to the following:

   (a) a clear statement of the conditions for withdrawal, including the amount of any charges levied, the period of any notice required and the extent of any interest forfeited;

   (b) where interest is forfeited on any withdrawal without notice, words such as 'instant access' or 'immediate withdrawals' must not be displayed together with the rate of interest without clear qualification;

   (c) accounts which do not allow withdrawals, even after notice, without forfeiture of interest, must include in advertisements a statement indicating that if a withdrawal is made the stated interest rate will not be achieved;

   (d) where a maximum or minimum amount must be deposited to achieve the stated interest rate, the text of the advertisement must include a clear statement to this effect;

(12) advertisements which invite deposits by immediate coupon response must:

   (a) include the full terms and conditions or state that they are available on request;

   (b) clearly state in the part of the advertisement to be retained by the customer a full postal address at which the advertiser can be contacted during normal business hours and the description and details of the advertised product including the information required by the code;

(13) a supplement to the code sets out the rules for calculation of compounded annual rates by reference to a formula and also to a table to be used for the calculation of the compounded annual gross, net or tax-free rate.

9.3   The Banking Code

The third edition of this voluntary code produced by the British Bankers' Association (BBA), the Building Societies' Association (BSA) and the Association for Payment Clearing Services (APCS) came into force on 1 July 1997.

The code governs banks and building societies in their relations with personal customers in the UK and sets standards of good practice which are followed as a minimum by its subscribers. The code is complemented by the Mortgage Code. The Independent Review Body for the Banking and Mortgage Codes monitors compliance with the code and oversees its periodic review.

The Banking Code sets out key commitments to which its subscribers agree to adhere and contains provisions under the general heads Information, Account Operations, Customer Protection and Customer Difficulties. On the subject of advertising, subscribers to the code undertake to ensure that all advertising and promotional material is clear, fair, reasonable and not misleading.

9.4   Banking Act 1987

We shall only consider this Act in the context of advertisements. The first point to note is that the Act restricts the use of banking names and descriptions. It provides that no person carrying on any business in the UK may use any name which indicates or may reasonably be understood to indicate that he is a bank or banker or is carrying on a banking business unless he is an authorised institution, as defined[2]. In addition to various exemptions the prohibition does not apply to the use by an authorised institution which is a company incorporated under the law of a country or territory outside the UK or is formed under the law of a member state of the European Union, if it is the name under which it carries on business in that country, territory or state[3]. There is an equivalent restriction on, and similar exemption from, any description of a person conducting banking business[4].

The Bank of England is given general power to control what it regards as misleading deposit advertisements by, or on behalf of, authorised institutions. On the publication or proposed publication of such an

---

2   Section 67, Banking Act 1987.
3   Section 68 *ibid.*
4   Section 69 *ibid.*

advertisement the Bank may by notice in writing give the institution a direction prohibiting the issue of advertisements of a specified kind, requiring that advertisements of a particular description be modified in a specified manner, prohibiting the repetition of any advertisements or requiring the institution to withdraw advertisements from display. The Bank must give the institution not less than seven days' notice of its intention to issue a direction in this regard and the institution may make representations in response to the Bank within seven days of the issue of the notice[4bis].

The Act authorises the Treasury, after consultation with the Bank of England and the Building Societies' Commission, to make regulations governing the issue, form and content of deposit advertisements. A deposit advertisement is any advertisement containing an invitation to make a deposit or information which is intended or might reasonably be presumed to be intended to lead directly or indirectly to the making of a deposit[5]. Any person who issues, or causes to be issued, in the UK an advertisement the issue of which is prohibited by the regulations commits an offence. An advertisement issued outside the UK is treated as issued in the UK if it is directed to persons in the UK or is made available to them otherwise than in a newspaper, journal, magazine or other periodical publication published and circulated principally outside the UK or in a sound or television broadcast transmitted principally for reception outside the UK[5bis].

9.5   Banking Act 1987 (Advertisements) Regulations 1988[6]

These are the only regulations which apply to deposit advertisements and are restricted to what is termed a 'controlled advertisement'.

The regulations apply to a deposit advertisement, unless it contains an invitation to make deposits only with offices of the deposit-taker in the UK or another member state of the European Union. They do not apply to a deposit advertisement which does not indicate the offices with which the deposits are invited to be made if the deposit-taker carries on a deposit-taking business in the UK or another member state of the European Union. In short, the regulations do not apply to advertisements for deposits to be made in the UK or the European Union.

4bis   Section 33 *ibid.*
5   Section 32(5) *ibid.*
5bis   Section 32(7) *ibid.*
6   SI 1988 No 645.

The regulations also do not apply to a deposit advertisement which is an investment business advertisement regulated by rules as to their form and content under or pursuant to the Financial Services Act 1986.

The following is a summary of the information required in a controlled advertisement:

(1) the full name of the deposit-taker;

(2) the country or territory in which the deposit-taker's principal place of business is situated;

(3) if the deposit-taker is a body corporate, the country or territory in which it is incorporated unless this is the same as that referred to in paragraph (2) above;

(4) the amount of the paid-up capital and reserves of the deposit-taker, if a body corporate, or the amount of the total assets less liabilities of the deposit-taker, if not a body corporate;

(5) if the advertisement contains any reference to the amount of the assets of the deposit-taker it must state with equal prominence the amount of the deposit-taker's liabilities;

> The statement as regards assets and liabilities is complied with if the advertisement states that the amount of any assets or paid-up capital and reserves exceeds an amount specified in the advertisement or that the amount of any liabilities does not exceed an amount specified;

(6) the advertisement may not contain any reference to the assets or liabilities of any person other than the deposit-taker;

(7) the advertisement must indicate the country or territory in which the offices of the deposit-taker are situated and unless it is an authorised building society within the meaning of the Building Societies Act 1986 the advertisement must contain a statement in a conspicuous position in the following terms:

> Deposits made with offices of [name of deposit-taker] in [name of country or territory] are not covered by the Deposit Protection Scheme under the Banking Act 1987;

(8) the advertisement may not state or imply that the deposits or their repayment, or that interest or the payment of interest in respect of them, will be guaranteed, secured, insured or the subject of any other form of protection unless it states the form of the protection, the extent of the protection and the full name of the person who will be liable to meet any claim by the depositor by virtue of the arrangements conferring the protection;

(9) where the advertisement specifies the rate of interest payable in respect of the deposit it must also state the relevant particulars, if any, in relation to the minimum amount which must be deposited to earn that rate of interest, the period of time during which that interest will be payable, the minimum period of time during which the deposit must be retained by the deposit-taker in order to earn that rate of interest and the minimum period of notice which must be given before repayment may be required of the deposit earning that rate of interest. The advertisement must also state the intervals at which interest will be paid;

(10) if the rate of interest specified is not an annual rate of simple interest the advertisement must state the basis on which it will be calculated;

(11) if the rate of interest specified may be varied during the period of the deposit this must be stated in the advertisement;

(12) if interest will or may not be paid in full at the rate specified in the advertisement this must be stated and the advertisement must state the nature and amount of or rate of any deductions which will or may be made;

(13) if the rate of interest specified is or may not be the rate at which interest will be payable on the date on which the advertisement is issued this must be stated in the advertisement and the advertisement must state the date on which interest is payable at the rate specified in the advertisement, such date being as close as reasonably practicable to the date on which the advertisement is issued;

(14) if an advertisement specifies more than one rate of interest payable in respect of deposits of a particular amount it must contain the information required by the regulations in respect of each such rate;

(15) where different rates of interest apply to deposits of different amounts the advertisement must contain the information required by the foregoing paragraphs in relation to each such rate;

(16) the advertisement must state the currency in which the deposits are to be made.

As regards the form of the advertisement, the information required by the regulations must be shown clearly and legibly or spoken clearly, as appropriate.

9.6 Permissive provisions

9.6.1 Description of the deposit-taker

The Bank of England is agreeable to deposit-taking institutions which are authorised under the Banking Act using the terms '(an) authorised (institution) under the Banking Act 1987'. However, it will not permit reference to the Bank of England so that words such as 'authorised/supervised by the Bank of England' are not acceptable[7].

9.6.2 The Deposit Protection Scheme

The Banking Act 1987 (Part II) made provision for the establishment of the Deposit Protection Scheme covering deposits up to a maximum amount made with authorised institutions in the UK. Part II was amended by the Credit Institutions (Protection of Depositors) Regulations 1995[8] following the European Union Directive on Deposit Guarantee Scheme[9]. The result is that certain banks are covered by the Deposit Protection Scheme, namely the following:

(1) banks authorised under the Banking Act 1987 incorporated in the UK including their branches in the European Economic Area (EEA);
(2) certain banks incorporated in other EEA States which have joined the UK scheme to supplement the cover available from the scheme operated in their home country in respect of deposits taken by their UK offices;
(3) certain banks incorporated outside the EEA in respect of deposits taken by their UK offices.

The foregoing regulations[10] set out the information to be supplied on request in explanatory literature and in advertisements in relation to the Deposit Protection Scheme or the Investor Protection Scheme in the UK or, where the institution or society participates in a relevant host state scheme, details of the protection afforded by that scheme.

As regards advertisements for deposits, they may include the following information but no more:

---

7 'Advertising for deposits'—Bank of England Notice BSD/1988/1 (April 1988).
8 SI 1995 No 1442.
9 94/19/EC.
10 Regulations 46 to 48 *loc cit.*

(1) if it relates to a UK institution or a building society, a statement to the effect that:
   (a) most relevant deposits with the institution or society are protected by the relevant UK scheme; and
   (b) where the institution or society participates in a host state scheme that supplemental protection is afforded to such deposits by that scheme;
(2) if it relates to an EEA institution, a statement to the effect that:
   (a) most relevant deposits with the institution are protected by its home state scheme; and
   (b) where the institution participates in a UK scheme that supplemental protection is afforded to such deposits by that scheme;
(3) if it relates to a non-EEA institution which is participating in the Deposit Protection Scheme a statement to the effect that most relevant deposits with the institutions are protected by that scheme;
(4) if it relates to a non-EEA institution which is not participating in the Deposit Protection Scheme a statement to the effect that most relevant deposits with the institution are protected by its home state scheme.

A deposit advertisement which includes a statement of the kind referred to above may also include:

(1) a statement as to the level of the protection afforded by the scheme or, as the case may be, each of the schemes referred to; and
(2) a statement to the effect that additional information about that scheme or each of those schemes may be obtained by any depositor or intending depositor on request.

A typical statement relating to the Deposit Protection Scheme appearing in an advertisement for deposits might read as follows:

> The ABC Bank is a member of the Deposit Protection Scheme established under the Banking Act 1987 (as amended). Payments under the scheme are limited to 90 per cent of a depositor's total deposits subject to a maximum payment to any one depositor of £18,000 (or ECU 20,000 if greater). Most deposits in Sterling and other European Economic Area Currencies and ECU made with offices of the bank within the European Economic Area are covered. Further details of the scheme are available upon request from any branch of the Bank.

Similar provisions apply to deposits with building societies under the

Building Societies' Investor Protection Scheme established under the Building Societies Act 1986. A typical deposit guarantee scheme notice might read as follows:

> The XYZ Building Society is a member of the Building Societies Investor Protection Scheme established under the Building Societies Act 1986. Payments under this scheme are limited to 90 per cent of an investor's total shares and/or deposits subject to a maximum payment to any one investor of £18,000 (or ECU 20,000 if greater). Most shares and deposits denominated in Sterling and other European Economic Area Currencies and ECU made with offices of the building society within the European Economic Area are covered. Further details are available upon request from the society.

9.7   Enforcement

Any person who issues or causes to be issued in the UK an advertisement which is prohibited under s 33, Banking Act or under regulations made under s 32 of the Act is guilty of an offence and liable to imprisonment and to a fine imposed under those sections. The advertisement is treated as issued or caused to be issued each day it is displayed or exhibited[11].

Voluntary codes are generally adhered to not only as a matter of principle but also because of the ultimate threat of legislative control should they fail to achieve their intended purpose.

Control of advertising for deposits by authorised institutions and building societies within the UK is generally effective. The system breaks down where there is no control by a UK or EU authority. A recent example is the case of the European Union Bank, based in Antigua, which advertised offshore banking services over the Internet and fell outside the control of the Bank of England.

9.8   Advertisements for overdrafts

Advertisements for overdrafts for personal customers or partnerships (ie 'individuals' as defined by the Consumer Credit Act 1974) are governed by the Consumer Credit Act and the Consumer Credit (Advertisement Regulations) 1989. This is so notwithstanding that the agreement for an overdraft on a current account is excluded from that Act's provisions in so far as form and formalities are concerned[12].

---

11   Section 32(6)(a), Banking Act 1987.
12   Section 74(1)(b) *ibid.*

Outside the advertising regime, for example in relation to the tariff of charges or the overdraft agreement itself, there is no prescribed uniform method of calculating or stating the applicable interest rate. In contrast to the APR in the case of regulated agreements, the interest rate may be expressed as a simple rate, as an effective annual rate ('EAR'), as a compound annual rate ('CAR') or in any other, hopefully intelligible, manner.

Chapter 10

Insurance Advertisements

10.1 Meaning of insurance advertisement

It is worthwhile considering the definition of an insurance advertisement, if only in order to highlight the variable definitions of an insurance advertisement as contained in the relevant statutes. One is tempted to attribute the different definitions to the time when the statutes were passed and the evolution of advertising. However, different definitions appear in statutes enacted at about the same time and more sophisticated definitions of advertisement can also be found in earlier statutes. It is rather a manifestation of the art of the draughtsman than of the state of the art of advertising at any particular time.

'Advertisement' is defined in the Insurance Companies Act 1982 as including every form of advertising, whether in a publication; by the display of notices; by means of circulars or other documents; by an exhibition of photographs or cinematograph films; by way of sound broadcasting or television, or by inclusion in any programme service (within the meaning of the Broadcasting Act 1990) other than a sound or television broadcasting service[1]. Similarly, and in contrast, 'advertisement' is defined in the Financial Services Act 1986 as including every form of advertising, whether in a publication, by the display of notices, signs, labels or show cards, by means of circulars, catalogues, price lists or other documents, by an exhibition of pictures or photographic or cinematographic films, by way of sound broadcasting or television or by inclusion in any programme service (within the meaning of the Broadcasting Act 1990) other than a sound or television broadcasting service, by the distribution of recordings,

---

1 Section 72(6).

or in any other manner[2]. Yet another definition of 'insurance advertisement' appears in the Insurance Companies Regulations 1994[2bis] where, for stated purposes (basically where the insurer is named in the advertisement) an insurance advertisement is defined as one which invites any person to enter into or offer to enter into, or which contains information calculated to lead directly or indirectly to any person entering into or offering to enter into, any contract of insurance other than a contract of reinsurance.

Whilst the Financial Services Act 1986 essentially relates to investments, which includes long-term insurance contracts, certain of its provisions relate to all types of insurance contracts. For the purposes of the Insurance Companies Act 1982 an insurance advertisement is an advertisement inviting persons to enter into or to offer to enter into contracts of insurance and includes an advertisement which contains information calculated to lead directly or indirectly to such result[3]. An investment advertisement, on the other hand, is any advertisement inviting persons to enter or offer to enter into an investment agreement or to exercise any rights conferred by an investment to acquire, dispose of, underwrite or convert an investment or containing information calculated to lead directly or indirectly to persons doing so[4].

It is worthwhile pointing out that, for the purposes of the Financial Services Act, an advertisement or other information issued outside the UK is treated as issued in the UK if it is directed to persons in the UK or is made available to them otherwise than in a newspaper, journal, magazine or other periodical publication published and circulating principally outside the UK or in a sound or television broadcast transmitted principally for reception outside the UK[5].

10.2 General control over the contents of insurance advertisements

Rather strangely, it is the Financial Services Act which outlaws misleading statements as to insurance contracts generally. Any person who makes a statement, promise or forecast which he knows to be misleading, false or deceptive or dishonestly conceals any material facts or recklessly makes, whether dishonestly or otherwise, a statement, promise or forecast which is misleading, false, or deceptive is guilty of an offence if he does so for the

---

2   Section 207(2), Financial Services Act 1986.
2bis   SI 1994/1516 reg 37(1).
3   Section 72(5), Insurance Companies Act 1982.
4   Section 57(2), Financial Services Act 1986.
5   Section 207(3) *ibid.*

purpose of inducing another person to enter into or refrain from entering into a contract of insurance or to exercise or refrain from exercising any rights conferred by a contract of insurance. A person is also guilty of such an offence if he acts recklessly with regard to the foregoing[6].

The offence is only committed if the statement, promise or forecast is made in or from or the facts are concealed in or from the UK; the person on whom the inducement is intended to or may have effect is in the UK or the contract is or would be entered into or the rights are or would be exercisable in the UK[7].

10.3   Contents of insurance advertisement

Like deposit advertisements, a radical distinction is drawn in the contents of advertisements between advertisements where the insurance company which issued the advertisement does not have its head office in a member state of the European Economic Area (EEA) and is not authorised to carry on an insurance business in the UK, and insurance companies which do meet such requirements. An advertisement by an insurance company which does not have its head office in an EEA State and is not authorised to carry on business in the UK must contain the following statement[8]:

> This advertisement relates to an insurance company which is not author-ised to carry on insurance business in the UK. This means that the manage-ment and solvency of the company are not supervised by Her Majesty's Government and you will not be protected by the Policyholders' Protection Act 1975 if the company should be unable to meet its liabilities to you.

The foregoing statement must appear prominently and, if the insurer is named, immediately after or alongside the statement of the name of the insurer or, if the insurer is stated more than once, immediately after or alongside the most prominent statement of the name[9]. If an insurer is named in such advertisement, its full name must be stated together with the country where it is registered and where its principal place of business is situated, if different[9bis].

Rather strangely, there is no requirement for the name of the insurer to appear in an insurance advertisement.

Any insurance advertisement which states the name of an insurance

---

6   Section 133(1) *ibid.*
7   Section 133(2) *ibid.*
8   Insurance Companies Regulations 1994 (SI 1994 No 1516), reg 35.
9   *Ibid* reg 37(3).
9bis   *Ibid* reg 36(3).

company to which Part II of the Insurance Companies Act 1982 applies (which, subject to exceptions, means all insurance companies established within or outside the UK carrying on insurance business within the UK and all UK companies carrying on insurance business in a member state other than the UK), or which contains the name of an EC company carrying on insurance business in the UK, if it is incorporated with a share capital and the advertisement states the amount of the authorised share capital, must also state the amount of share capital that has been subscribed and the amount which has been paid up at the time the advertisement is issued[10].

The requirements relating to the contents of advertisements set out in this section do not apply to advertisements which relate to a contract covering large risks only or if they are investment advertisements approved by an authorised person under s 57, Financial Services Act 1986[11].

10.4   Enforcement

Any person who issues an insurance advertisement which contravenes the Insurance Companies Regulations 1994 is guilty of an offence[12]. An advertisement issued by a person on behalf of or to the order of another person is treated as an advertisement issued by that other person[13]. A person who in the ordinary course of his business issues an advertisement to the order of another person shall not himself be guilty of an offence if he proves that the matters contained in the advertisement were not, wholly or in part, devised or selected by him or by any person under his direction or control[14].

10.5   Advertisements for long-term insurance contracts (investments)

A long-term insurance contract constitutes an investment within the meaning of para 10 of Sched 1 to the Financial Services Act 1986. Advertisements for such insurance are governed partly by the law already referred to in this chapter and partly by the regime set up under the Financial Services Act 1986.

---

10   *Ibid* reg 36.
11   *Ibid* reg 37(4); for the meaning of 'large risks' see s 96B, Insurance Companies Act 1982.
12   Insurance Companies Act 1982, s 72(3).
13   *Ibid* s 72(7).
14   *Ibid* s 72(4).

Classes of long-term insurance business are set out in Sched 1 to the Insurance Companies Act 1982 and include contracts of insurance relating to life and annuity, marriage and birth, linked long-term, permanent health, tontines, capital redemption, pension fund management, collective insurance and social insurance.

Generally speaking, credit protection insurance is excluded from the classification as long-term insurance by virtue of the statutory note to para 10 of Sched 1. This excludes from long-term insurance, insurance where the benefits under the contract are payable only on death or in respect of incapacity due to injury, sickness or infirmity; no benefits are payable under the contract on death unless it occurs within 10 years of the date of the insurance or before the insured attains a specified age not exceeding 70 years; the contract has no surrender value or the consideration consists of a single premium and the surrender value does not exceed that premium; and the contract does not make provision for its conversion or extension in a manner which would take it out of these provisions. Such insurance would therefore constitute general insurance and not long-term insurance. Likewise re-insurance contracts are excluded from long-term insurance.

Advertisements for long-term insurance contracts and advertisements for investments generally are governed by a separate regime set up under the Financial Services Act 1986. Investment advertisements are discussed in Chapter 11.

10.6 Advertisements by insurance brokers

The Code of Conduct[15] applying to insurance brokers specifically regulates advertisements made by them or on their behalf. Such advertisements must not contain statements which are misleading or extravagant. The advertisements must comply with the applicable parts of the British Code of Advertising Practice. Advertisements must distinguish between contractual benefits, namely those that the insurance contract is bound to provide and non-contractual benefits. Where the advertisement includes a forecast of non-contractual benefits it must be restricted to the forecast provided by the insurer concerned.

Advertisements made by or on behalf of insurance brokers should not be restricted to the policies of one insurer except where the reasons for

---

15   Code of Conduct drawn up by the Insurance Brokers' Registration Council and approved by the Insurance Brokers' Registration Council (Code of Conduct) Approval Order 1994 (SI 1994 No 2569).

such restriction are fully explained in the advertisement, the insurer is named in the advertisement and the prior approval of that insurer has been obtained.

When advertising their services, insurance brokers must disclose their identity, occupation and purpose before seeking information or giving advice.

Chapter 11

Investment Advertising

11.1 Meaning of an investment advertisement

An investment advertisement is an advertisement inviting persons to enter or offer to enter into an investment agreement or to exercise any rights conferred by an investment to acquire, dispose of, underwrite or convert an investment or containing information calculated to lead directly or indirectly to persons doing so[1]. Each element of the definition is, in turn, defined by the Act or subject to further definition at common law.

An advertisement is defined, for the purposes of the Financial Services Act 1986, as including every form of advertising, whether in a publication, by the display of notices, signs, labels or showcards, by means of circulars, catalogues, price lists or other documents, by an exhibition of pictures or photographic or cinematograph films, or by sound broadcasting or television or by inclusion in any programme service (within the meaning of the Broadcasting Act 1990) other than a sound or television broadcasting service, by the distribution of recordings, or in any other manner[2].

An investment agreement is any agreement the making or performance of which by either party constitutes an activity referred to in Part II of Sched 1 to the foregoing Act[3]. In broad general terms these activities comprise dealing in investments, safeguarding and administering or arranging for the safeguarding and administration of assets belonging to another where those assets include or could include investments, arranging deals in investments, custody of investments, managing investments, investment

---

1   Section 57(2), Financial Services Act 1986.
2   Section 207(2) *ibid.*
3   Section 44(9) *ibid* and note that an investment agreement is such notwithstanding the various exemptions in Sched 1, paras 17–27 (Parts III and IV of Sched 1).

advice, establishing, operating or winding up a collective investment scheme including acting as trustee of an authorised unit trust scheme or as a depositary or sole director of an investment company with variable capital[3bis]. Finally, investment business includes semi-dematerialised instructions relating to an investment eg by means of the CREST system. Part III of Sched 1 to the Financial Services Act excludes certain activities from constituting investment business and Part IV contains additional exclusions for persons without a permanent place of business in the UK.

'Investment' means any asset, right or interest falling within any paragraph in Part I of Sched 1 to the Financial Services Act[4]. In broad terms investments include shares, debentures (including debenture stock, loan stock, bonds, certificates of deposit and certain other instruments creating or acknowledging indebtedness) government and public securities, instruments entitling the holder to subscribe for shares or securities, certificates or other instruments representing securities or rights or interests in securities, units in collective investment schemes, options to acquire or dispose of investments, currency or certain precious metals, futures, contracts for differences, long-term insurance contracts (as to which see also Chapter 10) and rights and interests in investments. Currency, including foreign currency, is itself not an investment.

The definition of an investment advertisement, set out above, includes the words 'containing information calculated to lead directly or indirectly' to persons carrying out any of the activities referred to. The expression 'calculated to lead directly or indirectly' is also to be found in s 37(5) and (6) of the Act. It is submitted that these words are to be interpreted objectively, namely in the sense of whether the information is likely to give rise to the result referred to and independently of the intention of the person responsible for the advertisement. This interpretation would appear to accord with the mischief at which the restrictions on advertising in the Financial Services Act are aimed. Furthermore, if the expression 'calculated to lead' referred to the intention of the advertiser, it would render unnecessary s 57(4) of the Act. Finally, an objective interpretation of the word 'calculated' as meaning 'likely' rather than 'intended' has been supported by various decisions on statutes imputing criminal liability[5].

The words 'directly or indirectly' in the definition of investment

---

3bis   Part II of Schedule 1 as amended by SI 1996/1322 and SI 1996/2958. Custody of investments includes safeguarding and administering investments of another or arranging the same.
4   Section 1(1) *ibid.*
5   See, for example, *R v Davison* [1972] 3 All ER 1121, *Turner v Shearer* [1973] 1 All ER 397 and *Norweb plc v Dixon* [1995] 1 WLR 636.

advertisement are likely to be construed restrictively in the sense that any act resulting from or likely to result from the advertisement must be shown to be connected with or related back to the advertisement. Particularly in view of the criminal consequences attaching to an unauthorised advertisement, the word 'indirectly' is unlikely to be construed as limitlessly enlarging the scope of the words 'calculated to lead'[6].

Investment advertisements include an offering document, such as a private placing memorandum, unless it falls within one of the exempt categories listed below:

(1) an offer document for a life assurance policy;
(2) an invitation to subscribe for a unit trust scheme or a Personal Equity Plan ('PEP');
(3) an invitation to take out a personal pension.

The following are not investment advertisements as the underlying subject matter is not an investment:

(1) advertisements for bank or building society accounts or deposit accounts;
(2) advertisements for most types of payment protection insurance;
(3) advertisements for investment in works of art, coins, currency, stamps, silver or gold;
(4) advertisements for investment in land, buildings or timeshares.

11.2   Issue of an investment advertisement

Subject to the exceptions referred to in paras 11.5–11.8 below, no person other than an authorised person may issue or cause to be issued an investment advertisement in the UK unless its contents have been approved by an authorised person[7].

An advertisement or other information issued outside the UK is treated as issued in the UK if it is directed to persons in the UK or is made available to them otherwise than in a newspaper, journal, magazine or other periodical publication published and circulating principally outside the UK or in a sound or television broadcast transmitted principally for reception outside the UK[8]. This provision is also relevant to the operation of the Internet. Significant illustrations of the principles involved in

---

6   Compare *Green v Hoyle* [1976] 2 All ER 633 and *Potts' Executors v Inland Revenue Commissioners* [1951] AC 443 HL.
7   Section 57(1), Financial Services Act 1986.
8   Section 207(3) *ibid.*

unauthorised investment business from outside the UK are the unreported successful proceedings by SIB against the Spanish-based Anglo Scandinavian and the Danish-based Scandex Capital Management A/S. Both these companies conducted unauthorised investment business which involved making misleading statements to potential investors and unsolicited calls.

The approval of an investment advertisement by an unauthorised person must be effected through a firm which is authorised. An exception is made in respect of an EU operator, who is not authorised in the UK but is authorised in his home state, in respect of an advertisement issued by him in the course of investment business lawfully carried on by him in such state, and which conforms to rules made under s 48(2)(e) of the Act (the SIB's advertising rules)[8bis].

It is not sufficient that the advertisement is approved by an authorised person. The approving person must also possess appropriate expertise and be able to demonstrate that the advertisement is fair and not misleading.

Considerable debate surrounds the meaning of the expression 'cause to be issued' in the prohibition against unauthorised advertising contained in s 57 of the Act. At the one extreme the position might be reasonably self-evident, as where a person causes his employee, agent, appointed representative or contractor to issue an advertisement. The mere presence of other persons in the chain of issuance does not break the causal factor in the context of issuing an advertisement. On the other hand, the position is less clear in situations involving the uncontrolled and uncontrollable dissemination of an advertisement on the Internet.

It is submitted that to cause an advertisement to be issued means more than merely creating the circumstances which allow the advertisement to be published. It means doing or omitting to do something with the intention that the act or omission will procure the end result or acting recklessly with regard to the consequences in situations where, with due diligence, the end result could have been avoided[8quat].

The Securities and Investments Board has issued guidance on the use of the Internet. Its view is that, in general, it is unlikely that an access/site provider will fall foul of UK financial services' legislation if all he does is provide technical services and has no involvement in the marketing of the

8bis   Section 58(1)(c) *ibid.*
8quat   Compare *Kelly's Directories Ltd v Gavin and Lloyds* [1902] Ch D 631 re 'print or cause to be printed'; *Lovelace v Director of Public Prosecutions* [1954] 3 All ER 481 re 'cause to be acted or presented'; *Ross Hillman v Bond* [1974] 2 All ER 287; *Sopp v Long* [1969] 1 All ER 855.

products or services of someone to whom access or a site is provided. In the SIB's opinion it is unlikely that an access or site provider will be conducting investment business if it merely acts as a conduit through which persons or companies gain access to wide presence on the Internet and where it has no knowledge of, or control over, the information or services being provided.

The SIB acknowledges that where information held anywhere on the Net is made available to or can be obtained by someone in the UK that such information, if it takes the form of an investment advertisement, may be viewed as having been issued in the UK. In certain circumstances an access or site provider might seem to be issuing, or more likely, causing to be issued an advertisement by virtue of providing access or a site on the Net. However, it is SIB's view that if the access or site provider has:

(1) no knowledge or control over the information or service being put on to the Net; and

(2) no commercial interest, financial or otherwise, in the information or service being provided

it is unlikely that such person would be viewed as issuing or causing to be issued material put on to the Net by those for whom he provides access and/or a presence. In considering responsibility for unlawful investment advertising into the UK on the Internet, the SIB will also take into account the degree to which, given the nature of the Internet, someone had taken positive steps to avoid the material being made available to or receivable by persons in the UK. Positive steps include requiring preregistration to ensure that only those to whom the material was aimed had access. However, mere disclaimers stating that the material was not aimed at or meant to be viewed by persons in the UK are unlikely to be sufficient to avoid constituting a contravention of the Act[8quin].

The rules of certain SROs constrain the issue of personalised circulars so as to avoid implying that the advertiser knows a recipient sufficiently well to be able to recommend an investment. Accordingly, some investment circulars addressed to individuals by name will contain a statement to the effect that the addressee's personal circumstances may suggest that another investment product is more appropriate and invite addressees to contact the advertiser for information and advice.

8quin   SIB letters of December 1995 and June 1996 issued by the SIB Enforcement and Legal Services Division and para 16.5.4 *post*.

11.3   Authorisation and consequences of breach

11.3.1   Criminal consequences

Any person who issues or causes to be issued an investment advertisement without it being approved by an authorised person commits an offence and is liable to imprisonment, a fine or both[9]. 'Issuer' would automatically include the publisher whereas the person who caused the advertisement to be issued would ordinarily be the business engaging in investments.

An authorised person is a member of a recognised self-regulating organisation (SRO), a person holding a certificate issued for the purposes of conducting investment business by a recognised professional body (RPB), an insurer which is authorised to carry on investment business, a Friendly Society which is authorised to carry on investment business, the operator or member of a collective investment scheme constituted in an EU member state other than the UK if it satisfies the requirements prescribed by the Act in relation to it, a firm authorised by the Securities and Investments Board (SIB) and a person holding an authorisation granted by the Treasury[9bis]. In effect 'authorised person' also includes a European investment firm carrying on home-regulated investment business in the UK[9ter].

Authorisation may be limited in scope and activity. Indeed, many authorised persons, such as those authorised by RPBs, will not be empowered to approve investments as their authority to conduct investment business will be limited to that which is incidental to their mainstream activity. In other words, they will not be entitled to conduct discrete investment business.

An advertiser may itself approve an investment advertisement if it is an authorised person or procure its authorisation by an authorised intermediary. It will need to adopt the latter course if it is not itself authorised.

A defence is provided to the 'issuer' of an investment advertisement provided that he (a) acted in the ordinary course of a business other than an investment business, (b) issued the advertisement to the order of another person and (c) believed on reasonable grounds that the person to whose order the advertisement was issued was an authorised person, that the contents of the advertisement were approved by an authorised person, or that the advertisement was excluded from the restrictions on advertising (as to which see paras 11.4 and 11.5 below)[10].

---

9   Section 57(3), Financial Services Act 1986.
9bis   Chapter III *ibid.*
9ter   Investment Services Regulations 1995 (SI 1995 No 3275).
10   Section 57(4) *ibid.*

11.3.2 Civil consequences

A person issuing or causing to be issued an advertisement in breach of s 57 is not entitled (a) to enforce any agreement to which the advertisement relates and which was entered into after the issue of the advertisement or (b) to enforce any obligation to which a person is subject as a result of any exercise by him after the issue of the advertisement of any rights to which the advertisement relates. In each case the other party is entitled to restitution, to recover any money or other property paid or transferred by him as a result of entering into the transaction together with any profits made by the contravenor and compensation for any loss sustained[11]. An order can also be made against solicitors or any other persons who were knowingly concerned in the contraventions[11bis]. A court can also make a restitutionary order under s 6(2) imposing on a person carrying on investment business in the UK without authorisation (the contravenor) and any persons who were 'knowingly concerned' in the contravenor's breaches, liability to make payment to the investor so as to restore him to the position he was in before the transaction was made. The liability of those knowingly involved may only be secondary but there is a strong view in favour of their being jointly and severally liable with the contravenor[11ter].

A court may allow any agreement entered into or obligation to which a person has been subject as a result of an unauthorised advertisement to be enforced or money or property paid or transferred to be retained if the court is satisfied:

(1) that the person against whom enforcement is sought or who is seeking to recover the money or property was not influenced or not influenced to any material extent by the advertisement; or

(2) that the advertisement was not misleading as to the nature of the investment, the terms of the agreement, or, as the case may be, the

---

11   Section 57(5) and (6) and ss 5 and 6 *ibid.*
11bis   Section 61(1) *ibid* and see *Securities and Investments Board v Pantell SA (No 2)* [1993] Ch 256; [1993] 1 All ER 134 CA. This was a case brought by SIB under section 6(2). This case involved unauthorised investment business carried on by Pantell SA, incorporated in Switzerland, in the course of which it distributed in the UK advertisements for the purchase of shares in a USA company which were not approved by an authorsed person. In addition, salesmen for Pantell SA made unsolicited telephone calls to persons in the UK to persuade them to purchase the shares. Shares were so acquired in breach of section 3. The solicitors were held liable to *make restitution* even though they received nothing from the investors so that they had nothing to restore.
11ter   *Ibid* judgment of Steyn LJ at p 149.

consequences of exercising the rights in question and fairly stated any risks involved in those matters[12].

The Financial Services Act expressly provides that certain contraventions are actionable at the suit of a private investor who suffers loss as a result of the contravention[12bis]. A private investor is one whose cause of action arises as a result of anything he had done or suffered otherwise than in the course of investment business carried on by an individual, or of any kind of business, in the case of any other person[12ter]. Such action may be taken in relation to any breach of the SIB's Conduct of Business Rules or any breach of any restriction applying to certain exempt investment advertisements.

In the following circumstances an action may be brought at the suit of a person other than a private investor:

(1) circumstances in which the contravention in question is not of a kind mentioned in s 61(1) or (2) of the Act;

(2) circumstances in which the contravention is one of any rule, regulation, condition or requirement prohibiting a person from seeking to make provision excluding or restricting any duty or liability;

(3) circumstances in which the contravention is one of any rule, regulation, condition or requirement directed at ensuring that transactions in an investment are not effected with the benefit of unpublished information which, if made public, would be likely to affect the price of the investment; and

(4) circumstances in which the action would be brought at the suit of a person in a fiduciary or representative capacity where the cause of action arises as a result of anything done or suffered at a time when the person to whom the representative owed a duty or for whom he was acting was a private investor and recovery would be exclusively for the benefit of such a person and could not be effected through action brought otherwise than at the suit of the representative[12quat]. In addition, the Securities and Investments Board may take injunction proceedings against a delinquent person[12quin]. A court is also

---

12   Section 57(8) *ibid.*

12bis   Section 62 *ibid* read with s 62A.

12ter   The Financial Services Act 1986 (Restriction of Right of Action) Regulations 1991 (SI 1991 No 489), reg 2(1).

12quat   *Ibid* reg 3.

12quin   Section 61(1) *ibid.* And see *Securities and Investments Board v Pantell SA (No 2)* footnote 11bis *supra.*

empowered to grant a *Mareva* injunction in favour of the SIB in support of its right of action under s 6[12sext].

11.3.3   Disciplinary consequences

A breach of the advertising rules can give rise to disciplinary proceedings by the enforcement body of the relevant self-regulating organisation. The penalty may include a fine and ultimately expulsion from the organisation.

11.4   Excluded advertisements

Section 57 of the Financial Services Act, relating to restrictions on advertising, does not apply to excluded advertisements, namely those excluded by the Act or by orders made under the Act. These are known as exempt advertisements and are briefly set out below.

The fact that an advertisement has been approved by an authorised person does not necessarily and automatically mean that the advertisement is lawful. It may contain misleading or even fraudulent statements, with consequences discussed later.

11.5   Exempt advertisements

Section 57, which requires investment advertisements to be approved by an authorised person, does not apply to advertisements specified either in the Act or in regulations made under the Act[13], as being excluded from such restrictions[13bis]. An advertisement may be exempt by virtue of the issuer of the advertisement, the persons to whom the advertisement is addressed or the contents of the advertisement. We will now briefly consider the various categories of exempt advertisement.

11.5.1   Official bodies

Advertisements are exempt if they are issued or caused to be issued by, and relate only to investments issued by:

(1) the government of the UK, Northern Ireland or any country or territory outside the UK;

12sext   *Securities and Investments Board v Pantell SA* [1989] 2 All ER 673; *Securities and Investments Board v Lloyd-Wright* [1993] 4 All ER 210.
13   See Regulations SI 1995 No 1536 and SI 1996 No 1586 set out in Appendix 2.
13bis   Section 58 *ibid*.

(2) a local authority in the UK or elsewhere;
(3) the Bank of England or the central bank of any country or territory outside the UK; or
(4) any international organisation the members of which include the UK or another member state of the European Union[13ter].

11.5.2   Exempted person

This relates to advertisements issued or caused to be issued by a person who is exempt under the Financial Services Act provided the advertisement relates to matters in respect of which he is exempt. Such persons include the following:

(1) a recognised investment exchange;
(2) a recognised clearing house;
(3) the Society of Lloyd's and persons permitted by the Council of Lloyd's to act as underwriting agents in connection with insurance business at Lloyd's;
(4) listed money market institutions;
(5) an appointed representative as respects investment business carried on by him as such a representative and certain government officers[14].

The Secretary of State is also authorised to make an order under s 46 of the Act exempting other persons to a specified extent. Various orders have been made, including those set out in Appendix 2.

11.5.3   Investment business in an EU state

This exemption relates to advertisements issued or caused to be issued by a national of a member state of the European Union (other than the UK) in the course of the investment business lawfully carried on by him in such state and which conform to the form and content of advertisements set out in the SIB Rules[14bis].

11.5.4   Listed securities

This exemption relates to advertisements in connection with listed securities. Such advertisements rely for approval or authorisation on the London

---

13ter   Section 58(1)(a) *ibid.*
14   Section 58(1)(b) and ss 36, 38, 42, 43, 44 and 45 *ibid.*
14bis   Section 58(1)(c) *ibid.*

Stock Exchange which applies the Rules set out in the Yellow Book (the admission of securities to listing), pursuant to s 154 of the Financial Services Act. This exemption covers listing particulars, supplementary listing particulars, a prospectus, a supplementary prospectus, formal notice giving brief details of an issue, offer notice (including an application form to subscribe for shares), mini prospectus, summary particulars, announcements of admission to listing, publications of results and circulars to shareholders[14ter].

Press releases and other advertisements which merely refer to the admission to listing or a public offer do not require to be submitted to the London Stock Exchange[14quat] but must be approved under s 57 of the Financial Services Act unless otherwise exempt.

11.5.5   Unlisted securities

These are governed by the Public Offers of Securities Regulations 1995[15].

The foregoing 'POS' Regulations relate to any investment not admitted to official listings and include investments on the Alternative Investment Market (AIM)[16]. These regulations also apply to prospectuses approved in other member states provided they meet the other requirements of the regulations[17].

11.6   Exempt advertisements under subordinate legislation

Section 58(3) authorises the Secretary of State (now the Treasury) to exempt, by order, the requirement for certain advertisements to be authorised under s 57 of the Financial Services Act. These are advertisements which:

(1) appear to have a private character by reason of a connection between the person issuing them and those to whom they are issued or otherwise;

(2) appear to deal with investment only incidentally;

14ter   Section 58(1)(d)(i) and (ii) *ibid* and Rules 8.23 to 8.26 of the Yellow Book.
14quat   Rule 8.26 of the Yellow Book.
15   SI 1995 No 1537 especially regs 12 and 16 (known as the 'POS' Regulations),
Financial Services Act 1986 (Investment Advertisements) (Exemptions) (No 2) Order
1995 (SI 1995 No 1536) art 14. This is set out in Appendix 2.
16   Regulation 3(1) *ibid.*
17   See Sched 4, Part II, *ibid.*

(3) are issued to persons appearing to be sufficiently expert to understand any risks involved; or

(4) fall within such other classes of advertisement as he thinks fit.

The latter category appears to embrace all the foregoing and indeed does not appear to be circumscribed by the former categories. One might indeed ask why the draughtsman found it necessary to specify four categories when enumeration of the last class would clearly have sufficed.

The following is a brief summary of advertisements that have been exempted from section 57. The reader is referred to the order[18] for the details and conditions applying to the exemptions.

(1) Specific advertisements (essentially relating to the company's (or group company's) own shares, debentures and warrants) issued by a body corporate to existing members or creditors.

(2) Advertisements issued by a body corporate, other than an open-ended investment company, in relation to relevant securities provided that the advertisement does not contain any invitation or offer to persons in relation to any investments or to effect any transaction with or to make use of any services provided by the body corporate, does not contain any information calculated to lead to persons entering into an investment agreement or to exercise any rights conferred by an investment. Where the advertisement contains information about the price of securities or their yield, it must contain a prominent warning that past performance cannot be relied upon as a guide to future performance. Examples under this head include results advertisements.

(3) Advertisements issued by a body corporate other than an open-ended investment company, if they are addressed to persons entitled to relevant bearer securities issued by that body corporate, contain no invitation to enter into an investment agreement other than in relation to bearer securities and contain no information relating to any investment which is not a relevant security issued by the body corporate.

(4) Advertisements issued by a body corporate in connection with employee share schemes.

(5) Advertisements issued by one body corporate in a group to another body corporate in the same group.

---

18   The Financial Services Act 1986 (Investment Advertisements) (Exemptions) Order 1996 (SI 1996 No 1586). This is set out in Appendix 2.

(6) Advertisements issued by a participator in a joint enterprise to another participator in the same joint enterprise.

(7) Investment advertisements issued in connection with the sale of goods or supply of services provided that the supplier's main business is to supply goods or services.

(8) Advertisements issued by an 'overseas person', namely a person without a permanent place of business in the UK to persons with whom he has an existing relationship established abroad.

(9) Advertisements issued to certain persons sufficiently expert to understand the risks involved. These persons are the following:

   (a) an authorised person, or a European investment firm carrying on home-regulated investment business in the UK;
   (b) an exempted person;
   (c) a journalist;
   (d) a government, local authority or public authority;
   (e) a body corporate with 20 or more members, or a subsidiary of a body corporate with 20 or more members if it or its holding or subsidiary has a called up share capital or net assets of not less than £500,000;
   (f) a body corporate otherwise than as described in (e) which has a share capital or net assets of not less than £5 million;
   (g) an unincorporated association with net assets of not less than £5 million;
   (h) a person holding a permission granted by the Secretary of State pursuant to s 23 of and Sched 1 to the Act;
   (i) a director, officer or employee of any of the foregoing whose responsibilities involve him in investment business activities;
   (j) a trustee of a trust with assets totalling at least £10 million.

   The list is an exhaustive and not indicative one. It follows that ordinary experienced businessmen, companies not falling within the above parameters and trustees of smaller trusts would not qualify as persons sufficiently expert to understand the risks involved.

(10) Advertisements issued to persons regarded as having an existing and common interest in the subject-matter of the advertisement. This exception applies to an invitation made or information given with respect to shares in or debentures of a private company if the

advertisement states that the only persons entitled to enter into the offer or agreement are those within an identified group of persons who at the time of the issue of the advertisement might reasonably be regarded as having an existing and common interest with each other and with the company and the affairs of the company and in what is to be done with the proceeds of the offer. The advertisement must also contain a statement by the directors or the promoters:

(a) accepting responsibility for the statement without limitation of liability on the basis that they have all taken reasonable care to ensure that every statement whether of fact or opinion is true and not misleading;

(b) either accepting responsibility without limitation of liability that all reasonable care has been taken to ensure that the document contains all such information as the addressees or their professional advisers would reasonably require and expect to find for the purpose of making an informed assessment of the assets and liabilities, financial position, profits and losses and prospects of the company and the rights attaching to the shares or debentures to which the document relates or the words 'you should regard any subscription for shares in or debentures of his company as made primarily to assist the furtherance of its objectives (other than any purely financial objectives) and only secondarily, if at all, as an investment';

(c) that the advertisement contains prominently the words 'If you are in any doubt about this offer you should consult a person authorised under the Financial Services Act 1986 who specialises in advising on investments of the kind being offered' or other words to a like effect.

(11) Advertisements issued by trustees and personal representatives to fellow trustees or beneficiaries.

(12) Advertisements issued by operators of recognised collective schemes who are not authorised under the 1986 Act.

(13) Advertisements relating to publications or programmes containing advice not falling within Sched 1, para 15 to the Financial Services Act.

(14) Advertisements relating to the facilities offered by a specified market.

(15) Advertisements relating to shares in a private company established to manage the fabric or common parts of residential or business property or to supply services to such property.

(16) Advertisements issued for the purpose of remedying injustice

stated by the Parliamentary Commission of Administration to have occurred.

Each of the foregoing is subject to further qualification and amplification set out in the order and the reader is referred to the order for details of the same[18bis].

11.7 Further exempt advertisements

The range of advertisements exempted from the need for authorisation under s 57 of the Financial Services Act is extended by a further order[19]. This excludes certain types of advertisements, subject to the conditions and requirements set out in the order. Briefly, but without setting out the details, they can be identified as follows:

(1) specified investment advertisements relating to shares in or debentures of a private company for the purpose of promoting or encouraging industrial or commercial activity or enterprise in the UK. Such an advertisement must *inter alia* contain the following notice:

> Investment in new business carries high risks, as well as the possibility of high rewards. It is highly speculative and potential investors should be aware that no established market exists for the trading of shares in private companies. Before investing in a project about which information is given, potential investors are strongly advised to take advice from a person authorised under the Financial Services Act 1986 who specialises in advising on investments of this kind.
>
> The persons to whose order this advertisement has been issued have taken reasonable steps to ensure that the information it contains is neither inaccurate nor misleading;

(2) certain advertisements issued in connection with take-overs of private companies. The conditions include that the offer must be for all shares in the target company, must be recommended by all directors of the latter and the consideration must be cash, shares or debentures of the offeror or any combination of the same;

(3) certain advertisements issued in connection with sales of shares in a body corporate;

(4) advertisements issued by persons holding permissions granted by the SIB under para 23 of Sched 1 to the Financial Services Act;

18bis See Appendix 2.
19 The Financial Services Act 1986 (Investment Advertisements) (Exemptions) (No 2) Order 1995 (SI 1995 No 1536). See Appendix 2.

(5) advertisements sent to the placer of the advertisement or the publication in which the advertisement appears;

(6) advertisements directed at informing or influencing persons involved with public bodies or persons generally involved in the acquisition or disposal of investments;

(7) advertisements relating to an investment falling within any of paras 1–5 of Sched 1 to the Financial Services Act which is traded or dealt with on a relevant EEA market or a market established under the rules of a specified investment exchange, or if the advertisement is required or permitted by an appropriate regulatory body;

(8) advertisements issued by industrial and provident societies relating to their debentures;

(9) advertisements which are prospectuses or supplementary prospectuses issued in accordance with the Public Offers of Securities Regulations 1995 ('the POS Regulations'). This exemption, together with that referred to in paragraph (7) above, effectively excludes advertisements relating to AIM companies from the requirement of authorisation under s 57;

(10) advertisements required or authorised to be issued under other legislation.

The reader is referred to the specific wording of the exemptions as set out in the order, for their precise terms.

11.8   Investment advertisements in newspapers

A distinct exemption from the category of investment advice is provided for in relation to advice given in a newspaper, journal, magazine or other periodical publication if the principal purpose of the publication, taken as a whole and including any advertisements contained in it, is not to lead to persons to invest in any particular investment[20]. This would cover investment tips in investment magazines and the business pages of newspapers. There is yet another exemption in respect of advice given in any programme or advertisement included, or made for inclusion, in any television service, sound broadcast service or teletext service[21]. On the other hand, if the advice is given in a tipsheet or in replies to readers' letters it is likely to constitute investment business and to require authorisation[22].

---

20   Financial Services Act 1986, Sched 1, para 25 and SIB Guidance Release No 4/89.
21   *Ibid* para 25A.
22   See SIB Guidance Release No 4/89.

11.9   False and misleading statements

Subject to limited exceptions, the Control of Misleading Advertisements Regulations 1988 do not apply to investment advertisements[23]. The exceptions are any advertisement which relates exclusively to any matter in relation to which the authorised person is an exempted person (under Part I, Chapter 4 of the Financial Services Act) and any advertisement relating to listing particulars, supplementary listing particulars and supplementary prospectuses where required or permitted to be published by an approved exchange. The regulations also do not apply to a bank or investment firm authorised in another EEA member state and carrying on home-regulated business in the UK[24].

The Financial Services Act renders it an offence for any person to make a statement, promise or forecast which he knows to be misleading, false or deceptive or dishonestly conceals any material facts. It is likewise an offence for any person to recklessly make, whether dishonestly or otherwise, a statement, promise or forecast which is misleading, false or deceptive. In each case the statement, promise or forecast must be made for the purpose of inducing, or recklessly as to whether or not it may induce, another person (whether or not the person to whom the statement is addressed or the facts are concealed) to enter or offer to enter into, or refrain from entering or offering to enter into, an investment agreement or to exercise or refrain from exercising any rights conferred by an investment[25]. In each case there must be a connection with the UK, namely that the statement etc is made in or from or the facts are concealed in or from the UK, the person on whom the inducement is intended is in the UK or the agreement is or would be entered into or the rights would be exercised in the UK. The person affected will also have an action for damages at common law.

11.10   Form and content of investment advertisements

The form and content of investment advertisements are, broadly speaking, governed by the Core Conduct of Business Rules made by the Securities and Investment Board and which are incorporated in the rules of the various self-regulating organisations (SROs). The following is a summary of the relevant rules applying to advertisements[26]:

---

23   SI 1988 No 915, reg 3.
24   Investment Services Regulations 1995 (SI 1995 No 3275).
25   Section 47. See also *Securities and Investments Board v Pantell SA (No 2)*, footnote 11bis *supra*.
26   Rules 5 to 12.

(1) Where a firm issues or approves an investment advertisement it must apply appropriate expertise and be able to show that it believes on reasonable grounds that the advertisement is fair and not misleading. The advertisement must also identify the issuer or approver and its regulator (ie the relevant SRO).

(2) A firm must not approve a specific investment advertisement if it relates to units in an unregulated collective investment scheme.

(3) In relation to a direct offer advertisement, namely a specific investment advertisement (including a preprinted or off-the-screen advertisement) which contains an offer to enter into the investment with anyone who responds to the advertisement or an invitation to a person to make an offer to the firm and specifies the manner or indicates a form in which any response is to be made (eg by providing a tear-off slip) the advertisement must:

    (a) give information about the investments or investment services, the terms of the offer and the risks involved which is adequate and fair having regard to the UK or overseas regulatory protections which apply and the market to which the advertisement is directed; and

    (b) offer derivatives or warrants only where the firm itself issues the advertisement and only to a customer for whom it believes on reasonable grounds the investment or investment services are suitable.

(4) A firm must not issue or approve a specific investment advertisement which is calculated to lead directly or indirectly to an overseas person carrying on an investment business, which is not regulated business, with or for a private customer who is in the UK, unless the advertisement contains the prescribed disclosure and the firm has no reason to doubt that the overseas person will deal with investors in the UK in an honest and reliable way. The prescribed disclosure means a written statement that all or most of the protections provided by the UK regulatory system do not apply and, where the business is excluded from the Investors' Compensation Scheme, a statement that compensation under that scheme will not be available. Such prescribed disclosure must also be made in any communication made or advertisement issued to a private customer outside the UK in connection with investment business which is not regulated business.

(5) A firm's communications designed to promote the provision of investment services must be fair and not misleading and must be presented fairly and clearly.

(6) A firm must not recommend a transaction to a private customer or act as a discretionary manager for him unless it has taken reasonable steps to enable him to understand the nature of the risks involved.

(7) A firm must take reasonable steps to ensure that a private customer is given adequate information about its identity, business address, the identity and status of its employees and other agents, its regulator and, where the firm is promoting a packaged product, adequate information about the firm's polarisation status. The firm must also give a customer wishing to buy a packaged product sufficient information to enable him to make an informed decision.

(8) Comparisons and contrasts must be based on verified facts or on assumptions set out in the advertisement.

(9) Prescribed risk warnings must be set out.

Each self-regulating organisation also has its own rules which must be considered in relation to any investment advertisement published by it and this is the subject of Chapter 12.

Investment advertisements

Summary flowchart guide

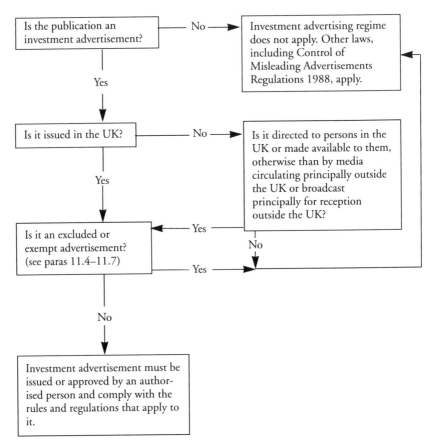

Chapter 12

Investment Advertising Rules

12.1 Definitions of advertisement types

It is important to recognise that the rules of the Securities and Investments Board (SIB) and the rules of each self-regulating organisation (SRO) contain their own definitions and interpretation of terms although fundamentally they bear the same meanings. We shall now turn to the principal categorisation of advertisements.

12.1.1 DIE advertisement[1]

A DIE advertisement is an advertisement issued by a designated investment exchange or required or permitted to be published by the rules of a designated investment exchange.

12.1.2 Direct offer advertisement[2]

A direct offer advertisement is a specific investment advertisement (some of which are discussed below[2bis]) (including a pre-printed or off-the-screen advertisement) which:

(1) contains an offer by the firm or another offeror to enter into an advertisement agreement with anyone who responds to the advertisement or an invitation to anyone to respond to the advertisement

---

1   SIB Rules: The Financial Services Core Glossary 1991 (3rd edn); SFA Rules: Definitions Chapter 9; IMRO Rules: Definitions Schedule.
2   *Ibid.*
2bis   para. 12.5.

by making an offer to the firm or another offeree to enter into an investment agreement; and

(2) specifies the manner or indicates a form in which any response is to be made eg a tear-off slip on a coupon, completion and return of an application form.

12.1.3   Exempt advertisement[3]

An exempt advertisement is an investment advertisement which can lawfully be issued in the UK by a person who is not an authorised person without approval of its contents by an authorised person.

An exempt advertisement includes advertisements exempted under s 58 of the Act and orders made under that section. The reader is referred to the previous chapter and the orders set out in Appendix 2.

12.1.4   Image advertisement[4]

An image advertisement is an advertisement which does no more than:

(1) promote public awareness of the advertiser;
(2) describe the services it provides or the products it markets;
(3) commend the advertiser in general, but not any particular service it provides or product it markets; or
(4) offer to supply further information on request.

12.1.5   'Off-the-page' or 'off-the-screen' advertisements

Off-the-page and off-the-screen advertisements are those which contain within them a mechanism by which an investor can make an immediate commitment to an investment or make such a commitment subject to satisfying any preconditions. The most common form is a coupon advertisement in a publication enabling a person to return the coupon with his investment cheque.

12.1.6   Packaged product[5]

Although this is not an advertisement type, it is thought appropriate to explain the meaning of 'packaged product' as it appears frequently in rela-

---

3   *Ibid.*
4   SIB Rules: Core Glossary 1991 *loc cit*; SFA Rules *loc cit*; IMRO Rules *loc cit.*
5   SIB Core Glossary 1991 *loc cit*; SFA Rules *loc cit*; IMRO Rules *loc cit.*

tion to advertisements. A packaged product is an investment contract which may lead to an investment in a life policy, units in a regulated collective investment scheme or in an investment trust savings scheme (including PEPs investing in such unit trusts).

12.1.7   Short form advertisement[6]

This is defined slightly differently in the various rules. In the SIB rules it means an advertisement which contains the advertiser's name and in respect of investment business does no more than some or all of the following:

(1) display the advertiser's address, telephone number, symbol or logogram;
(2) describe the advertiser's business and fees charged;
(3) contain one or both of a statement, or symbol approved by the Securities and Investment Board to show that the advertiser (or the firm approving the advertisement) is regulated in the conduct of investment business by the Board;
(4) state, in relation to investments which the advertiser will or may buy or sell (or arrange to buy or sell) their names, indicative prices, differences of prices from previous prices, their income and yields, their earnings (or price/earnings ratio);
(5) state, simply as a matter of fact, and not so as to imply any offer to deal, the advertiser (alone or with others) who is willing to arrange the issue of or a transaction in a particular investment.

Apart from the fact that different SRO rules have slightly different provisions, in each case the definition requires reference to a particular investment to be expressed in factual terms and not so as to imply any offer to deal or to arrange a deal in that investment. Short form advertisements include 'tombstones' and notices that transactions have taken place.

12.1.8   Specific investment advertisement[7]

This is an advertisement which identifies and promotes a particular investment or investment service. It may not be issued or approved without an accompanying statement of the name and regulator of the party approving it.

---

6   SIB: The Financial Services (Glossary and Interpretation) Rules and Regulations 1990; SFA Rules *loc cit*; IMRO Rules *loc cit*.
7   SIB Core Glossary 1991 *loc cit*; SFA Rules *loc cit*; IMRO Rules *loc cit*.

12.1.9   Takeover advertisement[8]

A takeover advertisement is an advertisement which is subject to the City Code on Takeovers and Mergers and the Rules Governing Substantial Acquisitions of Shares published by the Panel on Takeovers andMergers. It includes an advertisement to which such code would apply but for any exemption granted by the foregoing panel.

12.2   A note on direct offer advertisements

As already mentioned, these advertisements comprise off-the-page and off-the-screen advertisements. In an age when direct mail is so commonplace, they have assumed great popularity. Effectively they amount to 'execution-only business', namely business which does not involve the advertiser or the investment advisor providing any investment advice or assuming any knowledge of the customer or any responsibility in relation to the suitability of the product for the customer.

The Personal Investment Authority (PIA) Adopted FIMBRA Advertising Rules contain the requirement that the advertisement must include a statement that if the investor has any doubt as to whether the contract is suitable for him, he should contact the advertiser for independent advice. The addressee is also invited to contact the advertiser if he or she requires investment advice. Direct offer advertisements are required to contain more detailed information about the investment advertised than other investment advertisements. This is not unreasonable having regard to the fact that they can immediately result in the creation of investment agreements.

The disclosure requirements in direct offer advertisements for packaged products require a statement of the key features, as defined in the relevant rules. This may be a stand-alone document or be incorporated within the direct offer advertisement.

The key features must be typical or representative of the persons to whom the advertisement is addressed. They must also contain the commission or remuneration payable to a person if the contract is proceeded with. The PIA Adopted Lautro Rules contain separate provisions for direct offer advertisements.

The rules of the SIB permit direct offer advertisements in the form of off-the-screen advertisements provided that they are capable of being examined continuously for a reasonable period of time. Some of the SROs eg the PIA Adopted Lautro Rules, only permit a direct offer advertisement in the form of a printed document.

---

8   SIB *ibid*; SFA Rules *ibid*; IMRO Rules *ibid*.

The view of the SIB is that provided there is full and fair disclosure there need be no restriction on the freedom to issue direct offer advertisements. However, this view is qualified in relation to direct offer advertising of derivatives (options, futures and contracts for differences) and warrants. In these cases the SIB require the advertiser to satisfy itself first on the basis of 'know your customer'.

Rule 5.4 of the SIB Core Conduct of Business Rules provides that a firm must not issue or approve a direct offer advertisement for the sale of investments or the provision of investment services to a private customer unless the advertisement:

(1) gives information about the investments or investment services, the terms of the offer and the risks involved, which is adequate and fair having regard to the UK or overseas regulatory protections which apply and the market to which the advertisement is directed; and

(2) offers derivatives or warrants only where the firm itself issues the advertisement and does so only to a customer for whom it believes on reasonable grounds the investment or investment services to be suitable[8bis].

12.3   Advertising rules of self-regulating organisations

Each of the Securities and Investments Boards (SIB) and Self-Regulating Organisations (SRO) has its own advertising rules albeit that the rules are largely based upon the rules of the SIB and to a considerable extent replicate each other. Indeed, one would be justified in asking why the SROs cannot agree a standard set of advertising rules with particular variations applicable to the individual SROs.

As it would be a futile exercise to point out the distinctions between the different SRO advertising rules, the reader is referred to the source of these rules as set out below and the rules themselves in the Appendices.

12.3.1   Sources of advertising rules (the reader is referred to extracts from the Rules set out in Appendix 2)

(a)   Securities and Investments Board (SIB)

See Chapter III (B): Conduct of Business Rules 1990, Part 7.

8bis   See also Securities and Investment Board Policy Statement: Regulations of the Marketing of Investment Products and Services (March 1991).

(b)   Securities and Futures Authority (SFA)

See Chapter 5: Conduct of Business Rules, Sections 5–16 dealing with Advertising and Marketing.

(c)   Investment Management Regulatory Organisation (IMRO)

See Chapter 11: Conduct of Business Rules and in particular 11.1 as well as Appendix 1.1(1) dealing with Seeking Customers and Advertising for Business.

The Advertising Code in the Rule Book of IMRO merely has the status of formal guidance and does not constitute part of the rules of IMRO although compliance with it would be advisable.

(d)   Personal Investment Authority (PIA)

Rules relating *inter alia* to conduct of business including advertising have been adopted by the PIA on a transitional basis from the rule books of the other self-regulating organisations and also certain of the rules of the Securities and Investments Board. Applicants for membership of the PIA are notified which of these rules applies to them. In due course the PIA's own rules will replace these Adopted Rules. Former FIMBRA members will be governed by the Adopted FIMBRA Rules, former Lautro members will be governed by the Adopted former Lautro Rules and former IMRO members will be governed by the Adopted IMRO Rules.

The Adopted Rules of FIMBRA relating to advertising are to be found in Part 18 of the PIA Rules, Tables 18A–18C and Appendix 2B, including Notes 1–9.

The Adopted Rules of Lautro relating to advertisements are to be found in Part VI of the Adopted Rules of Lautro.

The advertising rules of IMRO and SIB are also adopted in the PIA Rulebook in respect of members to whom these rules apply. Readers are referred to the relevant IMRO and SIB Rules as the Adopted Rules are not set out in the Appendices.

12.3.2 Additional relevant rules

The rules of the PIA prescribe requirements for disclosure by appointed representatives and their investment staff in advertisements of their relationship to the PIA member and the fact that the member is regulated by the Personal Investment Authority. The member must secure compliance with these requirements. The PIA rules also set out the requirements for advertisements on stationery and where these are incompatible with the requirements for advertisements the advertising rules prevail[8ter].

8ter   PIA, rule 4.4.2.

12.4 Advertising rules of Recognised Professional Bodies (RPBs)

This text does not seek to deal with the separate advertising rules of RPBs. The RPBs are the Chartered Association of Certified Accountants, the Institute of Actuaries, the Institute of Chartered Accountants in England and Wales, the Institute of Chartered Accountants in Ireland, the Institute of Chartered Accountants of Scotland, the Insurance Brokers' Regulatory Council, the Law Society, the Law Society of Northern Ireland, and the Law Society of Scotland.

The reader should note that the rules of the various RPBs do specifically regulate the conduct of investment business including advertisements, the publication of recommendations and the like.

Ordinarily firms would make a specified individual responsible for ensuring compliance with the advertising requirements, retain a record of the advertisement for at least three years from publication showing who approved the advertisement and including a record of the evidence supporting its actual content. The rules of certain of the SROs make this mandatory.

12.5 Specific advertising rules applying to specific investment advertisements

12.5.1 Introduction

The reader is referred to the preceding chapter relating to the advertising of investments generally. This section sets out additional rules which govern specific investment advertisements. It also collates pertinent provisions under relevant product headings.

12.5.2 Pensions

The previous chapter alluded to rules applying to investment-based pension schemes. Set out below are separate provisions applying in the main to deposit-based pension schemes.

The Personal Pension Schemes (Advertisements) Regulations 1990[9] set out the requirements for advertisements relating to a deposit-based scheme, namely a scheme built on investment of contributions in an interest-bearing account. The regulations contain their own definitions of

---

9   SI 1990 No 1140.

'advertisement' and 'off-the-page advertisement'. They prescribe the requisite information and statutory warning notice where the advertisement contains projections, requirements of 'off-the-page advertisements' and that advertisements for deposit-based pension schemes shall not, in respect of their design, format or content:

(1) convey any information which is false or misleading;

(2) contain any statement of fact which the issuer does not at the time the advertisement is issued have reasonable grounds for believing will continue to be true for so long as it remains relevant to the subject-matter of the advertisement;

(3) make any comparison with any other personal pension scheme or occupational pension scheme or the state earnings-related pension scheme which is unfair or misleading;

(4) make any statement about the past performance of the scheme unless it also contains a warning that such information is not necessarily a guide to future performance; or

(5) contain, whether expressly or by implication, any statement to the effect that the advertisement has been approved by any government department or by the Occupational Pensions Board.

A breach of the regulations constitutes an offence.

The Pensions Schemes Act 1993 provides for regulations to be made relating to the form and content of advertisements issued by or on behalf of the trustees or managers of a personal or occupational pension scheme[10]. No regulations have been made to date.

The PIA rules specify additional requirements for specific investment advertisements for life policy or pension contracts including the need to insert prescribed warning notices regarding the return on investments.

12.5.3 Listed securities

Where listing particulars are to be published, any advertisement or other information of the kind specified by the listing rules must first be approved or authorised by the competent authority which, in the case of listings in the UK, is the International Stock Exchange of the UK and the Republic of Ireland Ltd[11]. An authorised person who contravenes this section can be sued by any person who suffers loss as a result of the contravention or, if the authorised person is a member of a recognised self-regulating organisa-

---

10   Section 117.
11   Section 154(1), Financial Services Act 1986.

tion, he is likely to be in breach of the rules of that organisation[12]. An unauthorised person who acts in breach of this provision is guilty of an offence[13].

As in the case of other investment advertisements, a defence is available to a person who in the ordinary course of a business other than an investment business issued an advertisement or other information to the order of another person where he believed, on reasonable grounds, that the advertisement or information had been approved or its issue had been authorised by a competent authority[14]. Where information has been approved or its issue has been authorised, neither the person issuing it nor any person responsible for it incurs any civil liability by reason of any statement or omission if the information and the listing particulars, taken together, would not be likely to mislead persons who are likely to consider the acquisition of the securities in question[15].

The foregoing provisions also apply in relation to a prospectus required by listing rules[16].

Separate provisions apply to false or misleading information in listing particulars but these fall outside the range of this text.

12.5.4 Public offers of unlisted securities

The Public Offers of Securities Regulations 1995 ('POS' Regulations) apply to any investment which is not admitted to official listing, is not the subject of an application for such listing and falls within para 1, 2, 4 or 5 of Sched 1 to the Financial Services Act 1986, namely, in general terms, falls within the category of shares, debentures, warrants relating to entitlement to or certificates representing securities. The regulations require a prospectus to be issued where securities are offered to the public in the UK for the first time and govern the form and content of the prospectus.

An advertisement, notice, poster or document (other than a prospectus) announcing a public offer of securities for which a prospectus is or will be required under the regulations may not be issued to or caused to be issued to the public in the UK by the person proposing to make the offer unless it states that a prospectus is or will be published and gives an address in the UK from which it can be obtained or will be obtainable[17]. A breach of such

---

12 Section 154(2), *Ibid.*
13 Section 154(3), *Ibid.*
14 Section 154(4), cf s 57(4).
15 Section 154(5).
16 Section 154A.
17 Regulation 12.

provision by an authorised person is tantamount to breach by him of the rules of the self-regulating organisation or recognised professional body to which he belongs. A breach of such provision by an unauthorised person constitutes an offence. In addition, any such breach is actionable at the hands of a person who suffers loss as a result of the contravention, subject to defences available for breach of statutory duty[18].

12.5.5   Securities advertisements addressed to sophisticated customers

Where a firm issues or approves a specific investment advertisement it must take reasonable care to ensure that it contains the requisite information prescribed by the rules. However this does not apply, for instance in the case of the SFA rules, to an advertisement which is addressed to persons who are not private customers or which states that the investment is not available to private customers or is contained in a publication circulating principally outside the UK or is a short-form advertisement[19].

12.5.6   Promotion of life policies

It is an offence to issue or cause to be issued in the UK an advertisement inviting a person to enter into or offer to enter into a contract of life assurance (namely an insurance contract which constitutes an investment under the Financial Services Act) or containing information calculated to lead directly or indirectly to any person doing so or, in the course of a business, advising or procuring any person in the UK to enter into such a contract, unless the insurance falls within certain categories[20]. The permitted categories are insurance with:

(1) a body authorised under s 3 or 4 of the Insurance Companies Act 1982 to effect and carry out such contracts of insurance;
(2) a body registered under enactments relating to friendly societies;
(3) an insurance company the head office of which is in a member state and which is entitled to carry on there insurance business of the relevant class;
(4) an insurance company which has a branch or agency in such a member state and is entitled under the law of that state to carry on there insurance business of the relevant class;

---

18   Regulation 16(1)–(4).
19   SFA Rules, rule 5.9(6)–(9).
20   Section 130(1).

(5) an insurance company authorised to effect or carry out such contracts of insurance in any country or territory which is designated for the purpose by an order made by the Secretary of State and any conditions imposed by the order have been satisfied[21].

12.5.7 Second-hand life policies

The rules of the Personal Investment Authority make express provision for the advertising of and recommendations about second-hand life policies. Rules for advertising such investments are set out in Appendix F2B and rules relating to the recommendations about such policies are contained in Appendix F6 to the PIA Rules.

12.5.8 Off-the-page advertisements[22]

(1) Off-the-page advertisements for life policies.
   The PIA Rules specify that information required in a Key Features Document prepared in accordance with the Adopted Lautro Rules must be set out in the advertisements.
(2) Off-the-page advertisements for regulated collective schemes.

Once again the PIA Rules stipulate that the advertisement must contain information set out, or required to be adopted, in a Key Features Document prepared in accordance with the Adopted Lautro Rules.

12.5.9 Collective investment schemes

A collective investment scheme is defined in s 75 of the Financial Services Act and essentially consists of three items. First, the collective participation by persons in property or profits from the property; secondly, the day-to-day management of the property by a third party; thirdly, the pooling of contributions and profits. The Act identifies two types of collective investment schemes. The unit trust scheme is a collective investment scheme under which the property is held on trust for the participants. An open-ended investment company is a collective scheme under which the property belongs beneficially to, and is managed by, a body corporate which invests the funds for the benefit of the members. The rights of the members are represented by shares in or securities in that body corporate.
   Only authorised unit trust schemes or overseas collective investment

---

21   Section 130(2) and (3).
22   PIA Rules, r 7.24, 7.25 and 7.26.

schemes recognised under ss 86–88 of the Financial Services Act 1986 may be freely promoted by authorised persons in the UK. Thus, it is only in respect of such schemes that an advertisement may be issued inviting persons to become participants or containing information calculated to lead directly or indirectly to persons becoming participants. Likewise it is only in respect of such schemes that an authorised person may advise or procure any person to become a participant[23].

Recognised schemes are those which may be promoted in the UK pursuant to recognition by the Securities and Investment Board under s 86 (the UCITS Directive), s 87 (designated countries or territories such as certain of the Channel Islands, Bermuda and the Isle of Man) or s 88 (other individually recognised overseas schemes).

The restrictions on promotion, including advertising, do not apply if the advertisment is issued or the advice is given to or the marketing is targeted at a person who is an authorised person or whose ordinary business involves the acquisition and disposal of property of the same kind as the property to which the scheme relates. Furthermore, the restrictions do not apply to persons listed in the Financial Services (Promotion of Unregulated Schemes) Regulations 1991 made by the Securities and Investment Board pursuant to its powers under s 76(3) of the Act.

There is no criminal or civil sanction for breach of s 76(1). However, a person who contravenes any provision of Chapter VIII of the Financial Services Act which relates to collective investment schemes is treated as having contravened the SIB's rules or the rules of the relevant SRO or RPB by which the person is authorised[24]. If an unauthorised person promotes a collective investment scheme he commits an offence under s 4 of the Act.

12.5.10   Advertising collective investment schemes

Scheme particulars will usually constitute investment advertisements and provided they comply with the regulations applying to scheme particulars, will not need to satisfy any additional advertising regulations.

A person in the European Union who has become an authorised person may issue an investment advertisement relating to his collective investment scheme in the UK provided the scheme has been recognised by the Securities and Investments Board. The investment advertisement must comply with the relevant rules.

---

23   Section 76(1), Financial Services Act 1986.
24   Section 98 *ibid.*

An investment advertisement by an unauthorised person requires the approval of an authorised person. However, a European Union operator who is not authorised may advertise the collective investment scheme if the advertisement is issued in the course of investment business lawfully carried on by him in his home state in the European Union, conforms with SIB's advertising rules and the operator is a national of a member state other than the UK[25].

---

25   Section 76(2) *ibid.*

Chapter 13

Miscellaneous Advertising

There are various products or services which can be described as financial or quasi-financial and the advertising of which is regulated in one form or another. This chapter is devoted to them.

13.1 Property

The Property Misdescriptions Act 1991 renders it an offence to make a false or misleading statement about a prescribed matter in the course of an estate agency business or a property development business, otherwise than in providing conveyancing services[1]. In accordance with the usual provisions in this type of legislation it is a defence for the accused person to show that he took all reasonable steps and exercised all due diligence to avoid commiting the offence[2]. It is specifically provided that the contract shall not be void or unenforceable and shall not give rise to a right of action in civil proceedings in respect of any loss, by reason only of the commission of such an offence[3].

Unusually in legislation of this kind, the material concepts are defined. Thus 'false' is defined as meaning false to a material degree and a statement is considered to be misleading if, though not false, what a reasonable person may be expected to infer from it or from any omission from it, is false[4].

---

1 Section 1(1).
2 Section 2(1). For a recent successful defence under this section see *London Borough of Enfield v Castle Estate Agents Ltd* (1997) 73 P & CR 343 QBD.
3 Section 1(4).
4 Section 1(5)(a) and (b).

The statement must be false or misleading about a prescribed matter and the following matters have been specified for that purpose[5]:

(1) location or address;
(2) aspect, view, outlook or environment;
(3) availability and nature of services, facilities or amenities;
(4) proximity to any services, place, facilities or amenities;
(5) accommodation, measurements or sizes;
(6) fixtures and fittings;
(7) physical or structural characteristics, form of construction or condition;
(8) fitness for any purpose or strength of any buildings or other structures on land or of land itself;
(9) treatments, processes, repairs or improvements or the effects thereof;
(10) conformity or compliance with any scheme, standard, test or regulations, or the existence of any guarantee;
(11) survey, inspections, investigation, valuation or appraisal by any person or the results thereof;
(12) the grant or giving of any award or prize for design or construction;
(13) history;
(14) person by whom any building, fixture or component was designed etc;
(15) the length of time during which land has been available for sale;
(16) price;
(17) tenure or estate;
(18) length of any lease or the unexpired term of any lease and the terms and conditions of the lease;
(19) amount of any ground rent, rent or premium and frequency of rent review;
(20) amount of any rent-charge;
(21) where all or any part of any land is let to a tenant or subject to a licence, particulars of the tenancy or licence;
(22) amount of any service or maintenance charge or liability for common repairs;
(23) council tax payable;
(24) rates payable;
(25) existence or nature of any planning permission or proposal for development, construction or change of use;

---

5   The Property Misdescriptions (Specified Matters) Order 1992 (SI 1992 No 2834).

(26) the passing or rejection of any plans of proposed building work;

(27) the granting of a warrant or certification of completion under the Building (Scotland) Act 1959;

(28) the application of any statutory provision which restricts the use of land;

(29) the existence or nature of any restrictive covenants;

(30) easements, servitudes or wayleaves;

(31) existence and extent of any public or private right of way.

Under the Estates Agents Act 1979 an estate agent who commits an offence relating to the misdescription of property may be declared an unfit person to carry on estate agents' work[6].

It is not unusual for estate agents, surveyors and the like to set out, in their property particulars a clause purporting to exclude liability. Any such disclaimer is subject to the test of reasonableness in the Unfair Contract Terms Act 1977 which prohibits a person from excluding or restricting his liability for negligence except in so far as the term or notice satisfies the requirement of reasonableness[7]. In addition, it is submitted that exclusion clauses in relation to consumer contracts will need to pass the hurdles set by the Unfair Terms in Consumer Contracts Regulations 1994[8].

13.2 Timeshares

The Timeshare Act 1992 has been extensively supplemented by the Timeshare Regulations 1997[9].

The regulations govern *inter alia* the advertising of timeshare rights and make it obligatory for an advertisement to indicate the possibility of obtaining a brochure or document containing the information prescribed by the Act and where it may be obtained. Such information includes a general description of the proposed accommodation. A person who contravenes the section is guilty of an offence. In the usual manner, it is a defence for the person to show that at the time when he advertised the timeshare rights he did not know and had no reasonable cause to suspect that he was advertising timeshare rights or that he had reasonable cause to believe that the advertisement complied with the requisite requirements[10].

---

6   Estate Agents Act 1979, s 3(1)(a), (3) read with The Estate Agents (Specified Offences) (No 2) (Amendments) Order 1992 (SI 1992 No 2833).

7   Section 2(2).

8   SI 1994 No 3159. See especially reg 4 and Sched III, para 1(b).

9   SI 1997 No 1081.

10   Regulation 4.

13.3 *Bureaux de change*

Bureaux de change are governed by regulations which do not specifically relate to advertisements but cover information relating to the subject matter of the transaction. They are briefly outlined below.

A person operates a *bureaux de change* if he operates an enterprise in the course of which he buys from or sells to consumers, and holds himself out to consumers generally as being prepared to buy and sell any foreign currency.

The relevant regulations[11] require the person to provide exchange rate information in writing, clearly and prominently, so as to be visible to each customer as he approaches the premises. Once an exchange rate transaction has been entered into the customer must be furnished with a receipt containing the prescribed information. Similar rules apply to coin exchange machines. Criminal penalties are provided for breach of the regulations.

13.4 Lotteries

In general, it is illegal to promote a lottery except for the National Lottery established under the National Lottery etc Act 1993. The prohibition in the Lotteries and Amusements Act 1976 includes advertising for sale or distribution of any tickets or chances in a lottery[12]. The Act does not define 'lottery' and resort should be had for this purpose to the relevant cases. A lottery has been defined as the distribution of prizes by chance where the persons taking part in the operation, or a substantial number of them, make a payment or consideration in return for obtaining their chance of a prize[13].

The range of pseudo-financial advertising governed by controls is extensive, ranging from holiday package brochures on the one hand, to advertisements for pre-paid funeral plans on the other. This work does not seek to be exhaustive of the entire range.

---

11   The Price Indication (*Bureaux de Change*) (No 2) Regulations 1992 (SI 1992 No 737).
12   Section 2(1)(b).
13   *Reader's Digest Association Ltd v Williams* [1976] 3 All ER 737 at 739. See the more detailed discussion on lotteries at Chapter 17, 17.2.

Chapter 14

Marketing of Credit and Hire Facilities

14.1 General observations

An investment by its very nature involves a long-term commitment on the part of the investor and hence one might expect the marketing of investments to be extensively regulated, as indeed is the case. Credit and hire facilities on the other hand tend to involve a short to medium-term commitment and obligations which are transparent or can be made reasonably transparent, by reference to the cost of the credit or hire facilities. The borrower or hirer has a reasonable opportunity of arriving at a fair estimate of his potential commitment at the outset by calculating the cost of credit or hire over the period of the loan or hire agreement. All this would dictate a fairly simple regime relating to the marketing of credit or hire facilities except for the fact that in recent times there has been legitimate pressure relating to mortgage lending. The Office of Fair Trading amongst others has been of the view that there is a significant imbalance in the advice proffered to borrowers in respect of long-term mortgage commitments as compared to the advice to which investors are entitled under the Financial Services regime in respect of investment advice. This defect has recently been remedied by a new voluntary Code of Mortgage Lending Practice which applies to loans, excluding overdrafts, secured on residential homes unless the loan is governed by the Consumer Credit Act 1974.

14.2   General statutory controls

14.2.1   Minors

It is an offence for a person, with a view to financial gain to send to a minor any document inviting him to borrow money, to obtain goods on credit or hire, to obtain services on credit or to apply for information or advice on borrowing money, obtaining credit or hiring goods[1].

Where a document is received by a minor at any school or educational establishment for minors, a person sending it to him at that establishment knowing or suspecting it to be such an establishment, shall be taken to have reasonable cause to suspect that he is a minor[2]. It is a defence to show that the person sending the document did not know and had no reasonable cause to suspect that the recipient was a minor.[3]

The leading case is that of the *Alliance and Leicester Building Society v Babbs*[4], a decision of the Divisional Court. The facts in this case were that a nine-year-old with a savings account with the Alliance & Leicester received in the envelope containing a statement of the account, an offer of a personal loan by way of a mail shot. The leaflet, at the foot of one of its pages, bore a statement that loans were not available to applicants under 18 years of age. It was submitted on behalf of the appellant Society that when one read the documents as a whole, including the foregoing notice, properly construed, it was not an invitation to any minor into whose hands it might fall to borrow money from the Society.

That argument was accepted by the court and was sufficient for the appeal to succeed. The court also found that the circular had not been sent to the minor by the Society with a view to obtaining financial gain from a person who at the time of receipt of the brochure was a minor, another requirement of the section, owing to the fact that the computer program was geared to rejecting such applications.

Circulars for loans sent to the public at large should contain a clear statement that loans are not available to persons under 18 years of age and require the applicant either to state his age or to declare that he is at least 18 years of age.

However, these precautions will not suffice if the trader, wittingly or unwittingly, grants applications received from minors pursuant to such written invitations.

---

1   Section 50(1), Consumer Credit Act 1974.
2   Section 50(2) *ibid.*
3   Section 50(3) *ibid.*
4   [1993] CCLR 77.

Both the Banking Code and the Mortgage Code caution lenders against sending marketing material indiscriminately. Subscribers to the codes are required to be selective and careful where borrowers are under 18 years of age and where material relates to loans.

14.2.2   Canvassing credit agreements

Subject to limited exceptions, it is an offence to canvass debtor-creditor agreements ie personal loan agreements, off trade premises[5]. A debtor-creditor agreement is a regulated consumer credit agreement being one of the following:

(1) a restricted-use credit agreement to finance a transaction between the debtor and the supplier, other than the creditor, not made by the creditor under pre-existing arrangements or in contemplation of future arrangements between himself and the supplier; or

(2) a restricted-use credit agreement to refinance any existing indebtedness of the debtor, whether to the creditor or another person; or

(3) an unrestricted-use credit agreement which is not made by the creditor under pre-existing arrangements between himself and the supplier in the knowledge that the credit is to be used to finance a transaction between the debtor and the supplier[6].

'Trade premises' means a place where a business is carried on, whether on a permanent or temporary basis, by the creditor or owner (under a hire agreement), a supplier, the canvasser, or the person whose employee or agent the canvasser is, or the consumer[7].

Canvassing consists of soliciting the consumer into a debtor-creditor agreement by making oral representations to the consumer or any other individual eg the individual's spouse, during a visit by the canvasser to premises which are not trade premises as described above, if such a visit is carried out for the purpose of making such oral representations and is not carried out in response to a signed written request by or on behalf of the person making it and made on a previous occasion[8].

It follows that it is quite permissible for a canvasser to solicit entry into personal loan agreements if he first calls on the proposed borrowers and

---

5   Section 49(1) and the Determination made by the Director General of Fair Trading under s 49(3).

6   Section 13 *ibid.*

7   Section 48(2) *ibid.*

8   Section 48(1), s 49(2) and s 153 *ibid.*

requests a signed written invitation to call on a subsequent occasion. There should be some realistic gap between the two visits, so that it is not merely artificial. Calling on consecutive days or even on the same day, say in the morning for the invitation and in the evening to solicit entry into the loan agreement, would ordinarily comply with the requirements. Likewise, if the call is made for purposes other than soliciting the entry of the individual into the credit agreement eg for selling him a life assurance policy and in the course of such visit the borrower requests a mortgage or personal loan facility, that would not contravene the prohibition.

A borrower in this situation is given 'belt and braces' protection because even if he subsequently enters into the credit agreement, it will, by definition, be a cancellable regulated agreement so that he will also have a limited opportunity to rescind the agreement once he has entered into it[9].

14.2.3   Unsolicited credit-tokens

It is an offence to give a person a credit-token if he has not asked for it. The request must be contained in a written document signed by the person making the request unless the credit-token relates to a small debtor-creditor-supplier agreement ie one which does not exceed a limit stipulated under s 17 of the Consumer Credit Act[10]. The prohibition does not apply to the giving of a credit-token to a person for use under a credit-token agreement already made or in renewal or replacement of a credit-token previously accepted by the person under an agreement which continues in force[11].

A credit-token is a card, cheque, voucher, coupon, stamp, form, booklet or other document or thing given to an individual by a person carrying on a consumer credit business, who undertakes:

(1) that on the production of it (whether or not some other action is also required) he will supply cash, goods and services (or any of them) on credit; or

(2) that where, on the production of it to a third party (whether or not any other action is also required) the third party supplies cash, goods and services (or any of them), he will pay the third party for them (whether or not deducting any discount or commission), in return for payment to him by the individual[12].

---

9   See s 67 *ibid.*
10   Section 51(1) and (2) *ibid.*
11   Section 51(3) *ibid.*
12   Section 14(1) *ibid.*

The use of an object to operate a machine, for example a cash machine or ATM provided by the person giving the object or by a third party is regarded as the production of the object[13].

The breadth of this provision requires extreme care to be exercised in relation to promotional letters and leaflets sent to borrowers or prospective borrowers inviting them to present such documents in order to qualify for the offer of a credit facility. The offence requires the 'production' of some or other object and will therefore not be committed if the customer or potential customer is merely required to disclose some information eg a reference number or password contained in the document sent to him (rather than the document's production), in order to qualify for the credit facility. In other words, the document will then not constitute a credit-token. It is also submitted that a credit agreement which is sent to a prospective borrower for signature by him does not constitute a credit-token even if signed in advance by the credit grantor so that it becomes an executed credit agreement once the borrower has signed it. To hold other-wise would be straining the meaning of 'production' and run counter to the definition of a credit-token agreement which is a regulated agreement for the provision of credit in connection with the use of a credit-token[14]. The latter definition makes it clear that a credit-token is something which is 'used', which clearly an agreement is not. Moreover, if a credit agreement were a credit-token, then all credit agreements would require prior signed written requests by individuals before entering into them. Clearly this would be a ridiculous conclusion.

In *Elliott v Director General of Fair Trading*[15] a company sent unsolicited advertisements enclosing a card which stated, falsely, that the production of the signed card with appropriate identification would entitle the holder to credit. In fact, the card was merely intended to induce customers to enter the retail premises. The customer still had to satisfy credit criteria before becoming entitled to credit. Notwithstanding the further requirements, the Divisional Court upheld the company's conviction for having sent out unsolicited credit-tokens since, on the facts, it had 'undertaken' to provide credit, even though further action on its part was required. Thus, 'undertaking' includes contractual offers and even 'invitations to treat'[16].

Various materials are used in the course of promoting credit and the following are not credit-tokens because they do not relate to credit: cheque

---

13   Section 14(4) *ibid.*
14   See s 189(1) *ibid.* It would also render s 63(2)(b) ineffective and meaningless.
15   *Elliott v Director General of Fair Trading* [1980] 1 WLR 977.
16   Goode: *Consumer Credit Legislation III* [15].

guarantee cards, debit cards, discount cards and so-called letters to privileged customers offering them a discount on the cash price of goods. A promotional letter sent by a retailer offering credit facilities by a third party upon its production would probably be tantamount to a credit-token on the grounds that the retailer would be deemed to be acting as the agent of the credit grantor. This must be the logical conclusion as otherwise the retailer would not be in a position to grant the undertaking for the supply of cash goods etc on credit on behalf of the third party.

14.2.4 Deemed agency provisions

In the context of credit marketing, s 56 of the Consumer Credit Act has particular significance. This deems the negotiator in certain negotiations to be the creditor's agent as well as acting in his own capacity. It applies to negotiations conducted by a credit-broker in relation to goods sold or proposed to be sold by him to the creditor before forming the subject matter of a debtor-creditor-supplier agreement between the creditor and his customer. The deemed agency provisions also apply to negotiations conducted by the supplier in relation to a transaction financed or proposed to be financed by a debtor-creditor-supplier agreement between the creditor and his customer. There are further specific limitations on the type of debtor-creditor-supplier agreement[17].

The negotiations referred to are antecedent negotiations. They are deemed to commence when the negotiator and the debtor first enter into communication (including communication by advertisement) and comprise any representations made by the negotiator to the debtor and any other dealings between them[18].

By virtue of a drafting error, the intended result of a credit-broker being the agent also in relation to a subsequent hire agreement, is not caught by the section; neither are negotiations conducted by the supplier in relation to a future hire agreement.

At common law the situation is well established by the leading case of *Branwhite v Worcester Works Finance Ltd*[19]. This established that unless some very exceptional factual material is present, a relationship of principal and agent does not arise between a finance company entering into a hire-purchase agreement and the dealer or retailer. The court also decided that the fact that the finance company had provided the supplier with a stock of its forms to enable him to provide one to a prospective customer

---

17   Section 56(1), Consumer Credit Act 1974.
18   Section 56(4) *ibid.*
19   [1969] AC 552.

and that it had provided the supplier with the information necessary to calculate and inform the customer of the payment amounts did not constitute the supplier of the agent of the finance company as a matter of law or amount to evidence of such agency relationship in fact. These conclusions apply equally to a leasing agreement, as held in *Woodchester Equipment (Leasing) v British Association of Canned and Preserved Foods Importers and Distributors Ltd*[20].

14.3   Documentary issues affecting marketing

There are extensive regulations which apply to regulated credit and hire agreements and copies of the agreements. This section merely focuses on certain issues which appertain to marketing.

14.3.1   Cancellable agreements

A regulated agreement, whether a credit or a hire agreement, preceded by antecedent negotiations which included oral representations made in the presence of the debtor or hirer by an individual acting as, or on behalf of the negotiator is cancellable by the debtor or hirer, as the case may be, unless:

(1) the agreement is secured on land, or is a restricted-use credit agreement to finance the purchase of land or is an agreement for a bridging loan in connection with the purchase of land; or

(2) the unexecuted agreement is signed by the debtor or hirer at premises at which any of the following is carrying on any business, whether on a permanent or temporary basis:

(a) the creditor or owner;

(b) any party to a linked transaction (as defined in s 19) other than the debtor or hirer or a relative of his; or

(c) the negotiator in any antecedent negotiations (as defined in s 56)[21].

A cancellable agreement must contain a statutory notice setting out the borrower's cancellation rights. Unless the creditor or owner signs first, in which case the signature by the borrower or hirer will convert the agreement into an executed agreement, the copy of the executed agreement which must be sent to the debtor or hirer within seven days of the making

---

20   Court of Appeal Division, 16 January 1995, unreported.
21   Section 67, Consumer Credit Act 1974. For 'negotiator' see para 14.2.4 *supra*.

of the agreement must, in the case of a cancellable agreement, be sent by post[22]. The debtor or hirer has five days commencing with the day after he received the copy of the agreement in which to notify the creditor or owner that he is cancelling the agreement[23]. Where the Act does not require a second copy of the agreement to be sent, the cancellation period is 14 days following the day on which he signed the unexecuted agreement[24].

14.3.2   Agreements secured on land

Agreements secured on land, unless exempt agreements, follow the reverse procedure to cancellable agreements. The borrower or hirer is sent an advance copy of the agreement ie a copy of the proposed credit or hire agreement which is to be secured on land. He is given at least seven days before the actual agreement ie the contract, is sent to him for his signature. After the latter has been sent, the creditor or owner must still refrain from approaching the debtor or hirer until the expiry of seven days after the day on which the agreement was sent to the debtor or hirer for his signature or, on its return by the debtor or hirer after signature by him, if a shorter period. In other words, in the case of a regulated agreement secured on land the customer is given a minimum of approximately 14 days in which to consider whether he wishes to enter into the agreement. He can ponder over it for a lengthier period of time but the 14 days is known as 'the consideration period'. During this period the creditor or owner must refrain from approaching the debtor or hirer, whether in person, by telephone or letter or in any other way except in response to a specific request made by the debtor or hirer after the beginning of the consideration period ie after the beginning of the sending of the advance copy[25].

A regulated agreement must embody all the terms of the agreement other than implied terms. The terms must therefore either be set out in the agreement or in another document referred to in the agreement[26].

The Office of Fair Trading requires customers to make a positive election if they wish to take up credit protection insurance. It may not be sold by negative option, namely in such a way that the customer is deemed to have contracted for credit protection insurance unless he indicates otherwise.

---

22   Section 63(3) *ibid.*
23   Section 68(a) *ibid.*
24   Section 68(b) *ibid.*
25   Section 58 and s 61(2) *ibid.*
26   Section 61(b) and s 189(4) *ibid.*

14.4   Voluntary controls

There are various voluntary controls in the form of codes of practice depending on the code to which a company subscribes. The codes include those of the Consumer Credit Trade Association, Consumer Credit Association of the United Kingdom, the code of practice of the Finance and Leasing Association and that association's Guidance Notes on Sales Aid Leasing, the Building Societies' Code of Practice relating to Linking of Services and on Certain Aspects of the Transfer of Mortgages by Building Societies or their Associated Bodies.

The lending organisations and credit reference agencies have put together the Guide to Credit Scoring 1993 which imposes obligations upon them in relation to credit scoring generally, information to be made available to consumers, the review of refusals to grant credit and a complaints' procedure.

The Banking Code, now in its third edition, governs the relations between banks and building societies on the one hand and personal customers in the UK on the other. It sets standards of good banking practice including in relation to the marketing of services and helping individuals choose a mortgage.

The Mortgage Code, produced by the Council of Mortgage Lenders, governs its subscribing members in their relations with personal customers in the UK. It sets standards of good mortgage lending practice in more detail than in the Banking Code. The codes contain the following relevant provisions:

14.4.1   Key Commitments

A set of Key Commitments which includes obligations to act fairly and reasonably in dealings with the customer, to give information on services and products in plain language, to help customers choose a product or service (and in the case of the Mortgage Code, an appropriate mortgage), to help customers understand the financial implications and to ensure that all services and products comply with relevant laws and regulations.

14.4.2   Provisions relating to the marketing of mortgages and, in the case of the Banking Code, of services generally

There is a prohibition on sending marketing material indiscriminately. In particular, subscribers agree to be selective and careful if the customer is under 18 years of age or where materials relate to loans and overdrafts.

14.4.3 Helping the customer to choose a mortgage

The codes provide for three levels of service by lenders and impose an obligation on them to tell customers which of the following levels of service is being offered:

(1) advice and a recommendation;
(2) information only on the different types of mortgage products; and
(3) information on a single mortgage product only.

The incorporation of this obligation follows criticism of mortgage lenders by the Office of Fair Trading, the Consumers' Association and others at the absence of an obligation on their part to give customers best advice, equivalent to that imposed on independent financial advisers in relation to investments.

The Mortgage Code extends its sweep beyond the mere choice of mortgage to encompass advice to mortgagors and potential mortgagors on alternative repayment methods, information on interest-only mortgages (encompassing means of repayment, adequacy of repayment vehicle etc), future potential repayment obligations, insurance obligations, mortgage indemnity insurance and the like.

14.4.4 The codes contain provisions relating to marketing which include:

(1) a prohibition on passing a customer's name and address to any company including other companies in the creditor's group for marketing purposes, unless the customer specifically requests it or expressly consents in writing;
(2) an obligation on the lender to give the customer an opportunity at the outset to say that he does not wish to receive marketing information on the lender's additional services and products;
(3) an obligation on the lender to remind the customer at least once every three years that he can ask not to receive such marketing information;
(4) a lender's ability to inform the customer about another company's services or products (so called 'host mailing') and if the customer responds positively, he may be contacted directly by that company.

14.5 Residual control

The Director General of Fair Trading is given the power under the Consumer Credit Act to keep under review and to advise the Secretary of

State about social and commercial developments in the UK and elsewhere relating to the provision of credit for hiring of goods to individuals and related activities[27]. This is not restricted to regulated credit or hire. Under this mantle and also under his duty to administer the licensing system created by the Act John Bridgeman, Director General of Fair Trading, issued a 'Warning to Lenders and Brokers' against certain malpractices. He stated *inter alia*:

> I expect enough time to be allowed for consideration of the terms and conditions of the loan and the opportunity for independent legal advice to be taken before signing. A cooling-off period of at least seven days would be good practice. The use of mobile phones and faxes by sales people may be convenient for the lender but not necessarily in the best interests of the borrower, who is rushed into signing a loan agreement[28].

The Office of Fair Trading subsequently issued Guidelines for lenders and brokers on Non-status lending[29].

14.6   Conclusion

Whilst the essential message in relation to the marketing of credit and hire facilities, namely engaging in fair and unoppressive marketing methods, is the central common theme to the various matters discussed in this chapter, the reader will observe that it is implemented by multifarious controls and controllers.

---

27   Section 61(b) and s 1(2) *ibid*.
28   20 February 1997.
29   July 1997.

Chapter 15

Marketing of Banking Products and General Insurance

15.1 Marketing of Banking Products

15.1.1 Regulation of deposit-taking business

Deposit-taking business is regulated by the Banking Act 1987. Subject to specified exceptions no person in the UK may accept a deposit in the course of carrying on, whether in the UK or elsewhere, a deposit-taking business unless it is an institution authorised by the Bank of England[1]. Certain institutions are exempted from such prohibition and they include the following: the central bank of a member state other than the UK, the National Savings Bank, a Penny Savings Bank, a municipal bank, a building society under the Building Societies Act 1986, a friendly society under the Friendly Societies Act 1974 in respect of transactions permitted by the rules of the society, an insurance company authorised under the Insurance Companies Act 1982 in respect of the acceptance of a deposit in the course of carrying on authorised insurance business, a credit union under the Credit Unions Act 1979 and a Local Authority.

Furthermore, by virtue of the 'European Passport' a European institution which is authorised to carry on deposit-taking business in its home state is permitted to carry on such activity in the UK as its host state[2]. The list of activities to which mutual recognition is granted includes the

---

1   Section 3(1), Banking Act 1987.
2   The Banking Coordination (Second Council Directive) Regulations 1992 (SI 1992 No 3218), reg 5.

following: acceptance of deposits and other repayable funds from the public, lending, financial leasing, money transmission services, issuing and administering means of payment (eg credit cards, travellers' cheques, and bankers' drafts), guarantees and commitments, trading for own account or for the account of a customer in money-market instruments, foreign exchange, financial futures and options, exchange and interest rate instruments and transferable securities. It also includes participation in securities issues and the provision of services relating to such issues, advice to undertakings on capital structure, industrial strategy and related questions, money-broking, portfolio management and advice, safekeeping and administration of securities, credit reference services and safe-custody services[3].

A deposit-taking business is defined as a business in the course of which money received by way of deposit is lent to others or any other activity of the business is financed, wholly or to any material extent, out of the capital of or the interest on money received by way of deposit. It is not a deposit-taking business for the purposes of the Banking Act[4] if the person carrying it on does not hold himself out as accepting deposits on a day-to-day basis and any deposits which are accepted are accepted only on particular occasions, whether or not involving the issue of debentures or securities[5]. It is an offence to conduct deposit-taking business unless the person is authorised or otherwise exempt[6].

In general terms a deposit is a sum of money paid on terms under which it will be repaid, with or without interest or a premium, and either on demand or at a time or in circumstances agreed by or on behalf of the person making payment and the person receiving it and which are not referable to the provision of property or services or the giving of security[7].

The prohibition on the acceptance of a deposit does not apply to certain transactions which have been exempted by order of the Treasury pursuant to its powers under s 4(4) of the Banking Act 1987. Such exempt transactions include the following[8]: acceptance by charities of certain deposits, certain church deposit funds, the acceptance by an industrial and provident society of certain deposits, the acceptance by certain associations and by certain industrial provident societies of specified deposits, acceptance of a deposit by a practising solicitor in the course

---

3 Sched I *ibid.*
4 Banking Act 1987, s 6(1).
5 Section 6(2) *ibid.*
6 Section 3(2) *ibid.*
7 Section 5(1) *ibid.*
8 Banking Act 1987 (Exempt Transactions) Regulations 1988 (SI 1988 No 646).

of his profession, the acceptance in the course of estate agency work of a deposit which is a pre-contract deposit, the acceptance of a deposit on terms involving the issue of any relevant debt security in specified circumstances and acceptance by an authorised person or an exempted person from the Financial Services Act 1986 of a deposit in the course of or engaging on behalf of specified activities.

In the case of *SCF Finance Co Ltd v Masri (No 2)*[9] on being sued for repayment of an outstanding balance Masri pleaded that SCF had conducted an unauthorised deposit-taking business. The business was that of licensed dealers in commodity and financial futures in the course of which they would, from time to time, enter into transactions on a client's behalf and demand from the client a 'deposit' to cover the transactions and 'margins' to cover the risk of loss on the transactions. Interpreting the similar provisions of the previous Banking Act 1979 the Court of Appeal held that the payments received were not deposits but were monies paid to SCF which could be used by way of security to protect them against the risk that Masri might default in reimbursing them for any expense which they had properly incurred. Moreover, even if they were deposits, SCF did not hold themselves out as accepting deposits on a day-to-day basis, as these were deposits accepted only on particular occasions and so did not involve a 'holding-out'.

15.1.2   Invitations to make deposits

The reader is referred to the earlier section on advertisements for deposits. The Banking Act makes provision for control by regulation of unsolicited calls for deposits (an unsolicited call being a personal visit or oral communication made without express invitation). Somewhat surprisingly no regulations have been made under the relevant section[10]. However, the Consumer Protection (Cancellation of Contracts Concluded Away From Business Premises) Regulations 1987 may apply to agreements for the making of deposits in the absence of regulations under the Banking Act[11].

A provision which is in force is the offence of fraudulently inducing a person to make a deposit[12]. Any person who makes a statement, promise or forecast which he knows to be misleading, false or deceptive, or dishonestly conceals any material facts or acts recklessly in that regard is

---

9   [1987] 1 All ER 175.
10   Section 34, Banking Act 1987.
11   See reg 3(2)(e).
12   Section 35, Banking Act 1987.

guilty of an offence if it is made for the purpose of inducing, or is reckless as to whether it may induce another person to make or refrain from making a deposit with him or with any other person. The offence must be connected to the UK in so far as the statement must be made in or from the UK or the person to whom the inducement is addressed must be in the UK or the deposit must be one which would be entered into in the UK.

15.1.3   Invitations for overdraft facilities

Overdraft facilities are treated as loans and if the applicable credit limit does not exceed £15,000 the facility is subject to the provisions of the Consumer Credit Act 1974 and the regulations made under it. However, the agreement itself does not need to comply with the provisions of the Act and the regulations made under it in so far as it is a debtor-creditor agreement enabling the debtor to overdraw on a current account if the creditor has informed the Office of Fair Trading in writing of its general intention to enter into such agreements. In addition, the Director General of Fair Trading requires that at the time or before the agreement is concluded the debtor is notified of the credit limit if any, of the annual rate of interest and applicable charges and the conditions under which these may be amended and of the procedure for terminating the agreement. This information must be confirmed in writing[13].

The reader is also reminded that it is an offence to canvass an overdraft facility, which is one type of debtor-creditor agreement, off trade premises[14].

15.1.4   The Banking Code[15]

This is a voluntary code followed by banks and building societies in their relations with personal customers in the UK. It sets standards of good banking practice which are followed as minimum by banks and building societies subscribing to it.

The code contains key commitments on the part of its subscribers who undertake *inter alia* to act fairly and reasonably in all their dealings with customers; to ensure that all services and products comply with the code

---

13   Section 74(1)(b) and (3), Consumer Credit Act 1974; and the Determination by the Director General of Fair Trading dated 21 December 1989.
14   See Chapter 14 on Marketing of Credit and Hire Facilities.
15   March 1997, effective on 1 July 1997.

even if they have their own terms and conditions; to give information on their services and products in plain language; to help customers choose a service or product to fit the customer's needs; to help the customer understand the financial implications of a mortgage, other borrowing, savings and investment products and card products; to help the customer understand how his account works, and to correct errors and handle complaints speedily.

The code provides that a customer will, on request, be given written information explaining the key features of any bank's main services and products; how the customer's account works; a tariff covering basic account services, interest rates, charges for using Automated Teller Machines (ATMs), charges for overdrafts and fixed-term products; a tariff of mortgage charges and charges for other services.

Importantly, and to be welcomed, the Banking Code imposes an obligation upon banks and other lenders subscribing to the code to furnish holders of savings or investment accounts (other than fixed rate accounts) which are no longer available to customers, annually with a summary of all their interest rates. In addition, to enable accountholders to compare interest rates and to consider whether or not to switch their deposits into another account, accounts which are no longer available to customers must be clearly marked.

On the marketing of services, the code provides that its subscribers will notify customers of additional services and products and give the customer an opportunity, including once every three years, to indicate that he does not wish to receive such information. Further, upon specific request of a customer, his name will not be passed to any company, including any other companies in the bank's group, for marketing purposes. The code permits its subscribers to inform customers about another company's services or products and if they respond positively, they may be contacted directly by that company.

Subscribers undertake not to send marketing material indiscriminately and in particular they will be selective and careful in respect of persons under 18 years of age or when material relates to loans and overdrafts.

Subscribers undertake to ensure that all advertising and promotional material is clear, fair, reasonable and not misleading.

In relation to mortgages, the code takes a leaf out of the Mortgage Code by setting out the three levels of service which may be provided and that its subscribers will inform customers at the outset which service they offer. The three services are: advice and a recommendation; information on the different types of mortgage products; information on a single mortgage product only.

The code requires its subscribers to give customers clear and appropriate information on the different types of savings and investment accounts to enable customers to make an informed choice.

All lending is made subject to the lender's assessment of the customer's ability to repay it. Key factors in this assessment are set out in the code.

The code requires lenders to encourage guarantors to take independent legal advice and all documents they are asked to sign must contain this recommendation as a clear and prominent notice. Guarantors must be advised of the limit of their liability; an unlimited guarantee may not be taken.

On the subject of foreign exchange services the code requires its subscribers to give an explanation of the service, details of the exchange rate and an explanation of the charges which apply.

The code contains provisions relating to confidentiality. Subscribers must treat all personal information about customers as private and confidential. Nothing about the customer's account, or his name and address, may be disclosed to anyone, including other companies in the same banking group except in exceptional cases permitted by law. These are where the bank is legally compelled to disclose; where there is a duty to the public to disclose; where the bank's interests require disclosure; and where disclosure is made at the customer's request or with his consent.

The code also restricts disclosure of information to credit reference agencies except in limited circumstances where the customer is in default or otherwise where the customer has given his consent.

Institutions subscribing to the code are obligated to make copies of it available to customers. Many lenders have made a virtue of necessity by presenting the code as a marketing tool. Banks and other lenders will generally make it available both at branches and as part of the 'Welcome Pack' which they send to customers when opening accounts.

There is no equivalent to the Banking Code in respect of the relationship between lenders and their corporate customers. Doubtless this will follow in due course.

15.2   Marketing of insurance

The reader is also referred to Chapter 16 on the marketing of investments, in relation to the marketing of life assurance which constitutes investment business.

15.2.1 Long-term insurance[16]

Long-term business or long-term insurance is defined in Sched 1 to the Insurance Companies Act 1982. Schedule 2E of that Act prescribes the information which UK insurers and EC companies conducting insurance business in the UK are required to provide to policyholders before the contract of long-term insurance is entered into and during the lifetime of a contract. This information includes the following:

(1) the definition of each benefit and option;
(2) the term of the contract and the means by which it may be terminated;
(3) the method of paying premiums and the duration of the payments;
(4) the method of calculating bonuses and the distribution of bonuses;
(5) an indication of surrender and paid-up values and the extent to which such values are guaranteed;
(6) an indication of the premiums for each benefit;
(7) in the case of a unit-linked policy a definition of the units to which benefits are linked and an indication of the nature of the underlying assets;
(8) information as to the period within which the policyholder may cancel the contract, the tax arrangements applicable to the policy, the arrangements for handling complaints and any compensation or guarantee arrangements if the insurer is unable to meet his liabilities under the contract;
(9) whether the parties to the contract are entitled to choose the law applicable to the contract and if so the law which the insurer proposes to choose and if not the law which will be so applicable.

In addition to the foregoing, information is required as to the name and legal form of the company, the company's home state and where appropriate, the member state of the branch through which the contract is to be entered into; the address of the company's head office and where required the address of the branch through which the contract is to be entered into; the complaints procedure.

The foregoing information must be furnished in English except that, where the other party to the contract so requests it may instead be furnished in the official language of another member state.

The information which is required to be furnished during the contract

---

16   Inserted by The Insurance Companies (Third Insurance Directive) Regulations 1994 (SI 1994 No 1696), reg 40(2), Sched 5.

of long-term insurance is essentially information regarding any change in the above information and information as to annual bonuses payable under the contract.

15.2.2　Contracts of general insurance

The following information is required by Sched 2E to the Insurance Companies Act 1982 to be notified to policyholders in respect of general insurance before entering into a contract:

(1) any arrangements which exist for handling complaints and the name and address of any body who deals with complaints from any party to the contract;

(2) that the existence of a complaints' body does not affect any right of action which any party to the contract may have against the insurer; and

(3) whether the parties to the contract are entitled to choose the law applicable to the contract and if so, the law which the insurer proposes to choose, and if not, the law which will be so applicable.

In addition, it is generally a requirement for the insurer to notify the address of the establishment through which the risk is to be covered and where the contract relates to relevant motor vehicle risks and the effecting of the contract constitutes the provision of insurance in the UK, the name and address of the claims representative.

15.3　Codes of conduct and statements of practice

Codes of conduct and statements of insurance practice play a vital role in the promotion and marketing of insurance contracts in the UK.

15.3.1　The Code of Conduct of the Insurance Brokers' Council[17]

This code sets out the fundamental principles governing the professional conduct of insurance brokers. It includes an obligation on brokers to provide advice objectively and independently, to do various things to satisfy the insurance requirements of their clients, including explaining and divulging costs and commission and the name of insurers with whom a contract of insurance is placed. Insurance brokers are also required to have proper regard to the wishes of a policyholder or client who seeks to termi-

---

17　Pursuant to s 10 of the Insurance Brokers (Registration) Act 1977.

nate any agreement with them. Any information acquired by an insurance broker may not be used or disclosed except in the normal course of negotiating, maintaining or renewing the contract of insurance for that client, unless the client's consent is obtained or information is required by a court.

The code also regulates advertisements by insurance brokers.

15.4   Codes and statements of practice of the Association of British Insurers (ABI)

15.4.1   General insurance business—code of practice for all intermediaries other than registered insurance brokers[18]

This code was introduced in 1989 to improve consumer protection in the selling of general insurance. It covers insurance products such as motor, household, private medical, creditor (payment protection), travel, extended warranty or mechanical breakdown, personal accident or sickness and the like. In relation to marketing of insurance, the code prescribes principles governing calls upon customers, identifying the status of its intermediary as either a company agent or an independent intermediary, ensuring that the policy meets customers' needs and resources and treating all information supplied by the customer as confidential to himself and to the company to which the proposal is introduced. The ABI strongly recommends to its members to join recognised adjudicator schemes to which ultimately complaints can be addressed eg the Insurance Ombudsman Bureau (IOB) or the Personal Insurance Arbitration Services (PIAS).

An intermediary may be an employee of an insurance company or an agent of one company or of up to six companies, for whose conduct the company or companies accept responsibility. Alternatively he may be an independent intermediary seeking to act on behalf of the prospective policyholder for whose conduct the intermediary accepts responsibility. Various specific exceptions are made to the limit of six insurers.

15.4.2   Life insurance (non-investment business) selling code of practice[18bis]

This code applies to intermediaries and introducers and contains general sales principles relating to long-term insurance contracts and permanent

---

18   SI 1994/1696.
18bis   August 1988.

health insurance which are not 'investments' under the Financial Services Act.

An associated Statement of Long-Term Insurance Practice, also issued by the ABI, regulates, *inter alia*, proposal forms, policies and accompanying documents. It advocates clarity. It directs that neither the proposal form nor the policy may contain any provision converting statements by the proposer as to past or present fact into warranties or guarantees, save for specific exceptions. Where the proposal form calls for the disclosure of material facts, a statement must be included in the declaration or prominently displayed in the proposal form drawing attention to the consequences of failure to disclose.

15.4.3   Statement of general insurance practice[18ter]

This Statement issued by the Association of British Insurers (ABI) applies to general insurances of policyholders resident in the UK and insuring in their private capacity. It contains similar provisions to the Statement of Long-Term Insurance Practice.

15.4.4   Payment protection insurance—statement of practice[18quat]

This code, also issued by the ABI, requires insurers to comply with the ABI General Insurance Business Code of Practice. Providers of this insurance are required to explain the suitability of the contract, to make available details of its main features and relevant restrictions and to furnish full details of the cover as soon as possible after completion of the contract. The policy must set out the insurers procedures for handling disputes.

15.4.5   Mortgage payment protection insurance—statement of practice[18quin]

This statement governs insurers offering mortgage payment protection insurance for loans for first charges on private dwellings. It obligates insurers to comply with the ABI General Insurance Business Code of Practice and the further requirements of this Statement, including explaining to the mortgagor the suitability of the policy, details of its main features and relevant restrictions.

18ter   January 1986.
18quat   June 1996.
18quin   June 1986.

15.5 Prescribed information to be supplied to policyholders

As already noted The Insurance Companies Act 1982, as amended by The Insurance Companies (Third Insurance Directives) Regulations 1994, requires certain information to be supplied to policyholders of UK insurers, EU companies and EFTA companies (companies in a state of the European Economic area which is not a member state of the European Union) before an insurance contract is entered into. The information to be supplied is dependent upon whether the contract is one of long-term insurance or of general insurance.

Whilst this work is not concerned with policy documents it should be mentioned that there are some policies, notably payment or credit protection insurance policies, which are commonly marketed concurrently with the credit agreement or hire agreement to which they relate. In other words, the borrower or hirer applies for such insurance at the time when he enters into the credit or hire agreement. In those circumstances it is necessary to furnish him with the prescribed information which would usually include:

> the name and legal form of the company, the company's home state, the address of the company's head office, the risks covered and the main exclusions, the premiums, any compensation or guarantee arrangements which will be available if the insurer is unable to meet its liabilities under the contract, the complaints procedure, whether the parties to the contract are entitled to choose the law applicable to the contract and, if so, the law which the insurer proposes to choose and, if not, the law which will be so applicable.[19]

As regards compensation arrangements, these are covered by the Policyholders Protection Act 1975, as extended by the Policyholders Protection Act 1997, and apply to qualifying persons under qualifying policies, including those issued by EU companies which provide insurance in the UK through an establishment elsewhere in the EEA.

15.6 Concluding reflections

The marketing of general insurance products has been, and generally speaking remains, lightly regulated by the relevant ABI Codes and Statements of Practice. This is workable not least because the Association

---

19   Sched 2E to the Insurance Companies Act 1982, inserted by Regulation 40 of SI 1994/1696.

of British Insurers represents some 430 insurance companies which between them account for over 95 per cent of the business of UK insurance companies. Self-regulation is supplemented by statutory controls, largely introduced at the behest of the European Commission in the form of Insurance Directives incorporated into UK statutes.

Long-term insurance is far more rigidly controlled under the Financial Services Act regime.

The nature of the marketplace and changing patterns in marketing have given rise to the twinning of banking and insurance products in the form of 'bancassurance', and are now frequently marketed together. Indeed, banking products are increasingly being marketed together with one or other free insurance, as an inducement to the prospective bank customer. Free banking as an incentive to taking up insurance will doubtless follow.

Chapter 16

Marketing of Investments

16.1 Introduction

This chapter is an outline of certain key features in the marketing of investments. Some aspects are already covered in the chapters on the advertising of investments.

16.2 Meaning of 'marketing'

The activities which fall under the heading 'marketing' in the financial services arena are encompassed by Part II of Sched 1 to the Financial Services Act 1986 under the headings dealing in investments, arranging deals in investments, managing investments, investment advice, establishing etc collective investment schemes and sending dematerialised instructions[1].

The principal part of the Act deals with various aspects of marketing, as set out below.

16.2.1 Misleading statements

The Act prohibits and creates liability for misleading statements and practices[2].

16.2.2 Unsolicited calls

Except as permitted by regulation, namely the Common Unsolicited Calls Regulations 1991, no person may in the course of or in consequence of an

---

1 Financial Services Act 1986, Sched 1, Part II, paras 12–16A.
2 Section 47 *ibid.*

unsolicited call made on a person in the UK or made from the UK on a person elsewhere, by way of business, enter into an investment agreement with the person on whom the call is made or endeavour to procure that person to enter into such an agreement[3]. Contravention of this section does not constitute an offence but, subject to certain exceptions, an investment agreement entered into in such a manner shall not be enforceable against the person on whom the call was made and that person is entitled to recover any money or other property paid or transferred by him under the agreement together with compensation for any loss sustained by him[4].

An unsolicited call is a personal visit or oral communication made without express invitation[5].

16.2.3   Restrictions on the promotion of collective investment schemes

An authorised person may not issue or cause to be issued an advertisement, advising or procuring any person in the UK to become a participant in a collective investment scheme which is not an authorised unit trust scheme or a recognised scheme[6] unless the advertisement is issued to or the person who is advised or procured to enter into the scheme is an authorised person or a person whose ordinary business involves the acquisition and disposal of property of the same kind as the property, or substantial part of the property, to which the scheme relates[7] or, if one or other exemption applies. The exemptions are set out in the Financial Services Act 1986 (Single Property Schemes) Exemption Regulations 1989 and the Financial Services (Promotion of Unregulated Collective Investment Schemes) Regulations 1991.

16.2.4   Restriction on promotion of contracts of insurance[8]

A person may not, in the course of a business, advise or procure any person in the UK to enter into a contract of insurance which constitutes an investment unless the contract of insurance is with a body authorised under the Insurance Companies Act 1982, a body registered under enactments relating to Friendly Societies, an insurance company the head office of which

---

3   Section 56(1) *ibid.*
4   Section 56(2) *ibid* and see exceptions under s 56(4).
5   Section 56(8) *ibid.*
6   Section 76(1) *ibid.*
7   Section 76(2) *ibid.*
8   Section 130(1)–(3) *ibid.*

or a branch or agency of which is in a member state other than the UK and which is entitled to carry on insurance business of the relevant class in that state or with an insurance company in any country which is designated by an order made by the Secretary of State.

Breach of the foregoing constitutes a criminal offence. It is a defence to prove that the alleged offender believed on reasonable grounds after due enquiry that one or other of the foregoing exemptions applied to the situation[9].

As regards the civil consequences of a contravention of s 130, the insurance company is not entitled to enforce any contract of insurance with which the offending advertisement, advice or procurement was concerned and the other party is entitled to recover any money or other property paid or transferred under the contract, together with compensation for any loss[10]. A court may in its discretion allow the contract to be enforced or money or property paid or transferred to be retained by the insurer if it is satisfied that the person against whom enforcement is sought or who is seeking to recover the money or property was not influenced, or not influenced to any material extent, by, as relevant, the advertisement or the advice in making his decision to enter into the contract or that, as relevant, the advertisement or the advice was not misleading as to the nature of the company with which the contract was to be made or the terms of the contract and fairly stated any risks involved in entering into it[11].

If there is a contravention of the foregoing by an authorised person an action lies at the suit of any person, including any third party, who suffers loss as a result[12].

The Securities and Investments Board is given powers to issue injunctions and restitution orders against a person contravening these provisions[13].

16.2.5 Restrictions applying to the marketing of listed securities

The restrictions applying to the marketing of listed securities, including the issue of prospectuses, is set out in ss 142–156B of the Act and the Listing Rules of the London Stock Exchange.

---

9   Section 130(6) and (8) *ibid.*
10   Section 131(1) *ibid.*
11   Section 131(30) *ibid.*
12   Section 131(7) *ibid.*
13   Section 131(8) read with s 61 *ibid.*

16.2.6   Restrictions on the marketing of unlisted securities

The marketing of unlisted securities is governed by the Public Offers of Securities Regulations 1995, known as the 'POS' Regulations 1995[14].

16.3   Core Conduct of Business Rules

16.3.1   Introduction

Sections 48 and 63A of the Financial Services Act make provision for Conduct of Business Rules as laid down by the Secretary of State, whose powers have since been transferred to the Securities and Investments Board. The latter has enacted the Core Conduct of Business Rules in its own rule-book which have also been adopted by IMRO, SFA and PIA. They are core rules so that the various SROs are free to expand upon them and indeed have done so in their various rulebooks.

16.3.2   Summary of the Core Conduct of Business Rules

(1)   Inducements

A firm must take reasonable steps to ensure that neither it nor any of its agents offers or gives, or solicits or accepts, in the course of regulated business or otherwise any inducement which is likely significantly to conflict with any duties owed by the recipient, or the recipient's employer, to customers in connection with regulated business.

(2)   Material interest

Where a firm has a material interest in a transaction to be entered into with or for a customer or a relationship which gives rise to a conflict of interest in relation to such a transaction, it must not knowingly advise or deal in the exercise of discretion in relation to that transaction unless it takes reasonable steps to ensure fair treatment for the customer.

(3)   Soft commission

A firm which deals for a customer on an advisory basis, or in the exercise of discretion, may not so deal through a broker pursuant to a soft commission agreement save in specified exceptional circumstances, which includes adequate prior and periodic disclosure of the same. A soft commission agreement is an agreement under which a firm which deals in securities on

---

14   SI 1995 No 1537.

an advisory basis or in the exercise of a discretion, receives goods or services in return for an assurance that not less than a certain amount of such business will be put through or in the way of another person.

(4) Polarisation

A firm which advises a private customer on packaged products must either be a product company or its marketing group associate or do so as an independent intermediary.

A firm which is a product company or its marketing group associate must not advise private customers to buy packaged products which are not those of the marketing group.

A firm which acts as a independent intermediary in advising a private customer on packaged products must act as an independent intermediary whenever it advises private customers on packaged products in the course of regulated business; but where a firm acts as an investment manager for a customer the firm may advise the customer on any packaged product.

Following the foregoing, a requirement of the regulator eg the PIA, is a statement in the terms of business relating to the advisor's status, along the following terms eg:

Regulator's Statement

Those who advise on life assurance, pensions or unit trust products are either representatives of one company or independent advisors.

Your advisor represents the ABC Marketing Group and acts on its behalf. Your advisor can only give advice on the life assurance, pensions and unit trust products of the ABC Marketing Group. Because your advisor is not independent he or she cannot advise you on the purchase of products of this type available from providers other than the ABC Marketing Group. ABC Assurance Ltd and ABC Unit Trust Managers Ltd are members of the ABC Marketing Group.

(5) Issue and approval of advertisements

The reader is referred to the discussion in Chapters 11 and 12.

(6) Overseas business for UK private customers

An authorised person must not carry on investment business which is not regulated business and with or for a private customer who is in the UK unless it has made the prescribed disclosure to the customer. It must also not give an introduction on advice, or make arrangements with a view to another person carrying on such business unless it has both made the prescribed disclosure and has no reason to doubt that the customer will be dealt with in an honest and reliable way.

The prescribed disclosure is a statement which makes it clear that all or most of the protections provided by the UK regulatory system do not apply and where the business is excluded from investor's compensation schemes by its territorial scope, a statement to that effect. A similar rule applies to communications issued to a private customer outside the UK in connection with business which is not regulated business.

(7)   Fair and clear communications

A firm, namely an authorised person, must communicate fairly and in a way which is not misleading and must take reasonable steps to ensure that any agreement, communication, notification or information which it sends to a private customer is presented fairly and clearly.

(8)   Customer's understanding

A firm must not recommend a transaction to a private customer or act as a discretionary manager for him unless it has taken reasonable steps to enable him to understand the nature of the risks involved.

(9)   Information about the firm

A firm must take reasonable steps to ensure that a private customer is given adequate information about its identity and business address, the identity and status with the firm of employees and other relevant agents with whom the customer has contact and the identity of the firm's regulator.

Unless a firm is acting as an investment manager it must take reasonable steps to ensure that a private customer it advises to buy a packaged product is also given adequate information about the firm's polarisation status, the buying process and information on the packaged products on which it can advise. An example of the foregoing would be a statement along the following lines:

> Members of the ABC Marketing Group are regulated by the Personal Investment Authority for Investment Business. Members of the marketing group are bound by the PIA's rules.
>
> The product range of the ABC Marketing Group includes life assurance, company and personal pensions, unit trusts and unit trust personal equity plans of that marketing group.

(10)   Information about packaged products

Before or when making a personal recommendation to a private customer to buy a packaged product a firm must give him information about the product which is adequate to enable him to make an informed investment decision. Before or as soon as is practicable after the customer buys a packaged product the firm must provide him with appropriate written product particulars unless the firm buys the packaged product as a discretionary investment or the transaction is effected or arranged on an execution-only basis.

(11) Appointed representatives

A firm must satisfy itself on reasonable grounds and on a continuing basis that any appointed representative it appoints is fit and proper to act for it in that capacity and that it has adequate resources to monitor and enforce compliance by its appointed representatives of high standards of business conduct.

A firm must ensure that any of its appointed representatives carry on regulated business for which the firm has accepted responsibility only in circumstances where the representative does not carry on or purport to carry on in the UK any investment business for which the representative is not an authorised or exempted person and in a way which ensures that the business for which the firm has accepted responsibility is, and is held out as being, clearly distinct from any financial business which the representative carries on which is not investment business.

(12) Customer agreements

Where a firm provides investment services to a private customer on written contractual terms, the agreement must set out an adequate detailed basis on which those services are provided.

(13) Customers' rights

A firm must not, in any written communication or agreement, seek to exclude or restrict any duty or liability to a customer which it has under the Financial Services Act or under the regulatory system.

(14) Suitability

A firm must agree simple steps to ensure that it does not make any personal recommendation to a private customer for an investment or investment agreement or effect or arrange a discretionary transaction unless the recommendation or transaction is suitable for that customer having regard to the facts disclosed by that customer and other relevant facts about the customer of which the firm is, or reasonably should be, aware.

(15) Standards of advice on packaged products

This rule specifies the standards which a firm should apply when recommending packaged products to private customers.

(16)   Charges and other remuneration

The amount of the firm's charges to a private customer must not be unreasonable. Before a firm provides investment services to a private customer it must disclose to him the basis or amount of its charges and other remuneration.

(17)   Confirmations and periodic information

A firm which effects a sale or purchase of an investment, other than a life policy, must ensure that the customer is sent with due dispatch a note containing the essential details of the transaction. A firm which acts as an investment manager must ensure that the customer is sent at suitable intervals a report of the value of the portfolio or account at the beginning and end of the period, its composition at the end, and in the case of a discretionary portfolio or account, changes in its composition between those dates.

(18)   Customer order priority

A firm should deal with customer and own account orders fairly and in due turn.

(19)   Timely execution

Unless a firm believes on reasonable grounds that it is in the best interests of the customer to postpone execution of an order, it should execute the order as soon as is reasonably practicable in the circumstances.

(20)   Best execution

Where a firm deals with or for a private customer, or fulfils an order from a non-private customer, it must provide best execution. A firm provides best execution if:

(1) it takes reasonable care to ascertain a price which is the best available for the customer in the relevant market at the time for transactions of the kind and size concerned; and

(2) unless the circumstances require to do otherwise in the interests of the customer, it deals at a price which is no less advantageous to him,

and in applying the core rule on best execution, a firm should leave out of the account any charges disclosed to the customer which the firm or its agent would make.

A firm need not provide best execution on a purchase of a life policy or on the purchase from the operator of a regulated collective investment scheme of units in the scheme.

(21)   Timely allocation

A firm must ensure that a transaction it executes is promptly allocated.

(22)   Fair allocation

Where a firm has aggregated an order for a customer with an order for an own account transaction or with another order for a customer transaction, in the subsequent allocation it must not give unfair preference to itself or to any of those for whom it has dealt and if all cannot be satisfied, it must give priority to satisfying orders for customer transactions unless it believes on reasonable grounds that without its participation it would not have been able to effect those orders either on such favourable terms or at all.

(23)   Dealing ahead of publication

Where a firm intends to publish to customers a recommendation it must not knowingly effect an own-account transaction in the investment concerned or any related investment until the customers for whom the publication was principally intended have had a reasonable opportunity to react to it.

(24)   Churning and switching

A firm must not make a personal recommendation to a private customer to deal, or deal or arrange a deal in the exercise of discretion for any customer, if the dealing would reasonably be regarded as too frequent in the circumstances.

A firm must not make a personal recommendation to a private customer to switch within a packaged product or between packaged products or effect such a switch in the exercise of a discretion for a private customer unless it believes on reasonable grounds that the switch is justified from the customer's viewpoint.

(25)   Certain derivatives only to be dealt with on a recognised exchange

A firm must not effect, arrange or recommend a contingent liability transaction (namely a derivatives transaction under which the customer will or may be liable to make further payments when the transaction fails to be completed or on the earlier closing out of his position) with, for or to a private customer unless it is made on a recognised or designated investment exchange or the firm believes on reasonable grounds that the purpose of the transaction is to hedge against currency risk involved in a position which the customer holds.

(26)   Market integrity

The Core Conduct of Business Rules relate to the preservation of market integrity including restrictions on insider dealing, obligations in connection with the stabilising of the price of securities, obligations in connection with the saleability and price of securities which are not quoted by a recognised or designated investment exchange and so on.

(27)   Administration and Chinese walls

The Core Conduct of Business Rules govern the safeguarding of customer investments, the requirement that a firm maintain a business profile describing its investment business, compliance obligations upon a firm, the need for a firm to maintain a complaints' procedure for the benefit of its customers and the obligation to maintain Chinese walls. Section 48(2)(h) of the Financial Services Act specifically makes provision for Chinese walls by authorising rules to be made enabling or requiring information obtained by an authorised person in the course of carrying on one part of his business to be withheld by him from persons with whom he deals in the course of carrying on another part and for that purpose enabling or requiring employees in one part of the business to withhold information from employees in another part.

(28)   Application

The Core Conduct of Business Rules apply subject to any exceptions contained in the rules of the relevant SRO which enable a firm to treat a customer as a non-private customer if:

(1)   it can show that it believes on reasonable grounds that the customer had sufficient experience and understanding to waive the protections provided for private customers;

(2)   it has given a clear written warning to the customer of the protections under the regulatory system which he will lose; and

(3)   the customer has given his written consent after having a proper opportunity to consider the warning.

The SRO rules can dispense with the need for consent in writing in the case of a customer not ordinarily resident in the UK and reasonably believed not to wish to consent in writing.

16.4 Certain features of investment business

16.4.1 'Best advice'

Certain Rules, most notably those of the Personal Investment Authority (PIA), impose an obligation of best advice in relation to the sale of certain products. Thus, a collective investment marketing firm may not recommend to any person a life policy, a certain type of personal equity plan (PEP) or units in a regulated collective investment scheme unless the PIA member reasonably believes that there is no other such investment which is likely to secure the customer's investment objectives more advantageously. An exception is made in relation to an advertisement which does not contain a recommendation that the investment is suitable for any particular person and where the member has given no advice in connection with its acquisition. A similar obligation is imposed on members which are not collective investment marketing firms[14bis].

The PIA recognises that a member may, in making comparisons have regard to non-financial as well as to financial considerations. These would include the quality and assurance of performance by the other party to the transaction and to the rigours of a life office's underwriting criteria, as well as the cost to the customer and the value of the benefits which he may receive. PIA expects a member to keep itself informed as to current terms available in the market generally and to survey the market at reasonably frequent intervals. In determining what to recommend to a customer a member may have regard to any reasonable charges which it would make to the customer for placing business with an office that does not pay commission.

Similar obligations to the foregoing are contained in the Adopted FIMBRA Rules. They set out the requirements of the financial adviser to 'know your client', to conduct 'fact-finds' of the customer, requiring him to obtain details of income and expenditure and reasons for wishing to enter into the transaction. The adviser may not advise a customer to buy a packaged product if he is aware of a packaged product which would better meet the customer's needs and circumstances, nor a packaged product issued or operated by a connected person of the financial adviser or its marketing group associate if he is aware of a generally available packaged product which is not one of such person or associate and which would equally meet the customer's needs. Before recommending other investments to a customer the financial adviser must provide him with enough

---

14bis   PIA Rule Book: Adopted SIB Rules s 5.02 and s 5.03.

information about the investments to give him an adequate basis upon which to decide whether or not to accept the recommendation[14ter].

The annual report for the Personal Investment Authority Ombudsman for the year to 31 March 1997 reveals that the majority of the 4,310 complaints received related to alleged breaches of the 'best advice' rules.

16.4.2   'Best execution'

This rule, which also features throughout the various SRO Rule Books, requires a member to take all reasonable steps to ensure that the terms of a transaction are such that it is effected on the best terms available in the market at the time the transaction is effected. The specific Rules may qualify this by reference to transactions of the kind and size concerned. The Adopted FIMBRA Rules provide that in deciding which are the best terms in the market for a particular investment, the financial adviser must consider all relevant factors, including the reputation of the other parties involved in the transaction. The Adopted SIB Rules bring into the equation the requirement that the terms are the best available at the time the transaction is effected, on the market generally for transactions with reliable counterparties of the same size and nature as the transaction in question[14quat].

16.4.3   Terms of business

SRO rules require member firms to prepare terms of business in the form of terms of business letters or of client agreements. Whilst client agreements require the firm to obtain the client's signature to the agreement, terms of business letters do not. The prescribed contents of terms of business letters are set out in the rules[15]. The required contents include a 'Regulator's Statement' in prescribed form to be set out more prominently than anything else in the terms of business letter. The statement refers to the two types of advisors, either representatives of one company or independent advisors and identifies the status of the particular advisor as any one of the following:

(1) an independent practitioner;
(2) an appointed representative of a product provider;
(3) a member of a marketing group;

14ter   Adopted FIMBRA Rules F29.4–F29.7.
14quat   Adopted FIMBRA Rules F29.16; Adopted SIB Rules s 5.04.
15   For example PIA rule 4.5.

(4) a representative of a firm which is a marketing associate; or

(5) a representative of a firm which is a product provider.

16.4.4   Key features document

Various SRO rules make provision for a Key Features Document containing key information about the product and which is to be supplied to the investor before he signs any application or proposal. These apply to both life and non-life products[16]. A typical Key Features Document would include a product description, information about the product provider, methods of payment, customer's cancellation rights, tax position, applicable law, complaints' procedure, available compensation if the product provider is unable to meet his liabilities, eg compensation under the Policyholders Protection Act 1975 and Common Questions and Answers. Where possible the Key Features Document must be tailored to the particular circumstances of the transaction but where it is contained in advertisements, eg direct offer or off-the-page advertisements, it must be based upon a fair example of the investor.

16.5   Unsolicited calls

16.5.1   Statutory provisions

An unsolicited call is a personal visit or oral communication without express invitation[17]. Such uninvited call is also known as 'cold calling'. The invitation can take any form eg returning a coupon attached to an advertisement or inviting a caller by telephone.

Whilst the Financial Services Act does not render unsolicited calls an offence, it prohibits a person in the course of or in consequence of an unsolicited call made on a person in the UK or made from the UK on a person elsewhere, by way of business, entering into an investment agreement with the person on whom the call is made or to procure or endeavour to procure that person to enter into such an agreement[18]. The consequences of entering into such agreement is that the investment agreement is unenforceable against the person on whom the call was made and that person is entitled to recover any money or other property transferred by him under the agreement together with compensation for any loss[19]. In addition, the Securities and

---

16   For example PIA rules, Sched L 5.8 and L 6A.
17   Section 56(8), Financial Services Act 1986.
18   Section 56(1) *ibid.*
19   Section 56(2) *ibid.*

Investments Board is empowered to seek an injunction and restitution order against the offender[20]. The foregoing provisions envisage circumstances where cold calling would be permitted and where the subsequent investment agreement would be enforceable eg where permitted by regulations made under the section or where a court concludes that the person on whom the call was made was not influenced to any material extent by anything said or done in the course of or in consequence of the call, the agreement was entered into following discussions between the parties and the person called upon was aware of the nature of the agreement and any risks involved in entering into it[21].

16.5.2   Common Unsolicited Calls Regulations 1991

These regulations were made by the Securities and Investments Board (SIB) and extended by SROs as amplified by their own rules[22] and do not apply to persons certified by recognised professional bodies ('RPBs').

The regulations commence by stating the effect of s 56 of the Act namely that no person shall in the course of or in consequence of an unsolicited call made on a person in the UK or made from the UK on a person elsewhere by way of business, enter into an investment agreement with the person on whom the call was made or procure or endeavour to procure that person to enter into such an agreement. The regulations must be read together with the definitions set out in the Financial Services Core Glossary 1991 set out in the SIB Rule Book.

The bulk of the regulations sets out exceptions and exemptions to the restrictions in s 56 and these are briefly summarised below.

(a)   Non-private investors

A non-private investor is defined in the Glossary as a person who is not a private investor, namely an individual investor who is not carrying on investment business and in the current context 'investor' is the party receiving the unsolicited call.

The regulations lift the restrictions where the call is made with a view to the investor entering into the investment agreement as a non-private investor and the investor enters into the investment agreement as a non-private investor.

Where the call is an overseas person call, the marketing restriction is lifted in the like circumstances.

---

20   Section 61(1) *ibid.*
21   Section 56(4) *ibid.*
22   Section 56(7A) *ibid.*

(b) Non-geared packaged products

The restriction is lifted in relation to the sale of non-geared packaged products as defined in the SIB Glossary. Generally speaking this covers life policies, units in authorised unit trust schemes and investment trust savings schemes except where they are, or are linked to, a high volatility product.

Where the call is to an overseas person, the restrictions are only lifted if the caller is a UK authorised or exempted person.

(c) Supply of callable investment services

The restrictions are lifted to the extent that the investment agreement relates to the provision by an authorised or exempted person to the investor of callable investment services, namely where the only investments involved are generally marketable non-geared packaged products and readily realisable securities other than warrants. In addition the agreement must be subject to (or exempted from) a cancellation or delayed entry procedure or provided under a cancellable customer agreement where the customer is notified that he has a seven-day cooling-off period.

(d) Existing customers

The restrictions are lifted where the investor has a legitimately established customer relationship with the caller and the relationship envisages unsolicited calls of the kind concerned.

(e) Acquisition of investment business

In the case of the acquisition of an investment business the restrictions are lifted to the extent necessary for the purposes of enabling the acquirer to invite customers of the business acquired to establish a customer relationship with him.

(f) Public takeovers

The restrictions are lifted in respect of calls made in connection with transactions which are subject to the City Code on Takeovers and Mergers and the Rules Governing Substantial Acquisitions of Shares. This would also include approaches to shareholders in a target company seeking their irrevocable commitments to accept an offer.

(g) Corporate acquisitions

The marketing restriction is lifted in relation to unsolicited calls made on an employee in connection with a management buy-out of his employer's business (MBO) or a management buy-in of a business in which he would fulfil management functions (MBI).

(h)   Connected individuals

The restrictions are lifted for calls between business partners, fellow directors or close relatives. They are also lifted for calls between the settler of a trust (other than a unit trust scheme), its trustees, beneficiaries and the agents of any of them, in so far as they relate to the settlement, management or distribution of the trust fund.

The restrictions are also lifted for calls between personal representatives, beneficiaries under a will or intestacy and the agents of any of them, to the extent that they are related to the management or distribution of the estate.

(i)   Employee share schemes

The restrictions are lifted in relation to certain dealings in investments to facilitate the buying, selling or holding of securities by a company or trustee for the benefit of employees or their relatives.

(j)   Occupational pension schemes

The restrictions do not apply to the extent that the investment agreement is a contract to manage the assets of an occupational pension scheme.

(k)   Calls made in non-commercial contexts

The restrictions do not apply where the call is made by a person who is not acting by way of business and who is not provided with an incentive to make the call.

(l)   Calls made in the course of a profession or non-investment business

No restrictions apply where the calls relate to giving investment advice or making arrangements, where this is a necessary part of other advice or services given in the course of carrying on professional business. They are not regarded as a necessary part of such other advice or services if they are separately remunerated.

(m)   Exempted persons

The restrictions are lifted in respect of exempted persons as defined in the Glossary.

(n)   Overseas persons

The restrictions are lifted in respect of certain overseas person calls. These are calls made on behalf of a person carrying on investment business which is not from a permanent place of business in the UK and where the overseas person is not an authorised person in relation to those services. The regulation sets out the parameters of the exemption. To the extent that any regulation does not specifically permit an overseas person call, the regulations lift the restrictions for such calls only to the extent that the marketing or dealing, as the case may be, is done through an authorised or exempted person.

(o)   Calls prohibited by telecommunications licence

Any prohibition in such a licence applies subject only to the lifting of restrictions in respect of public takeovers discussed above.

(p)   Unlawful business

This regulation simply states that the regulations do not permit any contravention of s 3 of the Financial Services Act save in respect of public takeovers referred to above.

(q)   Reasonable belief

The marketing restriction is lifted to the extent that the caller can demonstrate that he believes on reasonable grounds at the time of the call that the restrictions did not apply.

(r)   Reliance on guidance

A person is assumed to act in accordance with the regulations to the extent that the relevant regulator has issued formal guidance on compliance with them and in reliance on standards set out in that guidance the person concerned believes on reasonable grounds that he is acting in conformity with the regulations.

16.5.3   Telephone selling by telephone marketing agencies[23]

The Securities and Investments Board has issued a guidance release covering the activities of telephone marketing agencies which undertake telephone marketing campaigns relating to investments or investment services but which are not themselves authorised or exempted persons under the Financial Services Act. The guidance release, like other guidance releases by the SIB, is a statement of the SIB's views and does not necessarily constitute the law. The SIB's views include the following:

---

23   SIB Guidance Release No 3/91.

(1) a telephone call made without express invitation is an unsolicited call (s 56(8) of the Act);

(2) agencies making unsolicited calls must consider whether the calls fall within the scope of s 56(1) of the Act and where they do, the agency may only make the calls if permitted by the Common Unsolicited Calls Regulations 1991 (formerly the Financial Services (Unsolicited Calls) Regulations 1987);

(3) a call which is an unsolicited call under s 56 of the Act may also in some circumstances be an investment advertisement under s 57. Telephone marketing agencies must therefore make sure that any investment advertisement issued by them is issued to the order of or approved by an authorised person or permitted under s 58. In SIB's view, pre-recorded messages are likely to be advertisements, whereas scripted and guided messages and free-form calls (the structure and content of which is largely at the discretion of the agency's representative) are not likely to be advertisements;

(4) a telephone marketing agency needs authorisation or exemption if it carries on the business of dealing in investments, arranging deals in investments or giving investment advice.

16.5.4   Marketing investments on the Internet[24]

In its annual report for the year ending March 1996 the Securities and Investments Board (SIB) states that the Internet has emerged as a new and potentially significant medium for the promotion and carrying on of all aspects of investment business. It records that the view of the SIB is that the Internet is essentially no different from other media; the provisions of the Financial Services Act relating, for example, to investment advertisements, apply in the usual way.

SIB scans the Internet with a view to identifying unauthorised investments and unauthorised investment business and has pursued a number of potential breaches. As the Internet operates across national boundaries and jurisdictions, it raises a number of new issues which need to be addressed by regulators internationally and the SIB is playing a leading role in these discussions and in bilateral contacts with overseas regulators.

SIB is conscious of the fact that there may be a need for changes to the Financial Services Act in view of the way in which business can be transacted over the Internet and is in discussion with various UK regulators over the issues arising.

---

24   Circular letters issued by SIB in December 1995 and June 1996.

SIB has issued standard letters on the Internet both in respect of access or site providers and on advertising on the Internet[24bis].

(a)   Access or site providers on the Internet

In SIB's view, merely providing access or a site is unlikely to fall foul of the UK financial services legislation if all the provider does is to furnish technical services without having any involvement in the marketing of the products or services of someone on whose behalf access to the site is provided.

On the other hand, if the access or site provider is also commercially involved with an investment firm on whose behalf it is providing such access or site, the provider may in fact be engaged in carrying on investment business and, if not authorised, contravene s 3 of the Financial Services Act. This might arise where the provider:

(1)   provides access and/or an off-the-shelf Net site over which he has control as regards what was placed on the Net or over the nature of information about investments or investment services provided on the site;

(2)   has a joint venture arrangement with someone carrying on investment business, such as a firm providing share dealing services;

(3)   promotes an investment service under his own name; or

(4)   promotes another person's investment service or places investment material on the Net.

(b)   Marketing on the Internet

SIB is of the view that, subject to specific exclusions, promotional material circulated on the Net might fall within the definition of an investment advertisement. In its view, for the purposes of the Act, where information held anywhere on the Net is made available to or can be obtained by someone in the UK that information, if it takes the form of an investment advertisement, may be viewed as having been issued in the UK.

SIB goes no further than to state that it is possible that in certain circumstances an access or site provider might be seen to be issuing or, more likely, causing to be issued an advertisement by virtue of providing access or a site on the Net. This is less likely to be the case where the provider has no knowledge or control over the information or service which has been put onto the Net and no commercial interest, financial or otherwise, in the information or service being provided.

24bis   See further at para 11.2 *supra*.

It is SIB's view that where an advertisement held anywhere on the Internet is made available to or can be obtained by someone in the UK that advertisement may be viewed as having been issued in the UK at the point where it is made available to or is pulled up on a computer screen by a person in the UK. A mere statement of disclaimer eg that the advertisement is not directed at persons in the UK may have a practical consequence of putting off enquiries from the UK but, from the legal point of view, will generally not achieve its objective.

In determining whether an advertisement or other information on the Internet is to be treated as being directed to persons in the UK under s 207(3) of the Financial Services Act in contravention of s 57 of that Act, and possibly gives rise to civil proceedings by the SIB for injunction and restitution under s 61, the SIB will take into account the degree to which positive steps were taken to avoid the material being made available to or receivable by persons in the UK. Such steps might include requiring registration before access to any material was made available.

On-line trading on the Internet is, it is submitted, tantamount to conducting investment business in any jurisdiction in and from which the customer can access the Web site and enter into an agreement relating to an investment. The fact that the agreement is concluded by a person without a permanent place of business in the United Kingdom (an 'overseas person'), in that person's country, does not mean that the provider of such investment business can legally market, invite or enter into investments agreements in the UK, even if he is authorised to conduct investment business in the jurisdiction where he is situated. An overseas person may, however, conduct investment business in the UK with or through an authorised person or if he is an exempted person acting in the course of business in respect of which he is exempt[24ter]. Likewise an overseas person may not make or offer or agree to make arrangements with a view to another person buying, selling, subscribing for or underwriting a particular investment or with the view to a person who participates in the arrangements, doing so except with or in favour of an authorised person or an exempted person in relation to exempted transactions[24ter].

An overseas person may enter into investment agreements as principal with or as agent for a person in the UK if the transaction or agreement is the result of an approach made to the overseas person by or on behalf of the person in the UK which has not been solicited by the overseas person (or has been solicited by him in a way which does not contravene ss 56 or

---

24ter   Financial Services Act 1986, Sched 1, Part IV, para 26(1). See also Chapter IV of the Act on the meaning of 'exempted person'.

57 of the Financial Services Act 1986), or the result of an approach made by the overseas person which does not contravene either of those sections[24quat].

It certainly appears that the Internet is merely another medium for advertising and marketing investments and in due course new flesh will be added to the existing skeleton of rules and regulations that regulates financial advertising and marketing.

(c)   SFA and IMRO

The SFA and IMRO have issued guidance on how their rules apply to dealing on the Internet.

In general, all rules which apply ordinarily also extend to conducting business on the Internet. As regards advertising, SFA and IMRO take the view that an investment advertisement sent from overseas which is accessible on a computer screen in the UK is deemed to have been issued to persons in the UK. An Internet advertiser who wishes to rely on the exception that the advertisement was only issued to a restricted class of persons eg not private customers, will be required to show that the investment service was not available to private customers or that the password to gain access to the relevant Web site was only made available to non-private customers. IMRO recommends a password or customer status questionnaire to enable the investment firm to vet potential customers.

The Internet site advertisement must carry the name of the issuer or approver of the advertisement and identify the applicable SRO regulator. This need not be shown on each screen provided it is included on each new screen which refers to a fresh specific advertisement[24quin].

16.6   Cancellation rules

Section 51 of the Financial Services Act makes provision for the Secretary of State (whose functions have since been transferred to the SIB) to make rules enabling a person who had entered or offered to enter into an investment agreement with an authorised person to rescind the agreement or withdraw the offer.

The Financial Services (Cancellation) Rules 1989 apply in relation to unit trusts and PEPs. The purpose of the rules is to give investors the opportunity to make considered and well-informed investment decisions. They

---

24quat   Para 27 *ibid.*
24quin   SFA Board Notice 416, 25 April 1997; IMRO Notice to Registered Firms trading on the Internet.

grant investors 'a cooling-off' period in which to consider their decision and to reduce the incentive for salesmen to adopt hard-sell tactics.

The Financial Services (Cancellation) Rules 1994 apply to life policies including, in particular, with profits life policies, unit-linked life policies, personal pensions and annuities.

The Cancellation Rules also extend to European institutions operating under the 'passport' conferred by the Second Banking Co-ordination Directive[25].

16.7   PIA and the marketing of retail investments

The current PIA rulebook is in two volumes. The first contains material dealing with the processes of admission, compliance, discipline, prudential requirements and supervision; the second contains the business rules adopted from previous regulators namely FIMBRA, LAUTRO, IMRO and SIB.

Financial advisers are either appointed representatives ie tied to the companies that they represent, or independent financial advisers (IFAs). Company representatives advise only on the packaged products sold by their company or marketing group whereas independent financial advisers are not tied to any company. Where advice is sought on a product the IFA must comply with the twin requirements of 'know your customer' and 'suitability' of the product for the customer. Firms must maintain records containing sufficient information to show that a transaction was suitable for the customer. These records are known as 'factfinds'. The rules do not prescribe the content of a factfind which is left to the individual firms.

'Execution only' transactions are those carried out on the instructions of a customer where he has not sought the IFA's advice regarding the suitability of the product. Such business can be completed without a factfind.

Unsolicited calls, whether by way of personal visits or telephone calls, are generally covered by s 56 of the Financial Services Act and the Common Unsolicited Calls Regulations discussed above. The PIA rules add additional requirements such as, in the absence of agreement with the customer, that the calls must be made at a reasonable hour, the salesman must announce himself at the outset of the call by saying who he is, whom he represents and why he has called[26].

The issue of telemarketing under the PIA rules is complex. The PIA rules distinguish between Category A advertisements, Category B advertise-

---

25   SI 1992 No 3218, Sched 11, para 12.
26   PIA rules L, Sched 2, para 3.

ments and Category C advertisements. A Category A advertisement is equivalent to SIB's image advertisement; a Category B advertisement is one which identifies and promotes a specific product; a Category C advertisement is equivalent to SIB's off-the-page or direct-offer (eg mail pack) advertisements.

Category C advertisements which comply with the rules, will have given the customer sufficient information to make an informed decision about the suitability of the product. There is no need for a factfind unless advice is being sought.

The Key Features document is a relatively new document in the PIA information regime and currently applies to life and pension products. It describes the aims of the contract, what the investor must pay, the risks associated with the contract, an illustration of the possible future benefits under the policy and, where applicable, the amounts secured by the death benefit. It must be delivered at a specified stage depending upon how the product is marketed.

The PIA rules make provision for a third type of person, other than an appointed representative or independent financial adviser, namely an introducer. An introducer is an individual who is appointed by a firm which is a product provider or a marketing associate, or by an appointed representative or introducer firm of such a company, to carry out, in the course of business which is regulated by PIA, certain limited activities[27]. Introducers may effect introductions between customers and the firm and distribute advertisements. They may give factual information on investment contracts but they may not give investment advice. Thus, they may not advise customers on the merits of their purchasing, selling, subscribing for an investment or exercising any right which may be conferred by an investment.

At the time of writing the PIA is involved in a project entitled 'Evolution Project' in which it is evaluating its present rules and considering the nature of future rules by consulting its members and individuals[28]. The following is an indication of the PIA's current thinking:

(1) the existing legislation is too inflexible in accommodating changes in a dynamic market-place;

(2) the PIA would like to secure for consumers a regulatory body which is focused around the financial concerns of consumers rather than

---

27 PIA Glossary and rule 3.5.
28 PIA's Consultative Paper 23 published March 1927. This exercise is likely to be superseded by the wholesale overhaul of the financial services supervisory regime—see Chapter 1.

one which is a reflection of artificial boundaries between different types of products or services;

(3) the PIA believes that fewer and more focused rules are likely to be better observed, particularly by smaller firms;

(4) the PIA needs to overhaul the rule book generally to try to ensure that it is more intelligible, accessible and user friendly. This must be done within the constraints imposed by the Financial Services Act and the need to retain a legal effectiveness and certainty in its rules;

(5) the PIA must address and indeed take advantage of information technology developments. There is now electronic trading of life and pension products and possibilities of similar trading for unit trusts. The PIA is keen to explore possibilities of using electronic systems for various purposes including supervision of its members and enabling them to report transactions.

16.8   Concluding reflections

The regulation of investment marketing is so vast and complex that it is not possible, within this text, to refer, let alone cover, each aspect. It is hoped, however, that the reader will find that the text covers the fundamental aspects of investment marketing and provides a perspective and framework to the plethora of rules.

Chapter 17

Marketing Techniques and Considerations

In this chapter we consider certain marketing techniques and promotions and some constraints on marketing generally.

17.1 Prize competitions

Prize competitions are commonly used in the promotion of financial products. These must not offend the Lotteries and Amusements Act 1976 which renders it unlawful to conduct in or through any newspaper, or in connection with any trade or business or the sale of any article to the public:

(1) any competition in which prizes are offered for forecasts of the result either of a future event or of a past event the result of which is not yet ascertained or not yet generally known; or

(2) any other competition in which success does not depend to a substantial degree on the exercise of skill[1]. We will briefly consider the elements of the latter category.

The expression 'competition' is not defined in the statute but connotes persons striving against each other[1bis]. It is an unfortunate misuse of the term 'competition' for the foregoing Act to refer to games of chance as 'competitions'. In *Imperial Tobacco Co v Attorney General and Express Newspapers plc v Liverpool Daily Post and Echo plc*[2] the court found that the

---

1   Lotteries and Amusements Act 1976, s 14.
1bis   *Whitbread & Co Ltd v Bell* [1970] 2 All ER 64.
2   *Imperial Tobacco Ltd v Attorney General* [1980] 1 All ER 866 HL; *Express Newspapers plc v Liverpool Daily Post and Echo plc* [1988] 3 All ER 680.

particular games in question did not involve the exercise of any degree of skill and were therefore not competitions in the strict sense of the term. A pure game of chance can never constitute a prize competition[3].

In practice it is not always easy to establish whether success in a competition does depend to a substantial degree on the exercise of skill. A competition in which answers to questions can be obtained by searching in an encyclopaedia or making telephone calls does not, it is submitted, depend to a substantial degree on the exercise of skill. Interpreting and identifying a picture or completing a tie breaker is more likely to satisfy such a requirement.

The Direct Marketing Association has laid down detailed rules for prize competitions which bind the members subscribing to its Code of Practice.

17.2　Lotteries

As a general rule all lotteries (except those under the Gaming Act 1968 and National Lottery etc Act 1993) are unlawful, as are any activities related to their promotion[3bis].

In the leading case of *Reader's Digest Association Ltd v Williams*[4] the court defined a lottery as the distribution of prizes by chance where the persons taking part in the operation, or a substantial number of them, make a payment or consideration in return for obtaining their chance of a prize. The mere purchase of an item or the requirement to use a credit card account in order to qualify for participation in the chance of winning a prize is consideration for the foregoing purposes[5]. On the other hand, a free prize draw is quite legal.

Where a scheme is severable and one stage is dependent solely on chance but entitles the successful entrant to participate in the second stage which involves skill, the first stage will constitute an unlawful lottery if it also requires the entrant to make a payment or consideration as a condition of participating[6].

It was pointed out in the case of *In re Senator Hanseatische Verwaltungsgesellschaft mbH*[7] that, although lotteries have been unlawful for more than 200 years, Parliament has never attempted a definition of the term 'lottery' for the reason that there is no limit to the ingenuity of the devisers of pro-

---

3　*Whitbread & Co Ltd v Bell, loc cit.*
3bis　Sections 1 and 2, Lotteries and Amusements Act 1976.
4　[1976] 3 All ER 737 at 739.
5　*Imperial Tobacco Ltd, loc cit* at 872.
6　*Director of Public Prosecutions v Bradfute & Associates Ltd* [1967] 1 All ER 112.
7　[1997] 1 WLR 515 CA at 523.

jects and no end to the variety of schemes which may constitute a lottery. The courts have consistently held that what lies at the heart of the concept is the distribution of prizes by lot or chance. Any element of skill means that the scheme is not a lottery but it may still constitute an unlawful prize competition.

The Committee of Advertising Practice in its Sales Promotion Code[8] sets out recommended rules and provisions which are to apply to all promotions with prizes.

In addition to the substantive offence of conducting a lottery, it is an offence amongst other things, to advertise a lottery, tickets for sale or distribution in a lottery or to publish any inducement to participate in a lottery[8bis].

17.3 Trading stamps

An oft-ignored statute, because there have been so few prosecutions under it, is the Trading Stamps Act 1964 which regulates the issue, use and redemption of trading stamps.

A trading stamp is a stamp which is, or is intended to be delivered to any person on or in connection with the purchase of any goods or the hiring of any goods under a hire-purchase agreement and which is or is intended to be redeemable[9]. The definition must be read with the exceptions to it and the other definitions contained in the same section. These define the meanings of 'to redeem', 'stamp' and 'trading stamp scheme'. If a device is a trading stamp and the scheme is a trading stamp scheme, the requirements of the foregoing Act as to statements required on the face of trading stamps, the name and address of the promoter on catalogues and stamp books, statements in advertisements and the display of information in shops, must be adhered to. Failure to do so is an offence and any officer of a corporation who connives with the commission of an offence by that corporation is equally guilty of the offence.

If a device is a trading stamp it needs to state, on its face, in clear legible characters, a value expressed in or by reference to current coinage[10]. It is not uncommon to find a statement such as 'cash value 0.001p', or 'this stamp has no cash value or is not exchangeable for cash', though the latter is of questionable validity.

---

8   Sales Promotion Code, s 40, part of the British Codes of Advertising and Sales Promotion.
8bis   Section 2, Lotteries and Amusements Act 1976.
9   Section 10(1).
10   Section 2(1).

Within the purview of trading stamps fall certain Air Mile Coupons, labels collected from groceries, till receipts and ATM receipts carrying a particular promotion and coupons stating a certain amount off the next purchase or a certain amount by way of holiday vouchers offered on presentation when booking a holiday.

The Act, which was introduced in order to ensure that the cost of a gift was not simply loaded onto the price of goods or services, appears to have outlived its practical usefulness[11].

17.4   Distance selling

17.4.1   'Doorstep' selling and rights of cancellation

An almost constitutional right of cancellation now exists on the part of the consumer in relation to unsolicited goods or services sold to him at his doorstep or where the contract of purchase was concluded away from business premises. The reader will already have observed from previous chapters how this right has been conferred on the consumer in relation to offers of credit, hire facilities and investments. The general provisions governing the right of cancellation in relation to such contracts is embodied in the Consumer Protection (Cancellation of Contracts Concluded Away from Business Premises) Regulations 1987[12]. They have their origin in the EC Council Directive 85/577/EEC.

A consumer is given the right to cancel a contract within a period of seven days where the contract was for the supply by a trader of goods or services made during an unsolicited visit by the trader to the home of the consumer or of another person, or a visit to the consumer's place of work, or during a visit by the trader at the express request of the consumer where the goods or services are different to those to which the consumer's request related and the consumer did not know or could not reasonably have known that the supply of those goods or services formed part of the trader's business activities, or where the contract was made during an excursion organised by the trader away from premises on which he is carrying on any business.

A contract to which the regulations apply is unenforceable unless it contains a written notice in statutory form of the consumer's rights of cancellation.

---

11   See Richard Lawson: Loyalty Cards and the Trading Stamps Act, *Solicitors Journal,* 7 February 1997.
12   SI 1987 No 2117.

The regulations do not apply where rights of cancellation are provided under other Acts, such as regulated agreements under the Consumer Credit Act 1974, insurance contracts and investment agreements.

For the purposes of the regulations an 'unsolicited visit' is one which does not take place at the express request (whether oral or in writing) of the consumer and includes a visit which takes place after a trader telephones a consumer, otherwise than at his express request, indicating expressly or by indication that he is willing to visit the consumer[13].

17.4.2 Timeshares

The Timeshare Act 1992 embodies the customer's right to cancel a timeshare agreement and to cancel a timeshare credit agreement. Notice of such rights must be incorporated in the contract. These rights have been augmented by the Timeshare Regulations 1997[14].

The Timeshare Act confers a right on the offeree of a timeshare agreement and a timeshare credit agreement to cancel the agreement within 14 days of entering into it[15]. That period has been extended to up to three months and ten days if certain information was not provided to the purchaser[16].

The Timeshare Regulations 1997 amend the 1992 Act by providing for prescribed statutory information relating to the timeshare. An advertisement of a timeshare must make reference to the Act and indicate the availability of the agreement; the omission of such a statement constitutes an offence. Certain provisions only apply to timeshares in buildings and not to caravans or mobile homes. Some breaches of statutory duty also give rise to a claim in damages[16bis].

The application of the Timeshare Act 1992 has, by virtue of the European Directive, been extended to cover timeshare rights which arise by virtue of share ownership or collective investment schemes, whether or not the accommodation is situated in the UK or in another EEA State (the EU, Norway, Liechtenstein and Iceland), and the purchaser is ordinarily resident in the UK. A purchaser of a timeshare is entitled to receive the agreement in the language of the country of his residence or the country of which he is a national. In addition a purchaser resident in the UK is

---

13   Reg 3(3). See also Code of Practice of Direct Marketing Association, 2nd edn.
14   SI 1997 No1081 implementing EC Directive 94/47/EC.
15   Sections 2 and 3.
16   Section 5A of the Timeshare Act 1992 inserted by the Timeshare Regulations 1997, *loc cit* reg 9.
16bis   Section 10A.

entitled to the contract in English. A purchaser is also entitled to a translation in the language of the country where the property is situated.

The Timeshare (Cancellation Notices) Order 1992[17] prescribes the form of the notice of cancellation which must be set out in timeshare agreements and timeshare credit agreements.

17.4.3   Distance Selling directive

A natural evolvement of the rights of cancellation is embodied in the Distance Selling Directive[18] adopted by the Council of the European Union on 17 February 1997 and which is required to be implemented by Member States by mid-2000.

Distance selling contracts are contracts concerning goods or services concluded between a supplier and a consumer under an organised distance sale or service provision scheme run by the supplier who, for the purposes of the contract, makes exclusive use of one or more means of distance communication up to and including the moment at which the contract is concluded. It would therefore cover sales by direct mail, telesales, newspaper, radio, television, teleshopping, videophone, electronic mail (E mail) and Internet sales. Excluded from its provisions are sales of financial services in respect of which the Commission is expected to introduce separate legislation, and property sales.

The Directive requires consumers to be informed of the identity of the supplier, the main characteristics of the goods or services being sold, their price and the cost of using the relevant means of distance communication, arrangements for payment and the consumer's rights of withdrawal. The supplier must give certain information in writing. In most cases the consumer is given the right to withdraw within seven working days of receiving the written information or the receipt of the goods or conclusion of the contract in the case of services. The contract must generally speaking be performed within 30 days of the order.

17.4.4   Telephone selling and marketing (telesales) and taping of conversations

There are various controls on telephone selling by telephone marketing agencies and others.

In relation to investments, the Securities and Investments Board is of the

---

17   SI 1992 No 1942.
18   97/7/EC (OJ 1997 L1 44/19).

view that a telephone call made without express invitation is an unsolicited call so that making the same would contravene the Financial Services Act 1986, s 56(1), unless the agency is permitted to make such a call by the Common Unsolicited Calls Regulations 1991[19].

The Office of Telecommunications (OFTEL) has issued advice and recommendations relating to the use of telecommunications. These are notified when issuing licences to run telecommunications systems under the Telecommunications Act 1984. Provision is made for subscribers to request not to receive unsolicited sales calls *via* a particular medium, for example by telephone or fax. Where telephone conversations are recorded, the party must be given a brief introductory warning that this is taking place. This is frequently set out in the marketing literature of companies. Recordings are commonplace in the sale of investments under the Financial Services Act or in relation to deals made by principals and brokers which are governed by the Bank of England Code of Conduct.

The taping of telephone conversations is recommended in the conduct of business, including by the Bank of England, in respect of all conversations by dealers and brokers and back-office telephone lines used by those responsible for confirming deals or passing payment and other instructions. Where taping takes place, this should be supervised and reviewed periodically. Failure to tape will normally count against a firm if it seeks to use the arbitration procedure in the London Code of Conduct to settle a difference or if the firm is the subject of a complaint. When initially installing tape equipment, or taking on new clients or counterparties, firms should take the necessary steps to inform clients and counterparties that conversations will be recorded. This might be done by a warning included in their standard terms of business[19bis].

The Code of Practice of the Direct Marketing Association contains detailed rules governing telephone marketing[19ter].

17.5 Inducements

The giving of inducements is proscribed in various codes of conduct.

First, the Core Conduct of Business Rules of the Securities and Investments Board[20] provides that a firm must take reasonable steps to ensure that neither it nor any of its agents offers or gives or solicits or

---

19   SIB Guidance Release No 3/91.
19bis   The London Code of Conduct (July 1995), paras 48 and 49.
19ter   2nd edn, effective from October 1997.
20   Rule 1.

accepts any inducement which is likely significantly to conflict with any duties of the recipient (or his employer) owed to customers in connection with regulated business. 'Inducement' excludes any commission which the firm is obliged to disclose by virtue of the rules and goods or services provided under a 'soft commission agreement'. Similar provisions are found in the Rulebooks of the various self-regulating organisations[21].

The London Code of Conduct which regulates principals and broking firms in the wholesale markets has quite extensive provisions governing entertainment and gifts. Management and employees are prohibited from offering inducements to conduct business. Whilst the Bank of England recognises that entertainment and gifts offered in the normal course of business do not necessarily constitute inducements it receives a surprisingly high number of complaints about the excessive nature of entertainment being offered. Management is recommended to have a policy on entertainment and gifts and to review it periodically[22].

17.6   Data protection

17.6.1   Data Protection Act 1984

No marketing of financial services can disregard the provisions of the Data Protection Act 1994 which regulates the use of automatically processed information (ie information held on computers) relating to personal data (namely, information relating to individuals) and the provision of services in respect of such information.

'Personal data' is defined as data consisting of information which relates to a living individual who can be identified from that information (or from that and other information in possession of the data user) including any expression of opinion about the individual (eg as to his creditworthiness) but not any indication of the intentions of the data user in respect of that individual. 'Data' means information recorded in a form in which it can be processed by equipment operated automatically in response to instructions given for that purpose[23].

A 'data user' is a person who holds data and a person holds data if, briefly, the data form part of a collection of data processed or intended to be processed, the data user controls the contents and use of the data and the data

---

21   See, for example, SFA rules 5–7 and IMRO rule 1.6(1).
22   Paragraphs 61–64; July 1995 edn and see the circular letter issued by the Capital and Wholesale Markets Supervision & Surveillance Division of the Bank of England, 6 December 1996.
23   Section1(1) and (2).

are in the form in which they have been or are intended to be processed. A person carries on a computer bureau if he provides other persons with services in respect of data, briefly, as agent for other persons causing data to be processed or allowing other persons the use of the equipment in his possession for processing data. A 'data subject' is an individual who is the subject of personal data[24].

Data users and computer bureaux are required to register under the Act with the Data Protection Registrar and to comply with the Data Protection Principles referred to in s 2 of and set out in Sched I to the Act. In summary, the eight data protection principles prescribe that:

(1) personal data shall be processed fairly and lawfully;
(2) personal data shall be held only for one or more specified and lawful purposes;
(3) personal data shall not be used or disclosed in any manner incompatible with that purpose;
(4) personal data shall be adequate, relevant and not excessive in relation to the purpose for which it is held;
(5) personal data shall be accurate and kept up to date;
(6) personal data shall not be kept longer than is necessary for the purpose for which it is held;
(7) an individual shall be entitled at reasonable intervals and without undue delay or expense to be informed by any data user whether he holds personal data of which that individual is the subject and to access any such data held by a data user and, where appropriate, to have it corrected or erased;
(8) appropriate security measures shall be taken against unauthorised access to, alteration, disclosure or destruction of personal data and against its accidental loss or destruction.

17.6.2   European Union Data Protection Directive[25]

This new Directive must be implemented by Member States by 24 October 1998. The Directive has two objects. The first is to protect the fundamental rights and freedoms of natural persons and in particular their right to privacy with respect to the processing of personal data. Secondly, it requires that Member States shall neither restrict nor prohibit the free flow of personal data between Member States for reasons connected with the foregoing protection (ie the supply to the data subject of relevant information

---

24   Section 1(4), (5) and (6).
25   95/46/EC (OJ L 281/31).

and the data subject's right to object to the processing of personal data relating to him and to its disclosure for the first time to third parties).

Once the Directive has been implemented, the protection afforded by the Data Protection Act 1984 will extend beyond automatically processed information. The Directive applies protection to 'processing of personal data' which means any operation or set of operations which is performed upon personal data, whether or not by automatic means, such as collection, recording, organisation, storage, adaptation or alteration, retrieval, consultation, use, disclosure by transmission, dissemination or otherwise making available, alignment or combination, blocking, erasure or destruction[26].

17.6.3   Guidance notes issued by the Data Protection Registrar

The Data Protection Registrar has issued and continues to issue useful guidance notes on the application of the Data Protection Act. Those immediately relevant to the marketing of financial services are referred to below:

(1) Guidance Note 9: Implications of the Data Protection Act for direct marketing/direct mailing.

   This Guidance Note relates to the registration under the Act of persons involved in the use of lists of names for direct marketing. It gives directions as to the category under which the following persons should register: a list owner who decides to make a mailing list in his control available to third parties; a list broker who acts as an intermediary in making arrangements for the use of lists; a client advertiser whose promotional literature is to be mailed to those on the list; an advertising agency acting on behalf of the client advertiser in making arrangements for the mailing; and a mailing house or computer bureau which is to receive the list from the list owner and process it to produce labels, envelopes or personalised promotional material.

(2) Guidance Note 19: Fair obtaining—notification

   This Guidance Note relates to the First Data Protection Principle which requires that information to be contained in personal data shall be obtained fairly and applies such principle to the requirement that the persons from whom information is obtained must be notified as to how the information will be used. It recommends that the source should be told:

---

26   Article 2(b).

(a) what information it is intended will actually become personal data;

(b) by whom it will be held (namely, the identity of any relevant registered data user);

(c) who else will be able to use it (this can be described either by a name or by a general description);

(d) how it will be used.

A notification to a customer will not uncommonly take the following form:

> 'We will use information for credit assessment, including credit scoring and make such enquiries and take up such references as we may consider necessary. We may search the files of credit reference agencies which will keep a record of that request. We may pass details about the performance of your account to credit reference agencies. These details will be used by other lenders in assessing applications for credit by you and members of your household and occasionally for fraud prevention and debt collection.'

(3) Guidance Note 24: Guidance on the requirement in the First Data Protection Principle to 'obtain fairly' for firms advising on and selling financial investment products.

As with Guidance 19, this Guidance Note relates to the First Data Protection Principle. It includes a recommendation of statements, when appropriate, that information is needed to ensure appropriate financial advice is offered; that information will be retained on computer and for a stated purpose; that information will be disclosed to a third party who should preferably be named; that data will be used for direct marketing unless the customer elects otherwise (eg by ticking an opt-out box).

(4) Guidance Note 37: Advice on registration and compliance with the Eighth Data Protection Principle for the tied agents of insurance companies.

This Guidance Note explains the circumstances under which tied agents of insurance companies must register under the Data Protection Act, whether as data users or computer bureaux, and sets out their obligations to comply with the Eighth Data Protection Principle.

(5) Data Protection Guidance for direct marketers.

This Guidance Note is a comprehensive manual on data protection for those involved in direct marketing. It covers registration and the First Data Protection Principle, including fair obtaining, fair processes and lawful obtaining and processing. Under the latter head it discusses copyright, confidentiality, statutory limitations on disclosure and limitations placed on public sector organisations in the disclosure of personal data.

The Guidance Note acknowledges that UK law currently allows financial institutions to require the consent of individuals to the use of their data for cross marketing or host mailing purposes or, indeed, to the disclosure of their details to third parties, as a condition of business in the contract. However, the Data Protection Registrar draws attention to the Unfair Terms in Consumer Contracts Regulations which provide that unfair terms are not binding on the consumer and questions whether relying upon such contractual terms obliges customers to consent to the waiving of their rights to confidentiality. Whatever the position, it is clear that any such term must be expressed in plain, intelligible language as, where there is any doubt, the term will be interpreted in favour of the consumer[27].

(6) Data Protection Guidance on keeping customer information safe.

This Guidance Note provides advice on compliance with the Eighth Data Protection Principle for financial service providers that give out information about customers in response to enquiries. It is mainly aimed at banks and building societies which routinely provide detailed confidential customer information over the telephone. However, it is also of relevance to the insurance industry and the financial services industry. Its coverage includes the identification and verification of telephone callers. Under the latter category, it sets out the need for a verification procedure, the type of verification data (eg passwords and passnumbers), selecting and using the verification data, *ad hoc* telephone requests, automated information facilities and telephone banking. The Guidance Note also covers verification in person and in writing and verification of staff.

Whilst data protection is itself a legal imperative, the use of data is essential to any marketing activity. That activity must take cognisance of the Act, the guidelines produced relating to it and common law rules applying to the confidentiality of customer information particularly in the context of the banker–customer relationship[28]. Care must also be taken to avoid committing the tort of unlawful interference with the business interests of another person[29].

---

27   Paragraphs 94–96.
28   *Tournier v National Provincial and Union Bank of England* [1923] All ER Rep. 550; [1924] 1 KB 461.
29   *Indata Equipment Supplies Ltd v ACL Ltd* (1997) *The Times*, 14 August.

Chapter 18

The European Dimension

18.1 Introduction

No legal exposition can omit to mention the influence on English law of European law, ie law emanating from Brussels. This is no less true of financial advertising and marketing law. In previous chapters we mentioned various Directives and the enacting legislation in the UK. The reader will have observed that the Directives extend to misleading advertising, credit, financial services, insurance, banking, distance selling, timeshare sales, data protection and, more peripherally, unfair terms in consumer contracts.

There is little doubt that Directives and decisions of the European court will be of growing significance in the evolution of the law of the UK. Indeed, in areas which it covers, European Community law takes precedence over English law, whether statute or common law. The significance of this lies beyond the mere authority of European law, as the European Community to a large extent also dictates the timetable for change.

18.2 Evolution towards further European harmonisation

In financial services the European Commission's primary objective has been the creation of a single market putting into effect the principles of the Treaty of Rome of free movement of persons, goods, services and capital. That objective has now largely been achieved by the progressive adoption of some 50 Directives targeted at the providers of financial services, the Community's banks, insurance companies and securities' houses[1].

---

1   Green Paper of the Commission of the European Communities on Financial Services: Meeting Consumers' Expectations (22 May 1996), p 3.

The single market in financial services is based on the principle of home country control and mutual recognition founded on the implementation of agreed minimum standards of prudential supervision[2]. The European Court of Justice has always recognised that the need to protect the recipient of a service may justify limitations on the cross-border provision of services, so that consumers can legitimately be protected by their own domestic laws provided that these are non-discriminatory, necessary, non-duplicative and proportionate[3]. The Green Paper on Financial Services recognises the rapid growth in the distance selling of financial services, the need to grant cooling-off periods and the issue of inertia selling. Growth is especially anticipated in relation to cross-border business, facilitated in no small measure by the advent of electronic communications. The challenge will be to find means of regulating these without destroying or hampering initiative.

Concurrently with the Green Paper on Financial Services, the Commission issued a Green Paper on Commercial Communications in the Internal Market[4]. This covers all forms of advertising, direct marketing, sponsorship, sales promotions and public relations promoting products and services. It posits the following as preliminary observations:

(1) existing regulations may have to be reviewed where they are shown to hamper cross-frontier activity;

(2) the potential development of new barriers within the Internal Market needs to be tackled;

(3) future national and Community measures must be developed in conformity with both Internal Market and other Community objectives.

The Green Paper recognises that the advent of the Information Society has four implications for commercial communication services, namely:

(1) the new digital communication infrastructures represent a new carrier for such services which allows for the fusion of direct marketing techniques with creative advertising skills;

(2) speed of transmission and targeting possibilities will greatly facilitate trans-border commercial communications;

(3) they will lead to an integration of commercial communication services with distance retailing, allowing for interactive distance shopping, which is likely to revolutionise the whole concept of teleshopping;

---

2   *Ibid*.
3   *Ibid*, p 4.
4   Commercial Communications in the Internal Market (8 May 1996).

(4) the operators of other new Information Society services will seek out certain new commercial communication (eg interactive advertising) services to offer in order to make their services affordable[5].

The foregoing new developments will heighten the need to resolve existing trans-border regulatory problems and require a regulatory framework. Such a framework presumes a minimum degree of coherence and uniformity. The Green Paper reflects on the wide differences in national measures taken in implementing the Council Directive on Misleading Advertising and in its interpretation[6]. This creates real barriers to the flow of advertising services. In another area of advertising, the Green Paper observes that there are widely differing approaches to comparative advertising in certain Member States as a result of which advertisers are forced to entirely redesign their commercial communication campaigns in certain Member States.

There are other areas of disparity in commercial marketing. Promotional gifts and offers such as 'money off next purchase' are permitted in some Member States, restricted in others and prohibited altogether by a third group. The same pattern is found in the treatment by Member States of prize competitions. Such differences make it well nigh impossible to conduct a uniform trans-border campaign or prize competition.

The so called 'Television without Frontiers' Directive[7] has not produced uniformity between Member States. It provides for minimal harmonisation allowing Member States to apply rules to broadcasters established in their jurisdiction. The Commission has found considerable variance between Member States as to the levels of television advertising permitted by them and views the adoption of stricter measures by certain States, such as the UK, as creating barriers to the free movement of audio-visual advertising. The Commission is of a similar view in relation to the disparity in the approaches of different Member States to the advertising of financial products. Italy and the UK appear to stand out as the countries requiring prior approval to the issue of an investment advertisement. It is quite apparent that the European Commission is anxious to introduce greater uniformity across Member States.

18.3   European codes of practice

Lest it be thought that pan-European harmonisation is the sole prerogative of the European Parliament and the European Commission,

---

5   Pages 10–11.
6   Page 21; Council Directive 84/450/EEC.
7   Council Directive 89/552/EEC of 3 October 1989 (OJ 1989 L 298 p 23).

mention should be made of initiatives to introduce European Codes of Practice.

The European Advertising Standards Alliance (EASA) was established in Brussels in 1992 to bring together advertising self-regulatory bodies across Europe. Its main aims are to promote and support advertising self-regulation in Europe; to co-ordinate the handling of cross-border complaints; and to provide information and research on advertising self-regulation. It has published the EASA Guide to Self-regulation.

The Federation of European Direct Selling Associations (FEDSA) has produced the European Codes of Conduct for Direct Selling. One code is concerned with conduct towards consumers and the other with relations towards direct sellers by direct selling companies.

18.4   Applicable law and jurisdiction

In relation to torts, the Private International Law (Miscellaneous Provisions) Act 1995 now generally deems the law which is to apply to be the law of the country in which the events constituting the tort occurred[8]. Where elements of events occur in different countries, the applicable law where the cause of action is in respect of damage to property is the law of the country where the property was when it was damaged and in any other case (other than personal injury) the law of the country in which the most significant elements of the events constituting the tort occurred[9]. If, however, it appears in all the circumstances that it is substantially more appropriate for the applicable law to be the law of another country, the general rule is displaced and the applicable law for determining the issues is the law of that other country[10]. Further, where determining issues arising in any claim would either conflict with the principles of public policy or give effect to a penal, revenue or other public law which would not otherwise be enforceable under UK law, foreign law will not be applied[11].

The Private International Law (Miscellaneous Provisions) Act 1995 does not apply to defamation claims[12]. A defamation claim means any claim under the law of any part of the UK for libel or slander, slander of title, slander of goods or other malicious falsehood and any claim under the law of any other country corresponding to the foregoing. The law applicable to defamation claims will be the law which applies in the jurisdiction

---

8   Section 11(1), Private International Law (Miscellaneous Provisions) Act 1995.
9   Section 11(2)(b) and (c), *ibid.*
10   Section 12(1), *ibid.*
11   Section 14(3)(a), *ibid.*
12   Section 13(1), *ibid.*

in which the tort occurred. If it did not occur in a single jurisdiction, the law will be that where in substance the cause of action arose.

As a general rule a tort committed abroad will only be actionable in the UK if it would have been actionable as a tort if it had been committed in the UK and is actionable, though not necessarily as a tort, under the law of a foreign country[13].

It was held in *Shevill and Others v Presse Alliance SA*[14] that the Convention on Jurisdiction and the Enforcement on Judgments in Civil and Commercial Matters (the so-called Brussels Convention) which is set out in Sched 1 to the Civil Jurisdiction and Judgments Act 1982, permitted the victim of a libel in a newspaper distributed in states which were parties to the Convention to sue the publisher in the contracting state where the publisher was established or in any other contracting state where the publication was distributed and the victim claimed to have suffered injury to his reputation.

18.5   Concluding reflections

The essential characteristic of the European internal market is the freedom of movement throughout the European Union for goods, persons, services and capital, symbolised by the removal of internal frontiers. The European Court of Justice has echoed this claim by asserting that the aim is for transactions within the internal market to be treated in the same way as those within the territory of any individual Member State[15].

Financial advertising and marketing law is at the forefront of cross-border activity, if only by reason of the dramatic progress made in telecommunications. It is therefore inevitable that financial advertising and marketing law will become increasingly uniform across Member States of the European Union, a development which is merely a matter of time. The length of time this development takes is dependant upon the wills of politicians, legislators and the courts.

---

13   *Halsbury's Laws of England* Vol 8(1) paras 893 and 894 and Dicey & Morris: *The Conflict of Laws* (12th edn) Rule 203.
14   Decision of the European Court Case C 68/93: [1995] All ER EC 289: (1995) *The Times* 6 April and see the earlier discussion in Chapter 2 at para 2.2.
15   M Cremona in Goode: *Consumer Credit Legislation* at X[6].

Appendix 1

Credit and Hire Advertising

The Consumer Credit (Advertisements) Regulations 1989 (SI 1989 No 1125)

PART I
PRELIMINARY

1. Citation, commencement, interpretation and revocation

(1) These Regulations may be cited as the Consumer Credit (Advertisements) Regulations 1989 and shall come into force on 1st February 1990.

(2) In these Regulations, unless the context otherwise requires:—

'the Act' means the Consumer Credit Act 1974;

'advance payment' includes any deposit but does not include a repayment of credit or any insurance premium or any amount entering into the total charge for credit;

'the APR' means the annual percentage rate of charge for credit determined in accordance with the Total Charge for Credit Regulations and Schedule 3 to these Regulations;

'cash price' in relation to any goods, services, land or other things means the price or charge at which the goods, services, land or other things may be purchased by, or supplied to, persons for cash, account being taken of any discount generally available from the dealer or supplier in question;

'cash purchaser' means, in relation to any advertisement, a person who, for a money consideration—

  (a) acquires goods, land or other things; or

  (b) is provided with services,

under a transaction which is not financed by credit;

'Consumer credit tables' means tables contained in Parts 1 to 15 of 'Consumer credit tables' published in 1977 by Her Majesty's Stationery Office as modified by Correction Slips so published in December 1978 (being tables calculated in accordance with the principles set out in the Total Charge for Credit Regulations);

'contract of insurance' means a contract of insurance to which the Insurance Companies Act 1982 applies;

'credit advertisement' means an advertisement to which Part IV of the Act applies by virtue of it falling within section 43(1)(a) or which falls within section 151(1) of the Act in so far as section 44 is applied to such an advertisement;

'current account' means an account under which the customer may, by means of cheques or similar orders payable to himself or to any other person or by any other means, obtain or have the use of money held or made available by the person with whom the account is kept and which records alterations in the financial relationship between the said person and the customer;

'dealer' means, in relation to a hire-purchase, credit sale or conditional sale agreement under which he is not the creditor, a person who sells or proposes to sell goods, land or other things to the creditor before they form the subject matter of any such agreement and, in relation to any other agreement, means a supplier or his agent;

'hire advertisement' means an advertisement to which Part IV of the Act applies by virtue of it falling within section 43(1)(b) or which falls within section 151(1) of the Act is so far as section 44 is applied to such an advertisement;

'hire payment' means any payment to be made by a person in relation to any period in consideration of the bailment to him of goods, other than an advance payment;

'identified dealer' means, in relation to an advertisement—

(a) a dealer who is named in the advertisement or is identified in it by reference to a business connection he has with the advertiser; or

(b) a dealer upon whose premises the advertisement is published;

'premises' includes any place, stall, vehicle, vessel, aircraft or hovercraft at which a person is carrying on any business (whether on a permanent or temporary basis);

'supplier' has the meaning assigned to it by section 189(1) of the Act, except that it does not include, in relation to a hire-purchase, credit sale or conditional sale agreement, a creditor to whom goods, land or other things are sold or proposed to be sold by a dealer before becoming the subject matter of such an agreement;

'total charge for credit' shall be determined in accordance with the Total Charge for Credit Regulations and Schedule 3 to these Regulations; and

'the Total Charge for Credit Regulations' means the Consumer Credit (Total Charge for Credit) Regulations 1980.

(3) Any reference in these Regulations to bailment is in Scotland a reference to hiring.

(4) In these Regulations, references to repayment of credit are references to repayment of credit with or without any other amount.

(5) In these Regulations, any reference to the name of any person is—

(a) in the case of any person covered by a standard licence, a reference to any name of his specified in the licence; and

(b) in the case of any other person, a reference to any name under which he carries on business.

(6) Where any expression is used in these Regulations and in the Act, for the purposes of these Regulations that expression shall be construed as if in the Act (except section 8)

references to consumer credit agreements and to regulated agreements (being consumer credit agreements) included references to personal credit agreements.

(7) The Regulations specified in Schedule 4 to these Regulations are hereby revoked to the extent specified in the third column of that Schedule.

PART II
FORM AND CONTENT OF ADVERTISEMENTS

2. General rules

(1) The person who causes any credit advertisement to be published shall ensure that, subject to the following provisions of these Regulations, every such advertisement is:—

    (a) a simple credit advertisement that is to say a credit advertisement containing only the information set out in paragraphs 1 to 5 of Part I of Schedule 1 to these Regulations in whole or in part and any other information referred to in paragraph 6;

    (b) an intermediate credit advertisement that is to say a credit advertisement containing only the information set out in paragraphs 1 to 9 of Part II of Schedule 1 and no other information except as referred to in paragraph 10;

    (c) a full credit advertisement that is to say a credit advertisement containing, subject to sub-paragraph (d) below, at least the information set out in Part III of Schedule 1; or

    (d) a full credit advertisement which invites individuals (being individuals who, at the date the advertisement is published, are debtors under agreements made with the advertiser) to agree to a specified variation of those agreements, containing—

        (i) the name of the advertiser and a postal address of his and the information within Part III of Schedule 1 as varied in relation to those agreements if the invitation is accepted by the debtor; and

        (ii) the information, other than the name and a postal address of the advertiser, specified in that Part which the advertisement does not indicate will remain unaltered if the invitation is accepted.

(2) The person who causes any hire advertisement to be published shall ensure that, subject to the following provisions of these Regulations, every such advertisement is—

    (a) a simple hire advertisement that is to say a hire advertisement containing only the information set out in paragraphs 1 to 5 of Part I of Schedule 2 to these Regulations in whole or in part and any other information referred to in paragraph 6;

    (b) an intermediate hire advertisement that is to say a hire advertisement containing only the information set out in paragraphs 1 to 7 of Part II of Schedule 2 and no other information except as referred to in paragraph 8;

    (c) a full hire advertisement that is to say a hire advertisement containing, subject to sub-paragraph (d) below, at least the information set out in Part III of Schedule 2, but not containing the expression 'no deposit' or any expression to the like effect, except where no advance payments are to be made by the hirer; or

    (d) a full hire advertisement which invites individuals (being individuals who, at the date the advertisement is published, are hirers under agreements made with the advertiser) to agree to a specified variation of these agreements, containing:—

(i) the name of the advertiser and a postal address of his and the information within Part III of Schedule 2 as varied in relation to the hire facility if the invitation is accepted by the hirer; and

(ii) the information, other than a name and postal address of the advertiser, specified in that Part which the advertisement does not indicate will remain unaltered if the invitation is accepted;

but not containing the expression 'no deposit' or any expression to the like effect, except where no advance payments are to be made by the hirer.

(3) In the case of an advertisement relating to a debtor-creditor agreement enabling the debtor to overdraw on a current account under which the creditor is the Bank of England, an institution authorised under the Banking Act 1987, the Post Office for the purposes of a transaction entered into in the ordinary course of that part of the business of the Post Office which consists of the provision of banking services or a building society incorporated (or deemed to be incorporated) under the Building Societies Act 1986, for any reference in Schedule 1 to these Regulations to the APR there may be substituted a reference to the statement of—

(a) a rate, expressed to be a rate of interest, being a rate determined as the rate of the total charge for credit calculated on the assumption that only interest is included in the total charge for credit; and

(b) the nature and amount of any other charge included in the total charge for credit.

(4) Paragraphs 6 and 7 of Part II, and paragraph 6 of Part III, of Schedule 1 to these Regulations do not apply to an advertisement in so far as it relates to fixed-sum credit to be provided under a debtor-creditor-supplier agreement, where the cash price of the goods, services, land or other things to be supplied under a transaction financed by the agreement does not exceed £50.

(5) The APR referred to in Schedule 1 to these Regulations shall be denoted in advertisements as 'APR' or 'annual percentage rate' or 'annual percentage rate of the total charge for credit'.

(6) The specific information referred to in Schedules 1 and 2 to these Regulations in every credit advertisement or hire advertisement shall be clear and easily legible and, subject to the following provisions of these Regulations and except for the name and address or telephone number, shall be shown together as a whole.

(7) Any information in any book, catalogue, leaflet or other document which is likely to vary from time to time shall be taken for the purpose of paragraph (6) above to be shown together as a whole if—

(a) it is set out together as a whole in a separate document issued with the book, catalogue, leaflet or other document; and

(b) the other information in the credit advertisement or hire advertisement as the case may be is shown together as a whole in the book, catalogue, leaflet or other document.

3. Representative terms

(1) Where in any advertisement relating to credit to be provided under a consumer credit agreement or relating to a consumer hire agreement as the case may be—

(a) the advertisement refers to transactions of a particular class; and

(b) any item of information mentioned in paragraph (2) below which applies in relation to one transaction of a particular class differs from an item of the like information which applies in relation to another transaction of the same class,

there may be substituted for such an item in the advertisement representative information together with an indication that the information is representative information.

(2) The items of information referred to in paragraph (1)(b) above are—

(a) the APR in an intermediate credit advertisement or a full credit advertisement; or

(b) the cash price and the frequency, number or amount of any payment or charge included in Parts II and III of Schedules 1 and 2 to these Regulations or of any repayment of credit in any full credit advertisement, and the total amount payable by the debtor in any full credit advertisement including its constituent parts.

(3) In this Regulation 'representative information' means information shown as a typical example which the advertiser may reasonably expect at the date the information is published to be representative of transactions of the class in question, being transactions which he might then reasonably contemplate that he would enter into on or after that date.

PART III
SPECIAL PROVISIONS FOR CREDIT ADVERTISEMENTS

4.   Credit advertisements in dealers' publications covering a calendar or seasonal period

(1) Regulations 2 and 3 above shall not apply to a credit advertisement contained in, or in a separate document issued with, a publication published by or on behalf of a dealer which relates to goods or services which may be sold or supplied by him in a calendar or seasonal period specified in the publication if the advertisement contains the information specified in paragraph (2) below and no other indication that a person is willing to provide credit.

(2) The information referred to in paragraph (1) above is—

(a) the name of the creditor, credit-broker or dealer and a postal address of his with or without his occupation or a statement of the general nature of his occupation; and

(b) an indication that individuals may obtain on request a quotation in writing about the terms on which the advertiser is prepared to do business.

5.   Full credit advertisements in dealers' publications

Information contained in a full credit advertisement relating to credit to be provided under a debtor-creditor-supplier agreement, being an advertisement contained in a publication published by or on behalf of a dealer which relates to goods or services which may be sold or supplied by him, shall be taken for the purposes of regulation 2(6) above to be shown together as a whole—

(a) if—

(i) the cash price alone; or

(ii) the cash price, any advance payment and the information specified in paragraphs 12 to 14 of Part III of Schedule 1 to these Regulations, and (except in the case of agreements for credit under which the total amount payable by the debtor is not greater than the cash price of the goods or services, the acquisition of which is to be financed by credit under the agreement) the APR

is clearly indicated in close proximity to every description of, or specific reference to, goods or services to which the information in the publication relates;

(b) if the remaining information in the advertisement is so presented as to be readily comprehensible as a whole by a prospective debtor and an indication is given in close proximity to any of that information that it relates to all or specified descriptions of goods or services; and

(c) if, except as mentioned in paragraph (a) above, no information relating to the provision of credit is shown together with the cash price.

6. Credit advertisements on the premises of a dealer

(1) This regulation applies to an advertisement which does not contain either—

(a) the cash price alone; or

(b) each of the cash price, the information about the APR specified in sub-paragraphs (a) to (c) of paragraph 7 in Part II of Schedule 1 to these Regulations and the information about the total amount payable by the debtor specified in paragraph 14 in Part III of that Schedule,

but which would otherwise be an intermediate credit advertisement or a full credit advertisement.

(2) Subject to paragraph (3) below, an advertisement to which this regulation applies—

(a) which is conspicuously displayed on any part of the premises of a dealer; and

(b) which specifies goods or services the acquisition of which from that dealer may be financed by credit and which may be acquired from that part of those premises,

shall be treated as complying with these Regulations if the information in paragraph (1)(a) or (b) above as the case may be—

(i) in the case of goods, is clearly marked on or displayed in close proximity to the goods; and

(ii) in the case of services, is displayed at any place on the premises at which customers may enquire about them,

with an indication that other information relating to the supply of goods or services on credit is displayed on the premises but without any other information indicating that the goods or services are available on credit.

(3) An advertisement to which this regulation applies by virtue of paragraph (1)(b) above shall not be treated as complying with these Regulations by virtue of paragraph (2) above unless the total amount payable by the debtor in respect of the goods or services specified in the advertisement as goods or services the acquisiton of which from the dealer in question may be financed by credit is also in the case of goods clearly marked on or displayed in close proximity to the goods and, in the case of services, displayed at any place on the premises at which customers may enquire about them, the total amount payable in the case of an agreement for running-account credit being calculated on each of the following assumptions:—

(a) the debtor is provided with an amount of credit equal to the cash price of the goods or services less any advance payment required;

(b) there are no changes in the rates of interest on the credit which may be provided under the agreement;

(c) the debtor pays the amount stated in the advertisement or if none is stated the fixed or minimum sums payable under the agreement;

(d) all repayments of credit and of the total charge for credit are made on the due date under the agreement; and

(e) the debtor acquires no further goods or is provided with no further services under the agreement.

7. Restrictions on certain expressions in credit advertisements

A credit advertisement shall not include—

(a) the word 'overdraft' or any cognate expression as describing any agreement for running-account credit except an agreement enabling the debtor to overdraw on a current account;

(b) any indication whether express or implied that any of the terms of a credit agreement impose on customers a lesser expense or obligation than is being imposed by other persons, except in the case of a full credit advertisement which states, in close proximity to that indication with no less particularity and prominence, the other persons concerned and their comparable terms;

(c) the expression 'interest free' or any expression to the like effect indicating that a customer is liable to pay no greater amount in respect of a transaction financed by credit than he would be liable to pay as a cash purchaser in relation to the like transaction, except where the total amount payable by the debtor does not exceed the cash price; or

(d) the expression 'no deposit' or any expression to the like effect, except where no advance payments are to be made.

8. Prominence to be afforded to the APR in credit advertisements and wording of prescribed information

(1) The APR referred to in Schedule 1 to these Regulations shall be afforded in every credit advertisement—

(a) greater prominence than a statement relating to any other rate of charge; and

(b) no less prominence than a statement relating to—

(i) any period;

(ii) the amount of any advance payment or any indication that no such payment is required; or

(iii) the amount, number or frequency of any other payments or charges (other than the cash price of goods, services, land or other things) or of any repayments of credit.

(2) Where words are shown in capital letters in any prescribed form of statement set out in Schedule 1 or 2 to these Regulations and are reproduced in an advertisement they shall be afforded no less prominence than any other information relating to credit or bailment of goods which is required or permitted to be included under these Regulations in the advertisement except the APR.

PART IV
GENERAL

9. Application of Regulations

(1) These Regulations do not apply to any advertisement which

(a) whether expressly or by implication indicates clearly that a person is willing—

  (i) to provide credit; or

  (ii) to enter into an agreement for the bailment of goods,

  for the purposes of a person's business; and

(b) does not indicate (whether expressly or by implication) that a person is willing to do either of those things otherwise than for the purposes of such a business.

(2) References in paragraph (1) above to a business do not include references to a business carried on by the advertiser or any person acting as a credit-broker in relation to the credit or hire facility to which the advertisement relates.

10. Transitional provisions

(1) Subject to paragraph (2) below, a person shall not be guilty of an offence under section 47(1) or 167 of the Act for contravention of these Regulations if the advertisement would have complied with the requirements of the Consumer Credit (Advertisements) Regulations 1980 if those Regulations had not been revoked by these Regulations.

(2) This regulation only applies to advertisements published in a catalogue, diary or work of reference comprising at least 50 printed pages—

(a) of which copies are first published, or made available for publication in the ordinary course of business, before 1st May 1990; and

(b) which in a reasonably prominent position either contains the date of its first publication or specifies a period, being a calendar or seasonal period, throughout which it is intended to have effect.

SCHEDULE 1   Regulation 2(1)
INFORMATION IN CREDIT ADVERTISEMENTS

PART I
**MAXIMUM INFORMATION THAT MAY BE CONTAINED IN SIMPLE CREDIT
ADVERTISEMENTS IN WHOLE OR IN PART**

Name

1. The name of the advertiser.

Logo

2. A logo of his, of his associate and of his trade association.

Address

3. A postal address of his.

Telephone number

4. A telephone number of his.

Occupation

5. An occupation of his or a statement of the general nature of his occupation.

Other information

6. Any other information other than—

(a) information that a person is willing to provide credit; or

(b) the cash price, or other price, of any goods, services, land or other things.

PART II
MAXIMUM INFORMATION TO BE CONTAINED IN INTERMEDIATE CREDIT ADVERTISEMENTS

Compulsory information

Name and address or telephone number

1. The name of the advertiser and a postal address or telephone number of his (or a freephone number) except—

(a) in the case of advertisements in any form on the premises of a dealer or creditor (not being advertisements in writing which customers are intended to take away);

(b) in the case of advertisements which include the name and address of a dealer; and

(c) in the case of advertisements which include the name of a credit-broker and a postal address or telephone number of his (or a freephone number).

Security

2. A statement that any security is or may be required, and where the security comprises or may comprise a mortgage or charge on the debtor's home a statement in the following form:—

'YOUR HOME IS AT RISK IF YOU DO NOT KEEP UP REPAYMENTS ON A MORTGAGE OR OTHER LOAN SECURED ON IT'

Insurance

3. A statement of any contract of insurance required, not being a contract of insurance against the risk of loss or damage to goods or land or any risk relating to the use of the goods or land.

Deposit of money in an account

4. A statement of any requirement to place on deposit any sum of money in any account with any person.

Credit-broker's fee

5.   In the case of an advertisement published for the purposes of a business of credit brokerage carried on by any person, the amount of any fee payable by the debtor or an associate of his to a credit-broker or a statement of the method of its calculation.

Information about terms of business

6.   Either a statement that individuals may obtain on request a quotation in writing about the terms on which the advertiser is prepared to do business or a statement that individuals may obtain on request a document containing no less information than a full credit advertisement about the terms on which the advertiser is prepared to do business.

APR

7.   Where a cash price is given in the advertisement in relation to any specified goods, services, land or other things, having a particular cash price, the acquisition of which from an identified dealer may be financed by credit or where other information about financial and related particulars set out in paragraph 10(f) or (i) below is given in the advertisement—

(a)   the APR in relation to any actual or prospective agreement, other than an agreement specified in sub-paragraph (b) below, or a statement indicating that the total amount payable by the debtor is not greater than the total cash price of the goods, services, land or other things, the acquisition of which is to be financed by credit under the agreement;

(b)   the APR in relation to a debtor-creditor-supplier agreement for running-account credit under which the debtor agrees to pay the creditor an amount specified in the agreement on specified occasions, there is a credit limit and charges for credit are either a fixed amount in respect of each transaction or calculated as a proportion of the price payable under a transaction financed by the credit, the APR being calculated on each of the following assumptions respectively:—

   (i)   the debtor is provided with an amount of credit at the date of the making of the agreement which, taken with the amount of the charge for that credit ascertained at that date, is equal to the credit limit, and the debtor repays the sum of the said amounts by payments of the amounts specified in the agreement on the specified occasions and makes no other payment and obtains no further credit in relation to the account; and

   (ii)   a like assumption to that in sub-paragraph (i) above save that the said sum of the said amounts shall be taken to be one third of the credit limit; and

(c)   in relation to agreements under which the rate or amount of any item included in the total charge for credit will or may be varied, a statement indicating that the rate or amount will or may be varied.

Cash price

8.   In the case of an advertisement relating to credit to be provided under a debtor-creditor-supplier agreement, where the advertisement specifies goods, services, land or other things having a particular cash price, the acquisition of which from an identified dealer may be financed by the credit, the cash price of such goods, services, land or other things.

Foreign currency mortgages

9.   Where the advertisement is for a mortgage or other loan secured on property and repayments are to be made in a currency other than sterling, a statement in the following form:—

'THE STERLING EQUIVALENT OF YOUR LIABILITY UNDER A FOREIGN CURRENCY MORTGAGE MAY BE INCREASED BY EXCHANGE RATE MOVEMENTS'

Optional information

10.   Any other information, except that no information may be shown indicating that a person is willing to provide credit other than as follows:—

Logo
>   (a) a logo of his, of his associate and of his trade association;

Occupation
>   (b) an occupation of his or a statement of the general nature of his occupation;

Credit facilities
>   (c) a statement that credit facilities are, or that a specified category of credit facility is, available, and where applicable a statement indicating the period or the maximum period of availability;

Restricted offers of credit to class or group of persons
>   (d) in the case of any credit being available only to, or on terms which are applicable only to, persons who fall within any class or group, a statement of that fact identifying that class or group;

APR
>   (e) where not shown under paragraph 7 above, the information about the APR specified in paragraph 7(a) to (c);

Interest
>   (f) where the APR is specified in the advertisement, the rate of any interest on the credit;

Amount of credit
>   (g) the amount of credit which may be provided under a consumer credit agreement or an indication of one or both of the maximum amount and the minimum amount of credit which may be provided;

Nature of security not affecting debtor's home
>   (h) the nature of any security required where this does not comprise a mortgage or charge on the debtor's home;

Advance payment
>   (i) where the APR is specified in the advertisement, a statement as to whether an advance payment is required and if so the amount or minimum amount of the payment expressed as a sum of money or as a percentage;

Different treatment of cash and credit purchasers

(j) a statement indicating any respect in which cash purchasers are treated differently from those acquiring any goods, land or other things, or being provided with services, under a transaction which is financed by credit; and

Name and address or telephone number of creditor

(k) in the case of an advertisement to which paragraph 1(c) above applies, the name of the creditor and a postal address or telephone number of his (or a freephone number).

PART III

MINIMUM INFORMATION TO BE CONTAINED IN FULL CREDIT ADVERTISEMENTS

Name and address

1. The name and a postal address of the advertiser except—

(a) in the case of advertisements in any form on the premises of a dealer or creditor (not being advertisements in writing which customers are intended to take away);

(b) in the case of advertisements which include the name and address of a dealer; and

(c) in the case of advertisements which include the name and a postal address of a credit-broker.

Security

2. A statement that any security is or may be required, and where the security comprises or may comprise a mortgage or charge on the debtor's home a statement in the following form:—

'YOUR HOME IS AT RISK IF YOU DO NOT KEEP UP REPAYMENTS ON A MORTGAGE OR OTHER LOAN SECURED ON IT'

Insurance

3. A statement of any contract of insurance required, not being a contract of insurance against the risk of loss or damage to goods or land or any risk relating to the use of the goods or land.

Deposit of money in an account

4. A statement of any requirement to place on deposit any sum of money in any account with any person.

Credit-broker's fee

5. In the case of an advertisement published for the purposes of a business of credit brokerage carried on by any person, the amount of any fee payable by the debtor or an associate of his to a credit-broker or a statement of the method of its calculation.

Quotation

6.   A statement that individuals may obtain on request a quotation in writing about the terms on which the advertiser is prepared to do business.

APR

7.—(1) The APR in relation to any actual or prospective agreement, other than an agreement specified in sub-paragraph (2) below, or a statement indicating that the total amount payable by the debtor is not greater than the total cash price of the goods, services, land or other things, the acquisition of which is to be financed by credit under the agreement.

(2) The APR in relation to a debtor-creditor-supplier agreement for running-account credit under which the debtor agrees to pay the creditor an amount specified in the agreement on specified occasions, there is a credit limit and charges for credit are either a fixed amount in respect of each transaction or calculated as a proportion of the price payable under a transaction financed by the credit, the APR being calculated on each of the assumptions set out in paragraph 7(b) of Part II of this Schedule respectively.

(3) In relation to agreements under which the rate or amount of any item included in the total charge for credit will or may be varied, a statement indicating that the rate or amount will or may be varied.

Restricted offers of credit to class or group of persons

8.   In the case of any credit being available only to, or on terms which are applicable only to, persons who fall within any class or group, a statement of that fact identifying that class or group.

Nature of security not affecting debtor's home

9.   The nature of any security required where this does not comprise a mortgage or charge on the debtor's home.

Frequency, number and amount of advance payments

10.   A statement of the frequency and number of any advance payments required and of the amount or minimum amount expressed as a sum of money or as a percentage or a statement indicating the manner in which the amount will be determined.

Different treatment of cash and credit purchasers

11.   A statement indicating any respect in which cash purchasers are treated differently from those acquiring any goods, land or other things, or being provided with services, under a transaction which is financed by credit.

Frequency, number and amount of repayments of credit

12.—(1) In the case of an advertisement relating to an agreement for running-account credit, a statement of the frequency of the repayments of credit under the advertised transaction and of the amount of each repayment stating whether it is a fixed or minimum amount, or a statement indicating the manner in which the amount will be determined.

(2) In the case of other credit advertisements, a statement of the frequency, number and amount of repayments of credit.

(3) In the case of an advertisement relating to an agreement under which interest on the credit to be provided is of a type to which sections 369 to 376 of the Income and Corporation Taxes Act 1988 apply (which make provision for the deduction of income tax at the basic rate from certain loan interest):—

   (a) a further statement indicating whether the amount of any repayment of credit mentioned in the advertisement is calculated before or after the deduction of tax; and

   (b) where such an advertisement indicates the amounts of repayments both before and after deduction of tax, and in one or other such case not all the repayments would be equal for the purposes of sub-paragraph (1) above, a statement indicating the lowest and the highest amounts and the exact year or other period in respect of which each such amount is to be paid, unless such information is included in the statement required under sub-paragraph (1) above.

(4) The advertisement shall not include in relation to any repayment under this paragraph the expression 'weekly equivalent' or any expression to the like effect or any expression of any other periodical equivalent, unless weekly payments or the other periodical payments are provided for under the agreement.

(5) The amount of any repayment under this paragraph may be expressed as a sum of money or as a specified proportion of a specified amount (including the amount outstanding from time to time).

Other payments and charges

13.—(1) Subject to sub-paragraphs (2) and (3) below, a statement indicating the description and amount of any other payments and charges which may be payable under the transaction advertised.

(2) Where the liability of the debtor to make any payment cannot be ascertained at the date the advertisement is published, a statement indicating the description of the payment in question and the circumstances in which the liability to make it will arise.

(3) Sub-paragraphs (1) and (2) above do not apply to any charge payable under the transaction to the creditor or any other person on his behalf upon failure by the debtor or a relative of his to do or refrain from doing anything which he is required to do or refrain from doing, as the case may be.

Total amount payable by the debtor

14.—(1) Subject to sub-paragraphs (2) and (3) below, in the case of an advertisement relating to credit to be provided under a consumer credit agreement which is repayable at specified intervals or in specified amounts and other than cases under which the sum of the payments within sub-paragraphs (a) to (c) below is not greater than the cash price referred to in paragraph 15 below, the total amount payable by the debtor, being the total of—

   (a) advance payments;

   (b) the amount of credit repayable by the debtor; and

   (c) the amount of the total charge for credit.

(2) In the case of an agreement for running-account credit the total amount payable by the debtor under this paragraph shall be calculated on each of the following assumptions:

(a) the debtor is provided with an amount of credit equal to the cash price of the goods or services less any advance payment required;

(b) there are no changes in the rates of interest on the credit which may be provided under the agreement;

(c) the debtor pays the amount stated in the advertisement or if none is stated the fixed or minimum sums payable under the agreement;

(d) all repayments of credit and of the total charge for credit are made on the due date under the agreement; and

(e) the debtor acquires no further goods or is provided with no further services under the agreement.

(3) Sub-paragraph (1) above does not apply in the case of an advertisement relating to running-account credit to be provided under a consumer credit agreement where the advertisement does not specify goods, services, land or other things having a particular cash price, the acquisition of which may be financed by the credit.

Cash price

15.   In the case of an advertisement relating to credit to be provided under a debtor-creditor-supplier agreement, where the advertisement specifies goods, services, land or other things having a particular cash price, the acquisition of which from an identified dealer may be financed by the credit, the cash price of such goods, services, land or other things.

Foreign currency mortgages

16.   Where the advertisement is for a mortgage or other loan secured on property and repayments are to be made in a currency other than sterling a statement in the following form:—

'THE STERLING EQUIVALENT OF YOUR LIABILITY UNDER A FOREIGN CURRENCY MORTGAGE MAY BE INCREASED BY EXCHANGE RATE MOVEMENTS'

SCHEDULE 2   **Regulation 2(2)**
INFORMATION IN HIRE ADVERTISEMENTS

PART I
**MAXIMUM INFORMATION THAT MAY BE CONTAINED IN SIMPLE HIRE
ADVERTISEMENTS IN WHOLE OR IN PART**

Name

1.   The name of the advertiser.

Logo

2.   A logo of his, of his associate and of his trade association.

Address

3. A postal address of his.

Telephone number

4. A telephone number of his.

Occupation

5. An occupation of his or a statement of the general nature of his occupation.

Other information

6. Any other information other than—

(a) information that a person is willing to enter into an agreement for the bailment of goods by him; or

(b) the cash price, or other price, of any goods.

PART II
MAXIMUM INFORMATION TO BE CONTAINED IN INTERMEDIATE HIRE ADVERTISEMENTS

Compulsory information

Name and address or telephone number

1. The name of the advertiser and a postal address or telephone number of his (or a freephone number) except—

(a) in the case of advertisements in any form on the premises of a dealer or owner (not being advertisements in writing which customers are intended to take away);

(b) in the case of advertisements which include the name and address of a dealer; and

(c) in the case of advertisements which include the name of a credit-broker and a postal address or telephone number of his (or a freephone number).

Nature of transaction

2. A statement indicating that the transaction advertised is the bailment of goods.

Security

3. A statement that any security is or may be required, and where the security comprises or may comprise a mortgage or charge on the hirer's home a statement in the following form:—

'YOUR HOME IS AT RISK IF YOU DO NOT KEEP UP PAYMENTS ON A HIRE AGREEMENT SECURED BY A MORTGAGE OR OTHER SECURITY ON YOUR HOME'

Insurance

4.   A statement of any contract of insurance required, not being a contract of insurance against the risk of loss or damage to goods or any risk relating to the use of the goods.

Deposit of money in an account

5.   A statement of any requirement to place on deposit any sum of money in any account with any person.

Credit-broker's fee

6.   In the case of an advertisement published for the purposes of a business of credit brokerage carried on by any person, the amount of any fee payable by the hirer or an associate of his to a credit-broker or a statement of the method of its calculation.

Information about terms of business

7.   Either a statement that individuals may obtain on request a quotation in writing about the terms on which the advertiser is prepared to do business or a statement that individuals may obtain on request a document containing no less information than a full hire advertisement about the terms on which the advertiser is prepared to do business.

Optional information

8.   Any other information, except that no information may be shown indicating that a person is willing to enter into an agreement for the bailment of goods by him other than as follows:—

Logo

(a) a logo of his, of his associate and of his trade association;

Occupation

(b) an occupation of his or a statement of the general nature of his occupation;

Restricted offers of hire facilities to class or group of persons

(c) in the case of any hire facilities being available only to, or on terms which are applicable only to, persons who fall within any class or group, a statement of that fact identifying that class or group;

Nature of security not affecting hirer's home

(d) the nature of any security required where this does not comprise a mortgage or charge on the hirer's home;

Advance payment

(e) a statement as to whether an advance payment is required and if so the amount or minimum amount of the payment expressed as a sum of money or as a percentage;

Duration of hire

(f) in a case where goods are to be bailed under an agreement for a fixed period or a maximum or minimum period, a statement indicating that this is the case and the duration of that period; and

Name and address or telephone number of owner

(g) in the case of an advertisement to which paragraph 1(c) above applies, the name of the owner and a postal address or telephone number of his (or a freephone number).

PART III
MINIMUM INFORMATION TO BE CONTAINED IN FULL HIRE ADVERTISEMENT

Name and address

1. The name and a postal address of the advertiser except—

(a) in the case of advertisements in any form on the premises of a dealer or owner (not being advertisements in writing which customers are intended to take away);

(b) in the case of advertisements which include the name and address of a dealer; and

(c) in the case of advertisements which include the name and a postal address of a credit-broker.

Nature of transaction

2. A statement indicating that the transaction advertised is the bailment of goods.

Security

3. A statement that any security is or may be required, and where the security comprises or may comprise a mortgage or charge on the hirer's home a statement in the following form:—

'YOUR HOME IS AT RISK IF YOU DO NOT KEEP UP PAYMENTS ON A HIRE AGREEMENT SECURED BY A MORTGAGE OR OTHER SECURITY ON YOUR HOME'

Insurance

4. A statement of any contract of insurance required, not being a contract of insurance against the risk of loss or damage to the goods or any risk relating to the use of the goods.

Deposit of money in an account

5. A statement of any requirement to place on deposit any sum of money in any account with any person.

Credit-broker's fee

6. In the case of an advertisement published for the purposes of a business of credit brokerage carried on by any person, the amount of any fee payable by the hirer or an associate of his to a credit-broker or a statement of the method of its calculation.

Quotation

7.   A statement that individuals may obtain on request a quotation in writing about the terms on which the advertiser is prepared to do business.

Restricted offers of hire facilities to class or group of persons

8.   In the case of any hire facilities being available only to, or on terms which are applicable only to, persons who fall within any class or group, a statement of that fact identifying that class or group.

Nature of security not affecting hirer's home

9.   The nature of any security required where this does not comprise a mortgage or charge on the hirer's home.

Frequency, number and amount of advance payments

10.   A statement of the frequency and number of any advance payments required and of the amount or minimum amount expressed as a sum of money or as a percentage or a statement indicating the manner in which the amount will be determined.

Duration of hire

11.   In a case where goods are to be bailed under an agreement for a fixed period or a maximum or minimum period, a statement indicating that this is the case and the duration of that period.

Frequency and amount of hire payments

12.   The frequency and amount of each hire payment stating if it be the case that it is a minimum amount and, in the case where the amount of any hire payment will or may be varied, a statement indicating that the amount will or may be varied and the circumstances in which it would happen:

> Provided that the advertisement shall not include in relation to any hire payment the expression 'weekly equivalent' or any expression to the like effect or any expression of any other periodical equivalent unless weekly payments or the other periodical payments are provided for under the hire agreement.

Other payments and charges

13.—(1) Subject to sub-paragraphs (2) and (3) below, a statement indicating the description and amount of any payments and charge other than advance payments and hire payments which may be payable under the transaction advertised.

(2) Where the liability of the hirer to make any payment cannot be ascertained at the date the advertisement is published, a statement indicating the description of the payment in question and the circumstances in which the liability to make it will arise.

(3) Sub-paragraphs (1) and (2) above do not apply to any charge payable under the transaction to the owner or any other person on his behalf upon failure by the hirer or a relative of his to do or to refrain from doing anything which he is required to do or to refrain from doing, as the case may be.

Variable payments and charges

14. Where any payment or charge referred to in paragraph 12 or 13 above may be varied under the hire agreement except to take account only of a change in value added tax (including a change to or from no tax being charged), a statement indicating that this is the case.

SCHEDULE 3   Regulation 1(2)
PROVISIONS RELATING TO DISCLOSURE OF THE TOTAL CHARGE FOR CREDIT AND THE APR

Use of representative information in calculation of the total charge for credit and the APR

1. Where, in the case of an advertisement relating to credit to be provided under a consumer credit agreement—

  (a) the amount of any charge required to be included in the total charge for credit in respect of any transaction within a particular class of transactions is not ascertainable at the date when the advertisement is published or differs from the amount which applies in relation to another transaction within the same class; or

  (b) any other fact required for such calculation is not ascertainable at that date or is different from a comparable fact in relation to another transaction within the same class,

there shall be included in the total charge for credit an amount in respect of that charge which, having regard to the amounts and facts which apply to other transactions within the same class, is representative of the charges which the advertiser might reasonably expect at the date the advertisement is published would apply in relation to transactions of the class in question, being transactions which he might then reasonably contemplate he would enter into on or after that date.

(2) If this paragraph is applied in relation to the amount of any charge or to any other fact—

  (a) a sum in the determination of which any such amount or fact is employed shall not be taken to be the amount of the total charge for credit; and

  (b) a rate of charge in the determination of which any such amount or fact is employed shall not be expressed to be the APR,

unless the advertisement either—

    (i) identifies any such amount or fact and quantifies so far as practicable any such amount; or

    (ii) contains an indication that representative amounts have been included in calculating the total charge for credit.

(3) For the purposes of this paragraph, a class of transactions means a class determined by reference to the subject-matter of the transactions or to the time at which, the circumstances in which or the persons with whom they are made.

Permissible tolerances in disclosure of the APR

2. For the purposes of these Regulations, it shall be sufficient compliance with the requirement to show the APR if there is included in the advertisement—

(a) a rate which exceeds the APR by not more than one; or

(b) a rate which falls short of the APR by not more than 0.1; or

(c) in a case to which any of paragraphs 3 to 6 below applies, a rate determined in accordance with the paragraphs or such of them as apply to that case.

Tolerance where repayments are nearly equal

3.   In the case of an agreement under which all repayments but one are equal and that one repayment does not differ from any other repayment by more whole pence than there are repayments of credit, there may be included in an advertisement relating to the agreement a rate found under any of regulations 7, 9 and 10 of the Total Charge for Credit Regulations as if that one repayment were equal to the other repayments to be made under the agreement.

Tolerance where interval between relevant date and first repayment is greater than interval between repayments

4.   In the case of an agreement under which—

(a) three or more repayments are to be made at equal intervals; and

(b) the interval between the relevant date and the first repayment is greater than the interval between the repayments,

there may be included in an advertisement relating to the agreement a rate found under any of regulations 7, 9 and 10 of the Total Charge for Credit Regulations as if the interval between the relevant date and the first repayment were shortened so as to be equal to the interval between repayments; and in this paragraph 'relevant date' means, in a case where a date is specified in or determinable under the agreement at the date of its making as that on which the debtor is entitled to require provision of anything the subject of the agreement, the earliest such date and, in any other case, the date of the making of the agreement.

Tolerance where Consumer credit tables do not exactly apply

5.—(1) In a case where, in relation to any agreement the charge per pound lent, the flat rate or the period rate of charge, as the case may be, is not exactly represented by an entry in a table contained in the Consumer credit tables, there may be included in an advertisement relating to the agreement a rate found by applying the next greater entry appearing in those tables for the purposes of calculating that rate.

(2) In sub-paragraph (1) above 'charge per pound lent', 'flat rate' and 'period rate of charge' have the meanings assigned to them by the relevant Introduction or Instructions contained in the Consumer credit tables.

Tolerance where period rate of charge is charged

6.   In the case of an agreement to which regulation 7(1) of the Total Charge for Credit Regulations (agreements under which a period rate of charge is charged) applies, there may be included in an advertisement relating to the agreement a rate, being the APR determined as if no account were taken of any amount by which the total amount of the charges included in the total charge for credit in relation to each period is varied so as to bring that amount to the nearest whole penny, one half-penny being for this purpose expressed to the next higher whole penny.

SCHEDULE 4 **Regulation 1(7)**
REVOCATIONS

(1)	(2)	(3)
Regulations revoked	References	Extent of revocation
The Consumer Credit (Advertisements) Regulations 1980	SI 1980 No 54	The whole Regulations
The Consumer Credit (Advertisements) (Amendment) Regulations 1980	SI 1980 No 1360	The whole Regulations
The Consumer Credit (Advertisements and Quotations) (Amendment) Regulations 1983	SI 1983 No 110	Regulation 2
The Consumer Credit (Advertisements and Quotations) (Amendment No 2) Regulations 1983	SI 1983 No 1721	Regulation 2
The Consumer Credit (Advertisements and Quotations) (Amendment) Regulations 1984	SI 1984 No 1055	Regulation 2
The Consumer Credit (Advertisements and Quotations) (Amendment) Regulations 1985	SI 1985 No 619	Regulation 2

Appendix 2

Investment Advertising

The Financial Services Act 1986 (Investment Advertisements)
(Exemptions) Order 1996 (SI 1996 No 1586)

ARRANGEMENT OF ARTICLES

SCHEDULES

1. Citation and Commencement

This order may be cited as the Financial Services Act 1986 (Investment Advertisements) (Exemptions) Order 1996 and shall come into force on 15th July 1996.

2. Interpretation

(1) In this Order and in the Schedules hereto—

'the Act' means the Financial Services Act 1986;

'the 1985 Act' means the Companies Act 1985;

'the 1986 Order' means the companies (Northern Ireland) Order 1986;

'approved securities market' means any market which is established under the rules of an investment exchange specified in Schedule 2 to this Order;

'EEA State' means a State which is a Contracting Party to the Agreement on the European Economic Area signed at Oporto on 2nd May 1992 as adjusted by the Protocol signed at Brussels on 17th March 1993;

'private company', in relation to a body corporate which is a company within the meaning of the 1985 Act, means a private company within the meaning of section 1(3) of the 1985 Act and, in relation to a body corporate which is a company within the meaning of the 1986 Order, means a private company within the meaning of article 12(3) of the 1986 Order;

'relevant bearer security' means a relevant security title to which is capable of being transferred without notice of that fact being given to the body corporate issuing the security or any person acting on its behalf;

'relevant EEA market' means a market in an EEA State which is established under the rules of an investment exchange specified in Part I of Schedule 1 to this Order or which meets the criteria specified in Part II of that Schedule;

'relevant security' means shares and also means an investment falling within paragraphs 2 of Schedule 1 to the Act and any investment falling within paragraph 4 or 5 of that Schedule which confers rights in respect of an investment falling within paragraph 1 or 2 of that Schedule; and

'shares' means any investment falling within paragraph 1 of Schedule 1 to the Act.

(2) For the purposes of this Order, a relevant security falling within paragraph 4 or 5 of Schedule 1 to the Act shall be taken to have been issued by the person who issued the investment in respect of which the relevant security confers rights if it is issued by a body corporate in the same group as that person or by some other person acting on behalf of, or pursuant to arrangements made with, that person.

3. Investment advertisements issued by body corporate to members or creditors

(1) Section 57 of the Act shall not apply to an investment advertisement issued or caused to be issued by a body corporate other than an open-ended investment company if the only persons to whom the advertisement is issued, other than persons to whom it may otherwise lawfully be issued, are reasonably believed by the person who issued the advertisement or who caused it to be issued to be persons who fall within any one or more of the following categories—

(a) creditors or members of, or persons who are entitled to investments falling within paragraph 1, 2 or 4 of Schedule 1 to the Act issued by, the body corporate;

(b) creditors or members of, or persons who are entitled to investments falling within paragraph 1, 2 or 4 of Schedule 1 to the Act issued by, another body corporate which is not an open-ended investment company but which is in the same group as the first body corporate; and

(c) persons who are entitled, whether conditionally or unconditionally, to become members of the body corporate or to have title to an investment of a kind mentioned in sub-paragraph (a) or (b) have issued by the body corporate transferred to them but who have not yet become a member of the body corporate or, as the case may be, acquired title to the investment,

and the advertisement contains no invitation or information which would make it an investment advertisement other than an invitation or information relating to an investment of a kind described in this paragraph issued or to be issued by the body corporate or by another body corporate which is not an open-ended investment company but which is in the same group as the first body corporate.

(2) Section 57 of the Act shall not apply to an investment advertisement issued or caused to be issued by an open-ended investment company if the circumstances are that the only persons to whom the advertisement is issued, other than persons to whom it may otherwise lawfully be issued, are reasonably believed by the person who issued the advertisement or who caused it to be issued to be persons who fall within any one or more of the following categories—

(a) creditors or members of, or persons who are entitled to investments falling within paragraph 2, 4 or 6 of Schedule 1 to the Act issued by, the open-ended investment company; and

(b) persons who are entitled, whether conditionally or unconditionally, to become members of the open-ended investment company or to have title to an investment of a kind mentioned in sub-paragraph (a) above issued by the company transferred to them but who have not yet become a member of the company or, as the case may be, acquired title to the investment,

and the advertisement contains no invitation or information which would make it an investment advertisement other than an invitation or information relating to an investment of a kind described in this paragraph issued or to be issued by the open-ended investment company.

4. Investment advertisements relating to relevant securities

(1) Section 57 of the Act shall not apply to an investment advertisement issued or caused to be issued by a body corporate other than an open-ended investment company if the advertisement fulfils the conditions specified in paragraph (2) of this article and either—

(a) relevant securities issued by the body corporate, or, in a case in which the body corporate is a wholly-owned subsidiary within the meaning of section 736 of the 1985 Act, by its holding company, are permitted to be traded or dealt in on a relevant EEA market or an approved securities market; or

(b) the advertisement consists of or is accompanied by the whole or any part of the body corporate's annual accounts or by the directors' report prepared and approved under sections 234 and 234A of the 1985 Act or the corresponding Northern Ireland enactment or consists of or is accompanied by any report prepared and approved under the law of another EEA State corresponding to the said sections 234 and 234A.

(2) The conditions specified in this paragraph are that the advertisement—

(a) does not contain any invitation or offer to persons to underwrite, subscribe for, otherwise acquire, or dispose of any investments or advise persons so to do;

(b) does not contain any invitation or offer to persons to effect any transaction with, or to make use of any services provided by, the body corporate or any person named in the advertisement in the course of any activity falling within any of paragraphs 12 to 16A of Schedule 1 to the Act in which the body corporate or the relevant person engages;

(c) does not contain any information calculated to lead directly or indirectly to persons doing any of the things mentioned in section 57(2) of the Act in relation to any investment which is not a relevant security issued by the body corporate or another body corporate in the same group; and

(d) in a case in which the advertisement contains information about the price at which relevant securities issued by the body corporate have been bought or sold in the past or, except where the information is restricted to a statement as to earnings per share, dividend or nominal rate of interest payable, about the yield on such securities, it states prominently a warning that past performance cannot be relied upon as a guide to future performance.

(3) For the purposes of paragraph (1)(b) of this article, 'annual accounts' means any of the following, that is to say—

(a) accounts produced by virtue of Part VII of the 1985 Act or the corresponding Northern Ireland enactment including accounts produced by virtue of Part VII or the corresponding Northern Ireland enactment as applied by virtue of any enactment;

(b) a summary financial statement prepared under section 251 of the 1985 Act;

(c) accounts delivered to the registrar under Chapter II of Part XXIII of the 1985 Act; and

(d) accounts produced or published by virtue of the law of an EEA State other than the United Kingdom which correspond to accounts falling within sub-paragraph (a), (b) or (c) of this paragraph.

5. Investment advertisements relating to relevant bearer securities issued by body corporate

(1) Section 57 of the Act shall not apply to an investment advertisement which is issued or caused to be issued by a body corporate other than an open-ended investment company if the advertisement—

(a) is addressed to persons entitled to relevant bearer securities issued by the body corporate or by a related body corporate;

(b) contains no invitation to persons to enter into an investment agreement other than an invitation relating to relevant securities of a class which consists of or includes the relevant bearer securities or investments in respect of which the relevant bearer securities confer rights and which is capable of being accepted only by persons who are entitled to relevant securites issued by the body corporate or a related body corporate; and

(c) contains no information relating to any investment which is not a relevant security issued by the body corporate or by a related body corporate.

(2) Section 57 of the Act shall not apply to an investment advertisement which is issued or caused to be issued by a body corporate other than an open-ended investment company if the circumstances are that the advertisement is addressed to persons entitled to relevant bearer securities issued by the body corporate or by a related body corporate and would not otherwise be regarded as an investment advertisement but for the inclusion of information which the authorities of a relevant EEA market or an approved securities market on which relevant securities of a class which consists of or includes the relevant bearer securities are traded or dealt in require or permit be made known to the holders of securities in that class.

(3) In this article—

(a) the expressions 'holding company' and 'subsidiary' have the same meanings as in section 736 of the 1985 Act;

(b) in relation to a body corporate, the expression 'related body corporate' means a body corporate which is not an open-ended investment company but which is either the holding company of or a subsidiary of the first body corporate; and

(c) relevant bearer securities may be regarded as being in the same class as relevant securities which are not relevant bearer securities.

6. Investment advertisements issued in connection with employees' share schemes

(1) Section 57 of the Act shall not apply to an investment advertisement issued or caused to be issued by a body corporate, a body corporate connected with it or a relevant trustee if the only reason why it would be subject to the provisions of section 57 of the Act is because it contains an invitation made or information given for the purpose of enabling or facilitating transactions in shares in or debentures of the first mentioned body corporate between or for the benefit of any of the persons mentioned in paragraph (2) of this article or the holding of such shares or debentures by or for the benefit of any such persons.

(2) The persons referred to in paragraph (1) of this article are—

(a) the *bona fide* employees or former employees of the body corporate or of another body corporate in the same group; or

(b) the wives, husbands, widows, widowers, or children (including, in Northern Ireland, adopted children) or step-children under the age of eighteen of such employees or former employees.

(3) For the purposes of this article—

(a) the expressions 'relevant trustee', 'shares' and 'debentures' have the meanings ascribed to them in paragraph 20(3) and (4) of Schedule 1 to the Act taking the reference in paragraph 20(3) to sub-paragraph (1) of that paragraph to be a reference to paragraph (1) of this article;

(b) a body corporate is to be regarded as connected with another body corporate if it would be so regarded for the purposes of paragraph 20 of Schedule 1 to the Act; and

(c) a group shall be treated as including any body corporate in which any member of the group holds a qualifying capital interest within the meaning of paragraph 30 of Schedule 1 to the Act.

7. Groups

Section 57 of the Act shall not apply to an investment advertisement issued or caused to be issued by one body corporate in a group to another body corporate in the same group and for these purposes a group shall be treated as including any body corporate in which a member of the group holds a qualifying capital interest within the meaning of paragraph 30 of Schedule 1 to the Act.

8. Joint enterprises

(1) For the purposes of this article 'joint enterprise' has the meaning given in paragraph 31 of Schedule 1 to the Act and the expression 'participator' shall be construed in accordance with that paragraph.

(2) Section 57 of the Act shall not apply to an investment advertisement issued or caused to be issued by a participator or potential participator in a joint enterprise to another participator or potential participator in the same joint enterprise if the only reason why the advertisement would be subject to the provisions of section 57 of the Act is because it contains an invitation or information of the kind described in section 57(2) of the Act which is made or given in connection with, or for the purposes of, the joint enterprise.

9. Sale of goods and supply of services

(1) For the purposes of this article—

(a) the expressions 'supplier' and 'related sale or supply' shall be construed in accordance with paragraph 19 of Schedule 1 to the Act and the expression 'customer' shall also be construed in accordance with that paragraph except that it shall be construed as excluding references to an individual; and

(b) a group shall be treated as including any body corporate in which a member of the group holds a qualifying capital interest within the meaning of paragraph 30 of Schedule 1 to the Act.

(2) Subject to paragraph (3) below, section 57 of the Act shall not apply to an investment advertisement issued or caused to be issued by a supplier or a body corporate in the same group as a supplier to a customer or a body corporate in the same group as a customer if the only reason why the advertisement would be subject to the provisions of section 57 of the Act is because it contains an invitation or information of the kind described in section 57(2) of the Act which is made or given for the purposes of or in connection with the supplier selling or offering or agreeing to sell goods to the customer or supplying or offering or agreeing to supply him with services or is given for the purposes of or in connection with a related sale or supply provided that the supplier's main business is to supply goods or services and not to engage in activities falling within Part II of Schedule 1 to the Act.

(3) This article shall not apply to an advertisement which contains an invitation or information with respect to an investment falling within paragraph 6 or 10 of Schedule 1 to the Act or, so far as relevant to either of those paragraphs, paragraph 11 of that Schedule.

10. Overseas persons

(1) In this article 'overseas person' means a person who does not fall within section 1(3)(a) of the Act.

(2) Subject to the provisions of paragraph (3) below, section 57 of the Act shall not apply to an investment advertisement which an overseas person issues or causes to be issued to another person if that other person is either—

(a) a person with or for whom the overseas person has, in the course of carrying on investment business, effected or arranged for the effecting of a transaction within the period of twelve months ending with the date on which the investment advertisement was issued; or

(b) a person to whom the overseas person has, in the course of carrying on such business, provided custody services falling within paragraph 13A of Schedule 1 to the Act within that period; or

(c) a person to whom the overseas person has, in the course of carrying on such a business, given advice falling within paragraph 15 of Schedule 1 to the Act within that period; or

(d) a person on whose behalf the overseas person has, in the course of carrying on such business, sent or caused to be sent dematerialised instructions falling within paragraph 16A of Schedule 1 to the Act(a) within that period.

(3) The provisions of paragraph (2) shall not apply unless—

(a) in a case within paragraph (2)(a) above, the transaction was effected or arranged at a time when the other person was neither resident nor had a place of business in the United Kingdom; or

(b) in a case within paragraph (2)(b) above, the custody services were provided outside the United Kingdom at a time when the other person was neither resident nor had a place of business in the United Kingdom; or

(c) in a case within paragraph (2)(c) above, the advice was given outside the United Kingdom at a time when the other person was neither resident nor had a place of business in the United Kingdom; or

(d) in a case within paragraph (2)(d) above, the dematerialised instruction was sent, or caused to be sent when the other person was neither resident nor had a place of business in the United Kingdom; or

(e) in a case within paragraph (2)(a), (b), (c) or (d), if the transaction was effected or arranged, or the custody services were provided, or the advice was given or the dematerialised instruction was sent or caused to be sent otherwise than in the circumstances described in whichever is relevant of sub-paragraph (a), (b), (c) or (d) of this paragraph, the overseas person had, on a previous occasion and in the course of carrying on investment business—

(i) effected or arranged for the effecting of a transaction with or for the other person in the circumstances described in sub-paragraph (a) of this paragraph; or

(ii) provided to the other person custody services falling within paragraph 13A of Schedule 1 to the Act in the circumstances described in sub-paragraph (b) of this paragraph; or

(iii) given the other person advice falling within paragraph 15 of Schedule 1 to the Act in the circumstances described in sub-paragraph (c) of this paragraph; or

(iv) sent or caused to be sent, on behalf of the other person a dematerialised instruction falling within paragraph 16A of Schedule 1 to the Act in the circumstances described in sub-paragraph (d) of this paragraph.][1]

---

1   *Substituted by the Financial Services Act 1986 (Investment Advertisements) (Exemptions) Order 1997 (SI 1997 No 963).*

11. Advertisements issued to persons sufficiently expert to understand the risks involved

(1) In this article 'relevant person' means a person who is not an authorised person [nor a European investment firm carrying on home-regulated investment business in the United Kingdom][1] and who is not unlawfully carrying on investment business in the United Kingdom.

(2) Section 57 of the Act shall not apply to an investment advertisement issued or caused to be issued by a relevant person if either—

(a) in the case of an advertisement which takes the form of a document, the only persons, other than persons to whom the advertisement may otherwise lawfully be issued, to whom the relevant person issues or causes the advertisement to be issued are persons whom he reasonably believes to be persons of a kind described in paragraph (3) below and, in a case in which a person is described in paragraph (3) below as acting in a particular capacity, the advertisement was issued to that person in that capacity; or

(b) in any other case, the relevant person reasonably believes that the means by which the advertisement is issued are such that it will not generally be made available except to persons to whom the advertisement may otherwise lawfully be issued or who are of a kind described in paragraph (3) below and, in a case in which a person is described in paragraph (3) below as acting in a particular capacity, the relevant person intended the advertisement to be received by him in that capacity.

(3) A person falls within this paragraph if he is either—

(a) an authorised person; or

[(aa) a European investment firm carrying on home-regulated business in the United Kingdom; or][2]

(b) an exempted person; or

(c) a person who is acting in the course of a business or employment which involves the dissemination of information concerning investments or activities of the kind described in Part II of Schedule 1 to the Act through newspapers, journals, magazines or other periodical publications or by way of sound broadcasting or television; or

(d) a government, local authority or pubic authority within the meaning of Note 1 to paragraph 3 of Schedule 1 to the Act; or

(e) a body corporate or an unincorporated association which either—

   (i) if it is a body corporate and has more than 20 members or is the subsidiary of a holding company which has more than 20 members, it, or any of its holding companies or subsidiaries, has a called up share capital or net assets of not less than £500,000; or

   (ii) if it is a body corporate other than one described in sub-paragraph (e)(i) above, it or any of its holding companies or subsidiaries has a called up share capital or net assets of not less than £5 million; or

---

1   *Inserted by the Financial Services Act 1986 (Investment Advertisements) (Exemptions) Order 1997 (SI 1997 No 963), art 4(a).*

2   *Inserted by the Financial Services Act 1986 (Investment Advertisements) (Exemptions) Order 1997 (SI 1997 No 963), art 4(b).*

(iii) if it is an unincorporated association, it has net assets of not less than £5 million; or

(f) a person who holds a permission granted under paragraph 23 of Schedule 1 to the Act; or

(g) a person acting in his capacity as a director, officer or employee of a person of a kind described above in this paragraph being a person whose responsibilities, when acting in that capacity, involve him engaging in activities which fall within Part II of Schedule 1 to the Act or which would fall within that Part were it not for the provisions of Part III of that Schedule; or

(h) any trustee of a trust where the aggregate value of the cash and investments which form part of the trust's assets (before deducting the amount of its liabilities) is £10 million or more or has been £10 million or more at any time during the previous two years.

(4) In paragraph (3) above, the expression 'net assets' has the meaning assigned to it in section 264 of the 1985 Act [and in paragraphs (1) and (3)(aa) above, 'European investment firm' and 'home-regulated investment business' have the meanings given by regulation 2 of the Investment Services Regulations 1995].[3]

12.   Advertisements relating to matters of common interest

(1) Subject to the provisions of paragraph (2) of this article, section 57 of the Act shall not apply to an investment advertisement which contains an invitation made or information given with respect to shares in or debentures of a private company if the advertisement—

(a) states expressly that the only persons who may enter into or offer to enter into any agreement for or with a view to subscribing for shares in or debentures of the company on the basis of any invitation or information contained in the advertisement or any such agreement which might reasonably be expected to be entered into, directly or indirectly, as a result of the advertisement are within an identified group of persons who, at the time the advertisement was issued, might reasonably be regarded as having an existing and common interest with each other and with the company in the affairs of the company and in what is to be done with the proceeds of the offer; and

(b) the advertisement complies with the requirements of Schedule 4 to this Order.

(2) For the purposes of paragraph (1) above persons shall not be regarded as having an interest of the kind described in that paragraph if the only reason why they would be so regarded is because—

(a) they will have such an interest if they become members or creditors of the company; or

(b) they are persons all of whom carry on a particular trade or profession; or

(c) they are persons with whom the company has an existing business relationship whether by reason of their being its clients, customers, contractors or suppliers or otherwise.

---

3   *Inserted by the Financial Services Act 1986 (Investment Advertisements) (Exemptions) Order 1997 (SI 1997 No 963), art 4(c).*

13. Advertisements by trustees or personal representatives

Section 57 of the Act shall not apply to an investment advertisement issued or caused to be issued by a person when acting as a trustee or a personal representative to—

(a) a fellow trustee or personal representative if the advertisement is issued for the purposes of the trust or estate; or

(b) a beneficiary under the trust, will or intestacy if the advertisement concerns his interest in the trust fund or estate.

14. Advertisements issued by operators of schemes recognised under section 87 or 88 of the Act

Section 57 of the Act shall not apply to an investment advertisement issued or caused to be issued by a person who is not an authorised person but who is the operator of a scheme recognised under section 87 or 88 of the Act to persons in the United Kingdom who are participants in a scheme recognised under section 87 or 88 of the Act which is operated by the person by or to whose order the advertisement is issued if the only reason why the advertisement would be subject to the provisions of section 57 of the Act is because it contains an invitation or information relating to that recognised scheme or to units in it.

15. Publications and programmes containing investment advice

Section 57 of the Act shall not apply to an investment advertisement if the only reason why section 57 would otherwise apply to the advertisement is that it contains an invitation or information of the kind described in section 57(2) of the Act relating—

(a) to a newspaper, journal, magazine or other periodical publication which contains advice to which paragraph 15 of Schedule 1 to the Act does not apply by virtue of the provisions of paragraph 25 of that Schedule; or

(b) to a programme which contains advice to which paragraph 15 of Schedule 1 to the Act does not apply by virtue of the provisions of paragraph 25A of that Schedule.

16. Advertisements by certain markets

(1) Section 57 of the Act shall not apply to an investment advertisement which is issued or caused to be issued by a market which is a relevant EEA market or is established under the rules of an investment exchange specified in Schedule 2 or 3 to this Order, if the only reason why section 57 would would otherwise apply to the advertisement is that it contains information relating to the facilities provided by the relevant market.

(2) For the purposes of paragraph (1) of this article, information which identifies a particular investment as one which may be traded or dealt in on a market or which identifies particular persons as persons through whom transactions on a market may be effected shall not be regarded as information relating to the facilities provided by the relevant market.

17. Management companies

Section 57 of the Act shall not apply to an investment advertisement if the only reason why that section would otherwise apply to the advertisement is that it contains an invitation or information relating to an investment falling within paragraph 1 of Schedule 1 to the Act issued or to be issued by a private company established for the purpose of managing the common parts or the fabric of property used for residential or business purposes or of supplying services to such property being an investment which is to be acquired in connection with the acquisition of an interest in the property in question.

18.   Advertisements in respect of the Parliamentary Commissioner for Administration

Section 57 of the Act shall not apply in respect of any advertisement issued or caused to be issued by any person for the purpose of enabling any injustice stated by the Parliamentary Commissioner for Administration in a report under section 10 of the Parliamentary Commissioner Act 1967 to have occurred, to be remedied with respect to the person to whom the advertisement is issued.

19.   Revocations

The Financial Services Act 1986 (Investment Advertisements) (Exemptions) Order 1995 is hereby revoked.

SCHEDULE 1   **Article 2**
RELEVANT EEA MARKETS

PART I
EXCHANGES OPERATING RELEVANT EEA MARKETS

Asociacion de Intermediarios de Activos Financieros
[Amsterdam Exchanges AEX][1]
Amsterdam Financial Futures Market
Amsterdam Pork and Potato Terminal Market (NLKKAS—Amsterdam Clearing House)
. . .[2]
Antwerp Stock Exchange
Athens Stock Exchange
Barcelona Stock Exchange
Berlin Stock Exchange
Bilbao Stock Exchange
Bologna Stock Exchange
Bremen Stock Exchange
Brussels Stock Exchange
Copenhagen Stock Exchange (including FUTOP)
Deutsche Terminboerse
Dusseldorf Stock Exchange
. . .[2]
Finnish Options Mark
Florence Stock Exchange
Frankfurt Stock Exchange
Genoa Stock Exchange
Hamburg Stock Exchange

---

1   *Inserted by the Financial Services Act 1986 (Investment Advertisements) (Exemptions) Order 1997 (SI 1997 No 963), art 5.*
2   *Deleted by the Financial Services Act 1986 (Investment Advertisements) (Exemptions) Order 1997 (SI 1997 No 963), art 5.*

Hanover Stock Exchange
Helsinki Stock Exchange
Irish Futures and Options Exchange
The Irish Stock Exchange Limited
Lisbon Stock Exchange
The London Stock Exchange Limited
Luxembourg Stock Exchange
Madrid Stock Exchange
Marche a Terme International de France (MATIF)
MEFF Renta Fija
MEFF Renta Variable
Milan Stock Exchange
Marche des Options Negociables de Paris (MONEP)
Munich Stock Exchange
Naples Stock Exchange
OM Stockholm AB
Oporto Stock Exchange
Oslo Stock Exchange
Palermo Stock Exchange
Paris Stock Exchange
Rome Stock Exchange
Stockholm Stock Exchange
Stuttgart Stock Exchange
Trieste Stock Exchange
Turin Stock Exchange
Valencia Stock Exchange
Venice Stock Exchange
Wiener Bourse

PART II
CRITERIA RELEVANT TO DEFINITION OF 'RELEVANT EEA MARKET'

The criteria relevant for the purposes of the definition of 'relevant EEA market' in article 2 of this Order are the following—

(a) the head office of the market must be situated in an EEA State; and

(b) the market must be subject to requirements in the EEA State in which its head office is situated as to—

    (i) the manner in which it operates;

    (ii) the means by which access may be had to the facilities it provides;

    (iii) the conditions to be satisfied before an investment may be traded or dealt in by means of its facilities; and

    (iv) the reporting and publication of transactions effected by means of its facilities.

SCHEDULE 2   Articles 2 and 16
EXCHANGES RELEVANT TO DEFINITION OF APPROVED SECURITIES MARKET AND FOR THE PURPOSES OF ARTICLE 16

Alberta Stock Exchange
American Stock Exchange

Australian Stock Exchange
Basler Effektenbourse
Bolsa Mexicana de Valores
Boston Stock Exchange
Bourse de Geneve
Chicago Board Options Exchange
Cincinnati Stock Exchange
Effektenborsenverein Zurich
Fukuoka Stock Exchange
Hiroshima Stock Exchange
Johannesburg Stock Exchange
Korea Stock Exchange
Kuala Lumpur Stock Exchange
Kyoto Securities Exchange
Midwest Stock Exchange
The Montreal Exchange
Nagoya Stock Exchange
NASDAQ
New York Stock Exchange
New Zealand Stock Exchange
Niigata Stock Exchange
Osaka Securities Exchange
Pacific Stock Exchange
Philadelphia Stock Exchange
Sapporo Securities Exchange
Securities Exchange of Thailand
Singapore Stock Exchange
Stock Exchange of Hong Kong Limited
Tokyo Stock Exchange
Toronto Stock Exchange
Vancouver Stock Exchange
Winnipeg Stock Exchange

SCHEDULE 3   Article 16
OTHER MARKETS RELEVANT FOR THE PURPOSES OF ARTICLE 16

Australian Financial Futures Market
Chicago Board of Trade
Chicago Mercantile Exchange
Coffee, Sugar and Cocoa Exchange, Inc
Commodity Exchange, Inc
Hong Kong Futures Exchange
International Securities Market Association
Kansas City Board of Trade
Mid-America Commodity Exchange
Minneapolis Grain Exchange
New York Cotton Exchange (including the Citrus Associates of the New York Cotton Exchange)
New York Futures Exchange
New York Mercantile Exchange
New Zealand Futures Exchange

Philadelphia Board of Trade
Singapore International Monetary Exchange
South African Futures Exchange (SAFEX)
Swiss Options and Financial Futures Exchange (SOFFEX)
Sydney Futures Exchange
Toronto Futures Exchange

SCHEDULE 4   **Article 12**
**ADVERTISEMENTS RELATING TO MATTERS OF COMMON
INTEREST**

1.   An advertisements complies with the requirements of this Schedule if it complies with the requirements of paragraphs 2, 3 and 4 below.

2.   An advertisement complies with the requirements of this paragraph if it contains a statement made by the directors or the persons named therein as promoters of the company accepting responsibility therefor without any limitation of liability on the basis that they have taken all reasonable care to ensure that every statement whether or fact or opinion which it contains is true and not misleading in the form and context in which it is included.

3.   An advertisement complies with the requirements of this paragraph if it contains either—

(a) a statement by the directors or the persons named therein as promoters of the company also accepting responsibility therefor without any limitation of liability that they have taken all reasonable care to ensure that the document contains all such information as a person such as the person or persons to whom the advertisement is addressed and their professional advisers would reasonably require and reasonably expect to find there for the purpose of making an informed assessment of the assets and liabilities, financial position, profits and losses, and prospects of the company and the rights attaching to the shares or debentures to which the document relates; or

(b) the words 'you should regard any subscription for shares in or debentures of this company as made primarily to assist the furtherance of its objectives (other than any purely financial objectives) and only secondarily, if at all, as an investment'.

4.   An advertisement complies with the requirements of this paragraph if it contains prominently the words 'If you are in any doubt about this offer you should consult a person authorised under the Financial Services Act 1986 who specialises in advising on investments of the kind being offered' or other words to a like effect.

**The Financial Services Act 1986 (Investment Advertisements)
(Exemptions) (No 2) Order 1995 (SI 1995 No 1536)**

ARRANGEMENT OF ARTICLES

SCHEDULES

1.   Citation and Commencement

This Order may be cited as the Financial Services Act 1986 (Investment Advertisements) (Exemptions) (No 2) Order 1995 and shall come into force on 19th June 1995.

2.   Interpretation

In this Order and in the Schedules hereto—

'the Act' means the Financial Services Act 1986;

'the 1985 Act' means the Companies Act 1985;

'the 1986 Order' means the Companies (Northern Ireland) Order 1986;

'EEA State' means a State which is a Contracting Party to the Agreement on the European Economic Area signed at Oporto on 2nd May 1992, as adjusted by the Protocol signed at Brussels on 17th March 1993, but until that Agreement comes into force in relation to Liechtenstein does not include the State of Liechtenstein;

'private company', in relation to a body corporate which is a company within the meaning of the 1985 Act, means a private company within the meaning of section 1(3) of the 1985 Act and, in relation to a body corporate which is a company within the meaning of the 1986 Order, means a private company within the meaning of article 12(3) of the 1986 Order; and

'relevant EEA market' means a market in an EEA State which is established under the rules of an investment exchange specified in Part I of Schedule 1 to this Order or which meets the criteria specified in Part II of that Schedule.

3.   Investment advertisements issued for the purpose of promoting or encouraging industrial or commercial activity or enterprise

(1) Section 57 of the Act shall not apply to an investment advertisement issued or caused to be issued by a body corporate of the kind described in paragraph (2) below which—

(a) relates to shares in or debentures of a private company;

(b) contains no invitation or information which would make it an investment advertisement other than an invitation or information which it is reasonable to expect a person engaged in an activity of the kind described in that paragraph to give in the course of engaging in that activity; and

(c) complies with the requirements of paragraph (3) of this article.

(2) A body corporate falls within this paragraph if—

(a) it is a body corporate which has as its principal object or one of its principal objects the promotion or encouragement of industrial or commercial activity or enterprise in the United Kingdom or in any particular area of it or the dissemination of information concerning persons engaged in such activity or enterprise or requiring capital in order to become so engaged; and

(b) it has no direct or indirect pecuniary interest in any matters which are the subject of any investment advertisement it issues which is exempt by virtue of this article or in any investment agreement which may be entered into following such an advertisement.

(3) The requirements referred to in paragraph (1)(c) of this article are that the advertisement should contain the following statements presented in a manner which, depending upon the medium through which the advertisement is issued, are calculated to bring the contents of the statements prominently to the attention of recipients of the advertisement—

Investment in new business carries high risks, as well as the possibility of high rewards. It is highly speculative and potential investors should be aware that no established market exists for the trading of shares in private companies. Before investing in a project about which information is given, potential investors are strongly advised to take advice from a person authorised under the Financial Services Act 1986 who specialises in advising on investments of this kind.

The persons to whose order this advertisement has been issued have taken reasonable steps to ensure that the information it contains is neither inaccurate nor misleading.

4. Take-overs of private companies

(1) In this article and in Schedule 4 to this Order—

(a) the expressions 'debentures' and 'shares', when used—

(i) in relation to a body corporate which is a company within the meaning of the 1985 Act have the same meaning as in that Act;

(ii) in relation to a body corporate which is a company within the meaning of the 1986 Order have the same meaning as in that Order; and

(iii) in relation to any other body corporate, mean investments falling within paragraph 1 or 2 of Schedule 1 to the Act issued by that body corporate; and

(b) 'relevant offer' means an offer of the kind described in Part II of Schedule 4 to this Order for shares in or debentures of a body corporate of the kind described in Part III of that Schedule.

(2) Section 57 of the Act shall not apply to an investment advertisement if it falls within paragraph (3), (4), or (5) below.

(3) An investment advertisement falls within this paragraph if—

(a) it is issued in connection with a relevant offer;

(b) it fulfils the conditions specified in Part IV of Schedule 4 to this Order; and

(c) it contains no invitation or information which would make it an investment advertisement other than—

    (i) an invitation or information relating to a relevant offer; or

    (ii) an invitation or information relating to a relevant offer and an invitation or information relating to an offer for investments falling within paragraph 4 or 5 of Schedule 1 to the Act which confer an entitlement or rights with respect to shares or debentures which are subject of that relevant offer.

(4) An investment advertisement falls within this paragraph if—

  (a) it either accompanies or is issued after the issue of an investment advertisement which contains a relevant offer and which falls within paragraph (3) above; and

  (b) it contains no invitation or information which would make it an investment advertisement other than an invitation or information relating to investments falling within paragraph 4 or 5 of Schedule 1 to the Act which confer an entitlement or rights with respect to shares or debentures which are the subject of that relevant offer.

(5) An investment advertisement falls within this paragraph if it is issued in connection with a relevant offer and is a form of application for shares or debentures or for investments falling within paragraph 4 or 5 of Schedule 1 to the Act.

5. Sale of body corporate

(1) In this article—

  (a) 'a group of connected individuals', in relation to the party disposing of shares in a body corporate, means persons each of whom is, or is a close relative of, a director or manager of the body corporate and, in relation to the party acquiring the shares, means persons each of whom is, or is a close relative of, a person who is to be a director or manager of the body corporate;

  (b) 'close relative' means a person's spouse, his children (including, in Northern Ireland, his adopted children) and step-children, his parents and step-parents, his brothers and sisters, and his step-brothers and step-sisters and includes a person acting in the capacity of trustee or personal representative of any such relative; and

  (c) 'single individual' includes two or more persons acting in their capacity as the personal representatives of a single individual.

(2) Section 57 of the Act shall not apply to an investment advertisement if the invitation is made or the information is given by or on behalf of a body corporate, a partnership, a single individual or a group of connected individuals for the purposes of or with a view to the acquisition or disposal of shares in a body corporate other than an open-ended investment company between parties each of whom is a body corporate, a partnership, a single individual or a group of connected individuals, being shares which—

  (a) consist of or include shares carrying 75 per cent or more of the voting rights attributable to share capital which are exercisable in all circumstances at any general meeting of the body corporate; or

  (b) would, together with any shares already held by the person or persons by or on whose behalf the advertisement is issued, carry not less than that percentage of those voting rights.

6. Dealings in course of non-investment business

Section 57 shall not apply to an investment advertisement issued or caused to be issued by a person who holds a permission granted under paragraph 23 of Schedule 1 to the Act if the only reason why the advertisement would be subject to the provisions of section 57 of the Act is because it contains an invitation or information given for the purposes of or in connection with anything done in accordance with the terms and conditions of the permission.

7. Advertisements issued to persons of particular kinds

(1) In this article 'relevant person' means a person who is not an authorised person and who is not unlawfully carrying on investment business in the United Kingdom.

(2) Section 57 of the Act shall not apply to an investment advertisement issued or caused to be issued by a relevant person in circumstances in which either—

(a) it is contained in a copy of a publication being a copy which is issued to a particular person by reason of his having placed an advertisement in that publication; or

(b) it is issued to a person whose business it is to place, or arrange for the placing of, advertising and who is sent the advertisement for the purposes of that business.

8. Advertisements directed at informing or influencing persons of a particular kind

(1) Section 57 of the Act shall not apply to an investment advertisement to which it would, apart from this article or other applicable exemption, otherwise apply if the advertisement may reasonably be regarded as being directed at informing or influencing only persons who fall within any one or more of the following categories—

(a) a government, local authority or public authority;

(b) persons whose ordinary activities involve them, as principal or as agent, in acquiring, holding, managing or disposing of investments for the purposes of a business carried on by them or whom it is reasonable to expect will, as principal or agent, acquire, hold, manage or dispose of investments for the purposes of such a business;

(c) persons whose ordinary business involves the giving of advice which may lead to another person acquiring or disposing of an investment or refraining from so doing; and

(d) persons whose ordinary business involves making arrangements with a view to another person acquiring or disposing of investments.

(2) For the purposes of paragraph (1) of this article—

(a) the expression 'government, local authority or public authority' has the meaning given in Note (1) to paragraph 3 of Schedule 1 to the Act; and

(b) an advertisement may be regarded as directed at informing or influencing a person of a kind specified in paragraph (1) if it is addressed to some other person in his capacity as an employee of that person, and, for these purposes, employment includes employment otherwise than under a contract of service.

9.—(1) For the purposes of article 8 of this Order, each of the following is an indication that an advertisement is directed at informing or influencing persons of a kind specified in paragraph (1) of that article—

(a) the advertisement expressly states that it is directed at persons of a kind specified in article 8(1) of this Order and that it would be imprudent for persons of any other kind to respond to it;

(b) the advertisement expressly states that any investment or service to which it relates is available only to persons having professional experience in matters relating to investment;

(c) the manner in which the advertisement is disseminated is such that it is unlikely to come to the attention of persons who are not professionally experienced in matters relating to investment; and

(d) any invitation or information contained in the advertisement is unlikely to appeal to persons who do not have professional experience in matters relating to investment.

(2) None of the indications given in paragraph (1) above is to be taken as showing conclusively that an advertisement is directed as there mentioned and, equally, the fact that an advertisement contains none of those indications is not to be taken to indicate that it is not so directed.

10.—(1) For the purposes of article 8 of this Order, each of the following is an indication that an advertisement is directed at informing or influencing persons of a kind not specified in paragraph (1) of that article—

(a) the advertisement concerns an investment which is likely to be of interest mainly to persons acting in their personal capacity;

(b) the minimum amount which may be expended in order to enter into any transaction to which the advertisement relates is sufficiently small that it is unlikely to deter persons who do not have professional experience in matters relating to investment from responding to the advertisement; and

(c) the advertisement is a direct-offer advertisement within the meaning given to that expression for the purposes of the core rules for the conduct of investment business.

(2) None of the indications given in paragraph (1) above is to be taken as showing conclusively that an advertisement is directed as there mentioned and, equally, the fact that an advertisement contains none of those indications is not to be taken to indicate that it is not so directed.

11. Advertisements required or permitted to be published by exchange or market rules

Section 57 of the Act shall not apply to any advertisement relating to any investment falling within any of paragraphs 1 to 5 of Schedule 1 to the Act which is permitted to be traded or dealt in on a relevant EEA market or a market established under the rules of an investment exchange specified in Schedule 2 to this Order, if the advertisement consists of or of any part of a document which is required or permitted to be published by the rules of the relevant market, or by a body which regulates such a market or which regulates offers or issues of investments to be traded on such a market.

12. Advertisements by certain markets

Section 57 of the Act shall not apply to an investment advertisement which is issued or caused to be issued by a market which is a relevant EEA market or is established under the rules of an investment exchange specified in Schedule 2 or 3 to this Order if the only reason why section 57 would otherwise apply to the advertisement is that it contains information which identifies a particular investment falling within paragraph 7, 8 or 9 of Schedule 1 to the Act as one which may be traded or dealt in on the market.

13. Industrial and provident societies

Section 57 of the Act shall not apply to an investment advertisement which is issued or caused to be issued by an industrial and provident society with respect to investments falling within paragraph 2 of Schedule 1 to the Act which it has issued or proposes to issue.

14. Public offers of securities

Section 57 of the Act shall not apply to an investment advertisement which—

(a) is a prospectus, or supplementary prospectus, issued in accordance with Part II of the Public Offers of Securities Regulations 1995;

(b) relates to a prospectus or supplementary prospectus published or to be published in accordance with Part II of the Public Offers of Securities Regulations 1995, and which contains no invitation or information which would make it an investment advertisement other than—

    (i) the name and address of the person by whom the investments to which the prospectus or supplementary prospectus relates are to be offered (within the meaning of the Public Offers of Securities Regulations 1995), or other particulars for communicating with him;

    (ii) the nature and the nominal value of the investments to which the prospectus or supplementary prospectus relates, the number offered and the price at which they are offered;

    (iii) a statement that a prospectus or supplementary prospectus issued in accordance with Part II of the Public Offers of Securities Regulations 1995 is or will be available and, if it is not yet available, when it is expected to be; and

    (iv) instructions for obtaining a copy of the prospectus or supplementary prospectus; or

(c) is required by a relevant EEA market for admission of an investment to trading on that market which—

    (i) contains the information which would be required by Part II of the Public Offers of Securities Regulations 1995 if it were a prospectus; and

    (ii) does not contain any information other than information required or permitted to be published by the rules of the relevant EEA market.

15. Advertisements required or authorised under enactments

Section 57 of the Act shall not apply to an investment advertisement if its issue is required or authorised by or under any enactment other than the Act.

16. Revocations

The Financial Services Act 1986 (Investment Advertisements) (Exemptions) (No 2) Order 1988 and the Financial Services Act 1986 (Investment Advertisements) (Exemptions) (No 2) Order 1992 are hereby revoked.

SCHEDULE 1   Article 2
RELEVANT EEA MARKETS

PART I
EXCHANGES OPERATING RELEVANT EEA MARKETS

Asociacion de Intermediarios de Activos Financieros
Amsterdam Financial Futures Market
Amsterdam Pork and Potato Terminal Market (NLKKAS—Amsterdam Clearing House)
Amsterdam Stock Exchange
Antwerp Stock Exchange
Athens Stock Exchange
Barcelona Stock Exchange
Berlin Stock Exchange
Bilbao Stock Exchange
Bologna Stock Exchange
Bremen Stock Exchange
Brussels Stock Exchange
Copenhagen Stock Exchange (including FUTOP)
Deutsche Terminboerse
Dusseldorf Stock Exchange
European Options Exchange
Finnish Options Market
Florence Stock Exchange
Frankfurt Stock Exchange
Genoa Stock Exchange
Hamburg Stock Exchange
Hanover Stock Exchange
Helsinki Stock Exchange
The International Stock Exchange of the United Kingdom and the Republic of Ireland Limited
Irish Futures and Options Exchange
Lisbon Stock Exchange
Luxembourg Stock Exchange
Madrid Stock Exchange
Marche a Terme International de France (MATIF)
MEFF Renta Fija
MEFF Renta Variable
Milan Stock Exchange
Marche des Options Negociables de Paris (MONEP)
Munich Stock Exchange
Naples Stock Exchange
OM Stockholm AB
Oporto Stock Exchange
Oslo Stock Exchange
Palermo Stock Exchange
Paris Stock Exchange
Rome Stock Exchange
Stockholm Stock Exchange
Stuttgart Stock Exchange
Trieste Stock Exchange
Turin Stock Exchange

Valencia Stock Exchange
Venice Stock Exchange
Wiener Bourse

PART II
CRITERIA RELEVANT TO DEFINITION OF 'RELEVANT EEA MARKET'

The criteria relevant for the purposes of the definition of 'relevant EEA market' in article 2 of this Order are the following—

(a) the head office of the market must be situated in an EEA State; and

(b) the market must be subject to requirements in the EEA State in which its head office is situated as to—

    (i) the manner in which it operates;

    (ii) the means by which access may be had to the facilities it provides;

    (iii) the conditions to be satisfied before an investment may be traded or dealt in by means of its facilities; and

    (iv) the reporting and publication of transactions effected by means of its facilities.

SCHEDULE 2   Articles 11 and 12
NON-EEA EXCHANGES RELEVANT FOR THE PURPOSES OF ARTICLES 11 AND 12

Alberta Stock Exchange
American Stock Exchange
Australian Stock Exchange Limited
Basler Effektenbourse
Bolsa Mexicana de Valores
Boston Stock Exchange
Bourse de Geneve
Chicago Board Options Exchange
Cincinnati Stock Exchange
Effektenborsenverein Zurich
Fukuoka Stock Exchange
Hiroshima Stock Exchange
Johannesburg Stock Exchange
Korea Stock Exchange
Kuala Lumpur Stock Exchange
Kyoto Securities Exchange
Midwest Stock Exchange
The Montreal Exchange
Nagoya Stock Exchange
NASDAQ
New York Stock Exchange
New Zealand Stock Exchange
Niigata Stock Exchange
Osaka Securities Exchange
Pacific Stock Exchange
Philadelphia Stock Exchange
Sapporo Securities Exchange

Securities Exchange of Thailand
Singapore Stock Exchange
Stock Exchange of Hong Kong Limited
Tokyo Stock Exchange
Toronto Stock Exchange
Vancouver Stock Exchange
Winnipeg Stock Exchange

SCHEDULE 3   **Article 12**
**NON-EEA EXCHANGES RELEVANT FOR THE PURPOSES OF
ARTICLE 12**

Australian Financial Futures Market
Chicago Board of Trade
Chicago Mercantile Exchange
Coffee, Sugar and Cocoa Exchange, Inc
Commodity Exchange, Inc
Hong Kong Futures Exchange
International Securities Market Association
Kansas City Board of Trade
Mid-America Commodity Exchange
Minneapolis Grain Exchange
New York Cotton Exchange (including the Citrus Associates of the New York Cotton Exchange)
New York Futures Exchange
New York Mercantile Exchange
New Zealand Futures Exchange
Philadelphia Board of Trade
Singapore International Monetary Exchange
South African Futures Exchange (SAFEX)
Swiss Options and Financial Futures Exchange (SOFFEX)
Sydney Futures Exchange
Toronto Futures Exchange

SCHEDULE 4   **Article 4**
PART I

1. In this Schedule—

'date of the offer' means the date specified in an investment advertisement to which article 4(3) of this Order applies as the date on which the advertisement was issued to recipients of the offer;

'equity share capital' 'holding company', 'subsidiary', and 'wholly owned subsidiary' have the same meanings as in the 1985 Act when used in relation to a body corporate which is a company within the meaning of that Act and have the same meanings as in the 1986 Order when used in relation to a body corporate which is a company within the meaning of that Order;

'offer document' means an investment advertisement to which article 4(3) of this Order applies;

'offeree company' means a body corporate of the kind specified in paragraph 3 of this Schedule shares in or debentures of which are the subject of an offer; and

'offeror' means a person by or on behalf of whom an offer is made;

and for the purposes of this Schedule shares or debentures are to be regarded as being held by or on behalf of an offeror if the person who holds them, or on whose behalf they are held, has agreed that an offer should not be made in respect of them.

PART II

2. An offer is an offer of the kind referred to in article 4(1)(b) of the Order if it is an offer for all the shares in, or all the shares comprised in the equity or non-equity share capital of, an offeree company or is an offer for all the debentures of an offeree company other than, in each case, shares or debentures held by or on behalf of the offeror, and—

(a) its terms have been recommended by all the directors of the offeree company other than any director who is the offeror or a director of the offeror;

(b) in the case of an offer for debentures or for non-equity share capital where, at the date of the offer, shares carrying 50 per cent or less of the voting rights attributable to the equity share capital are held by or on behalf of the offeror, the offer includes or is accompanied by an offer made by the offeror for the rest of the shares comprised in the equity share capital;

(c) in the case of an offer for shares comprised in the equity share capital where, at the date of the offer—

  (i) shares carrying 50 per cent or less of the voting rights then exercisable in general meetings of the offeree company; and

  (ii) shares carrying 50 per cent or less of the voting rights attributable to the equity share capital;

  are held by or on behalf of the offeror, it is a condition of the offer that sufficient shares be acquired or be agreed to be acquired by the offeror pursuant to or during the offer to result in shares carrying more than the said percentages of voting rights being held by him or on his behalf;

(d) except insofar as it may be totally withdrawn and all persons released from any obligation incurred under it, the offer is open for acceptance by every recipient for the period of at least 21 days beginning with the day after the day on which the document was issued to recipients of the offer;

(e) the acquisition of the shares or debentures to which the offer relates is not conditional upon the recipients approving, or consenting to, any payment or other benefit being made or given to any director or former director of the offeree company in connection with, or as compensation or consideration for, his ceasing to be a director or to hold any office held in conjunction with any directorship or, in the case of a former director, to hold any office which he held in conjunction with his former directorship and continued to hold after ceasing to be a director;

(f) the consideration for the shares or debentures is cash or, in the case of an offeror which is a body corporate other than an open-ended investment company, is either cash or shares in or debentures of the offeror or any combination of cash, such shares and such debentures; and

(g) copies of the following documents are available during normal office hours and free of charge at the place specified in the offer document by virtue of paragraph 10 of this Schedule—

  (i) the memorandum and articles of association of the offeree company and, if the offeror is a body corporate, the memorandum and articles of association of the offeror or, if it has no memorandum and articles of association, any instrument constituting or defining the constitution of the offeror, and, if such document is not written in English, a certified English translation of the instrument;

(ii) in the case of an offeree company which does not fall within sub-paragraph (iv) below, the audited accounts of the offeree company in respect of the last two accounting reference periods for which the laying and delivering of accounts under the 1985 Act or the 1986 Order has passed and, if accounts have been delivered to the relevant registrar of companies in respect of a later accounting reference period, copies of those accounts;

(iii) in the case of an offeror which is required to deliver accounts to the registrar of companies and which does not fall within sub-paragraph (iv) below, the audited accounts of the offeror in respect of the last two accounting reference periods for which the laying and delivering of accounts under the 1985 Act or the 1986 Order has passed and, if accounts have been delivered to the relevant registrar of companies in respect of a later accounting reference period, copies of those accounts;

(iv) in the case of an offeree company or an offeror which was incorporated during the period of three years immediately preceding the date of the offer or which has, at any time during that period, passed a resolution in accordance with section 252 of the 1985 Act or Article 260 of the 1986 Order, the information described in whichever is relevant of sub-paragraph (ii) or (iii) with respect to that body corporate need be included only in relation to the period since its incorporation or since it last ceased to be exempt from the obligation to appoint auditors as the case may be;

(v) all existing contracts of service entered into for a period of more than a year between the offeree company and any of its directors and, if the offeror is a body corporate, between the offeror and any of its directors;

(vi) any report, letter, valuation or other document any part of which is exhibited or referred to in the offer document;

(vii) if the offer document contains any statement purporting to have been made by an expert, that expert's written consent to the inclusion of that statement; and

(viii) all material contracts (if any) of the offeree company and of the offeror (not, in either case, being contracts which were entered into in the ordinary course of business) entered into during the period of two years immediately preceding the date of the offer.

PART III

3. A body corporate is a body corporate of the kind referred to in article 4(1)(b) of this Order if—

(a) it is a private company; and

(b) no shares comprised in the equity share capital of the company are or have, at any time within the period of ten years immediately preceding the date of the offer, been—

(i) listed or quoted on an investment exchange whether in the United Kingdom or elsewhere; or

(ii) shares in respect of which information has, with the agreement or approval of any officer of the company, been published for the purpose of facilitating deals in them, indicating prices at which persons have dealt or were willing to deal in them other than persons who were, at the time the information was published, existing members of a relevant class; or

(iii) subject to a marketing arrangement which accorded to the company the facilities referred to in section 163(2)(b) of the 1985 Act or article 173(2)(b) of the 1986 Order; or

(iv) the subject of an offer (whether in the United Kingdom or elsewhere) in relation to which a copy of a prospectus was delivered to the relevant registrar of companies in accordance with section 41 of the Companies Act 1948, section 41 of the Companies Act (Northern Ireland) 1960, section 64 of the 1985 Act or article 74 of the 1986 Order or Part II of the Public Offers of Securities Regulations 1995.

4. For the purposes of paragraph 3(b)(ii) of this Schedule a person shall be regarded as being a member of a relevant class if he was, at the relevant time, an existing member or debenture holder of the offeree company, or an existing employee of that company, or a member of the family of such a member or employee and for these purposes 'family' in relation to a person means that person's husband or wife, widow or widower and children (including step-children and, in Northern Ireland, adopted children) and their descendants and any trustee (acting in his capacity as such) of a trust the principal beneficiary of which is that person or any of those relatives.

PART IV

5. An advertisement fulfils the conditions specified in article 4(3)(b) of this Order if it takes the form of a document which complies with the requirements of paragraphs 6 to 11 of this Schedule and is accompanied by the material specified in paragraph 12.

6. The document must state on its face the identity of the offeror and, if the offer is being made on behalf of another person, the identity of that person.

7. The document must state on its face the fact that the terms of the offer are recommended by all the directors of the offeree company other than (if that is the case) any director who is the offeror or a director of the offeror.

8. The document must contain prominently the following words: 'If you are in any doubt about this offer you should consult a person authorised under the Financial Services Act 1986 who specialises in advising on the sale of shares and debentures' or other words to like effect.

9. The document must state clearly the matters referred to in paragraph 2(d) and (e) of this Schedule and the date on which it was issued to recipients of the offer.

10. The document must name a place in the United Kingdom at which copies of the documents specified in paragraph 2(g) of this Schedule may be inspected and state that those documents may be inspected at that place free of charge.

11. The document must contain the following information—

(a) particulars of all shares in or debentures of the offeree company and of all investments falling within paragraphs 4, 5 or 7 of Schedule 1 to the Act which relate to shares in or debentures of the offeree company held by or on behalf of the offeror or each offeror if there is more than one or, if none are so held, an appropriate negative statement;

(b) a statement as to whether or not the offer is conditional upon acceptances in respect of a minimum number of shares or debentures being received and, if the offer is so conditional, what the minimum number is;

(c) where the offer is conditional upon acceptances, the date which is the latest date on which it can become unconditional;

(d) if the offer is, or has become, unconditional the fact that it will remain open until further notice and that at least 14 days' notice will be given before it is closed;

(e) if applicable, a statement as to whether or not, if circumstances arise in which an offeror is able compulsorily to acquire shares of any dissenting minority under Part XIIIA of the 1985 Act or articles 421 to 423 of the 1986 Order, that offeror intends so to acquire those shares;

(f) if shares or debentures are to be acquired for cash, the period within which payment will be made and the method of payment;

(g) if the consideration or any part of the consideration for the shares or debentures to be acquired is shares in or debentures of an offeror—

  (i) the nature and particulars of the offeror's business, its financial and trading prospects and its place of incorporation;

  (ii) in respect of any offeror which is a body corporate, and in respect of the offeree company, its turnover, profit on ordinary activities before and after tax, extra-ordinary items, tax on extraordinary items and its profit and loss and the rate per cent of any dividends paid adjusted as appropriate to take account of relevant changes over the period and the total amount absorbed thereby for, in each case, the period of five years immediately preceding the date of the offer; provided that in the case of a body corporate which was incorporated during the period of five years immediately preceding the date of the offer or which has, at any time during that period, passed a resolution in accordance with section 252 of the 1985 Act or article 260 of the 1986 Order, the information described in this sub-paragraph with respect to that body corporate need be included only in relation to the period since its incorporation or since it last ceased to be exempt from the obligation to appoint auditors, as the case may be;

  (iii) particulars of the first dividend in which any such shares or debentures will participate and of the rights attaching to them (including, in the case of debentures, rights as to interest) and of any restrictions of their transfer;

  (iv) an indication of the effect of acceptance on the capital and income position of the holder of shares in or debentures of the offeree company; and

  (v) particulars of all material contracts (not being contracts which were entered into in the normal course of business) which were entered into by each of the offeree company and the offeror during the period of two years immediately preceding the date of the offer;

(h) particulars of the terms on which shares in or debentures of the offeree company acquired in pursuance of the offer will be transferred and of any restrictions on their transfer;

(i) whether or not it is proposed, in connection with the offer, that any payment or other benefit be made or given to any director or former director of the offeree company in connection with or as compensation or consideration for his ceasing to be a director or to hold any office held in conjunction with a directorship or, in the case of a former director, to hold any office which he held in conjunction with his former directorship and which he continued to hold after ceasing to be a director and, if it is so proposed, details of each such payment or benefit;

(j) whether or not there exists any agreement or arrangement between the offeror or any person with whom the offeror has an agreement of the kind described in section 204 of the 1985 Act or article 212 of the 1986 Order and any director or shareholder of the offeree company or any person who has been such a director or shareholder at any time during the period of twelve months immediately preceding the date of the offer, being an agreement or arrangement which is connected with or dependent on the offer, and if there is any such agreement or arrangement particulars of it;

(k) whether or not the offeror has reason to believe that there has been any material change in the financial position or prospects of the offeree company since the end of the accounting reference period to which the accounts referred to in paragraph 12 of this Schedule relate, and if the offeror has reason to believe that there has been any such change particulars of it;

(l) whether or not there is any agreement or arrangement whereby any shares or debentures acquired by the offeror in pursuance of the offer will or may be transferred to any other person together with the names of the parties to any such agreement or arrangement and particulars of all shares and debentures in the offeree company held by such persons;

(m) particulars of any dealings in the shares in or debentures of the offeree company, and, if the offeror is a body corporate, the offeror during the period of twelve months immediately preceding the date of the offer by every person who was a director of either of them at any time during that period, or, if there have been no such dealings, an appropriate negative statement;

(n) in a case where the offeror is a body corporate which is required to deliver accounts under the 1985 Act or the 1986 Order, particulars of the assets and liabilities as shown in its audited accounts in respect of the latest accounting reference period for which the period for laying and delivering accounts under the relevant legislation has passed or, if accounts in respect of a later accounting reference period have been delivered under the relevant legislation, as shown in those accounts and not the earlier accounts;

(o) where valuations of assets are given in connection with the offer, the basis on which the valuation was made and the names and addresses of the persons who valued them and particulars of any relevant qualifications; and

(p) if any profit forecast is given in connection with the offer, a statement of the assumptions on which the forecast is based.

12. The document must be accompanied by the following—

(a) the audited accounts of the offeree company in respect of the latest accounting reference period for which the period for laying and delivering accounts under the 1985 Act or the 1986 Order has passed, or, if accounts in respect of a later accounting reference period have been delivered under the relevant legislation, those accounts and not the earlier ones;

(b) a letter advising the directors of the offeree company on the financial implications of the offer from a competent person who is independent of and has no substantial financial interest in the offeree company or the offeror, being a letter which sets out the advice that person has given in relation to the offer;

(c) a statement by the directors of the offeree company, acting as a board, stating—

    (i) whether or not there has been any material change in the financial position or prospects of the offeree company since the end of the accounting reference period to which the accounts accompanying the offer document relate and, if there has been any such change, particulars of it;

    (ii) any interests, in percentage terms, which any of the directors have in the shares in or debentures of the offeree company or any offeror which is a body corporate being interests which, in the case of the offeree company, are required to be entered in the register kept by the company under section 325 of the 1985 Act or article 333 of the 1986 Order or, in the case of an offeror, would be required to be so entered if the director were a director of the offeror and in the case of an offeror which is not a company within the meaning of the 1985 Act or the 1986 Order if the offeror were such a company;

    (iii) any material interest which any director has in any contract entered into by the offeror and in any contract entered into by any member of any group of which the offeror is a member;

(d) a statement as to whether or not each director intends to accept the offer in respect of his own beneficial holdings in the offeree company;

(e) a statement by the directors of any offeror which is a body corporate shares in or debentures of which are the consideration or any part of the consideration for the offer that the information concerning the offeror and those shares or debentures contained in the document is correct;

(f) if the offeror is making the offer on behalf of another person, a statement by the offeror as to whether or not he has taken any steps to ascertain whether that person will be in a position to implement the offer and, if he has taken any such steps, what those steps are and his opinion as to whether that person will be in a position to implement the offer; and

(g) a statement that each of the directors of the offeree company, the offeror or, if the offeror is a body corporate, each of the directors of the offeror, are responsible for the information contained in the document insofar as it relates to themselves or their respective bodies corporate and that, to the best of their knowledge and belief (having taken all reasonable care to ensure that such is the case), the information is in accordance with the facts and that no material fact has been omitted.

The Financial Services Act 1986 (Investment Advertisements) (Exemptions) Order 1997 (SI 1997 No 963)

1. Citation and Commencement

This Order may be cited as the Financial Services Act 1986 (Investment Advertisements) (Exemptions) Order 1997 and shall come into force on 1st June 1997.

2. Interpretation

In this Order—

'the Act' means the Financial Services Act 1986;

'the 1996 Order' means the Financial Services Act 1986 (Investment Advertisements) (Exemptions) Order 1996.

3.   Overseas Persons

(*Amends the Financial Services Act 1986 (Investment Advertisements) (Exemptions) Order 1996 (SI 1996 No 1586, art 10.)*)

4.   Advertisement issued to persons sufficiently expert to understand the risks involved

(*Amends the Financial Services Act 1986 (Investment Advertisements) (Exemptions) Order 1996 (SI 1996 No 1586), art 11.)*)

5.   Exchanges operating relevant EEA markets

(*Amends Sched 1, Pt I to the Financial Services Act 1986 (Investment Advertisements) (Exemptions) Order 1996 (SI 1996 No 1586).*)

ADVERTISING RULES REFERRED TO IN CHAPTER 12 AT 12.3.1
(Relevant extracts only)

SIB CONDUCT OF BUSINESS RULES 1990

Part 7: Advertisements

7.01. Application

(1) This Part of these rules applies to advertisements in respect of investment business other than:

    a   an advertisement which is excluded from paragraph (e) of section 48(2) of the Act by virtue of section 48(5) of the Act, and

    b   an advertisement which contains matter required or permitted to be published:

        (i)   by or under any enactment, or

        (ii) by or under any provision of the law of a member State other than the United Kingdom corresponding to section 85 of the Act, or

        (iii) by an exchange which is:

            (A) a recognised investment exchange, or

            (B) a designated investment exchange, or

            (C) an approved exchange under Part V of the Act,

        and contains no other matter, and

    c   an advertisement offering any securities within the meaning of section 159(1) of the Act, an advertisement offering securities which is a primary or secondary offer within the meaning of section 160 of the Act and an advertisement offering securities which is exempted from sections 159 and 160 of the Act by virtue of section 161 of the Act, and

    d   an advertisement issued in such circumstances that it is unlikely that it will be communicated to persons who are neither business investors nor persons who carry on investment business.

Practice Note
The Board considers that a person within sub-paragraph d who by way of business passes on an advertisement which he receives as such will be issuing an advertisement and so is subject to section 57 of the Act and, if a firm, this Part of these rules.

(2) Except where the context otherwise requires references in this Part of these rules to an advertisement are references to an advertisement to which this Part of these rules applies.

7.02. [*Not used*]

7.03. Issue of advertisements by a firm

A firm shall not issue an advertisement unless the requirements of this Part of these rules are complied with in relation to that advertisement.

7.04. Approval by a firm of advertisements issued by unauthorised persons

(1) [*Not used*]

(2) A firm shall not approve for the purposes of section 57 of the Act the contents of an investment advertisement to be issued or caused to be issued by a person who is not an authorised person unless the requirements of this rule are compiled with in relation to that advertisement.

(3) In the case of an advertisement which relates to a collective investment scheme the requirements of this rule are that:

a   all the requirements of this Part of these rules are compiled with in relation to the advertisement as if the unauthorised person were a firm, and

b   if the approval is required for the purpose of the advertisement's being issued by an overseas person, that person is the operator of a regulated collective investment scheme and the advertisement relates to units in that scheme.

(4) In the case of an advertisement which relates to a life policy the requirements of this rule are that:

a   all the requirements of rule 5.11 (if applicable) and of this Part of these rules are complied with in relation to the advertisement as if the unauthorised person were a firm, and,

b   if the life policy is to be issued by a life office which is an overseas person:

   (i)   that life office is one referred to in section 130(2)(c) or (d) of the Act, or

   (ii) that life office is one referred to in section 130(3)(a) of the Act and the requirements of section 130(3) of the Act have been fulfilled.

(5) In the case of an advertisement which does not relate to a collective investment scheme or to a life policy and is an image advertisement or a short form advertisement, the requirements of this rule are that all the requirements of this Part of these rules are complied with in relation to the advertisement as if the unauthorised person were a firm.

(6) In the case of an advertisement which does not relate to a collective investment scheme or to a life policy and is not an image advertisement or a short form advertisement and is not an advertisement to which rule 7.23 applies, the requirements of this rule are:

a   if the approval is required for the purpose of the advertisement's being issued by an overseas person who is an associate of the firm in circumstances in which the advertisement is not likely to be received by anyone other than an established customer with whom the firm or the associate has a continuing relationship governed by a written agreement, that the firm has no reason to believe that any matter in the advertisement is inaccurate, unfair or misleading, or

b   if the approval is not required for the purpose and in the circumstances mentioned in sub-paragraph a:

   (i)   that all the requirements of this Part of these rules are complied with in relation to the advertisement as if the unauthorised person were a firm, and

  (ii) if the approval is required for the purpose of the advertisement's being issued by an overseas person:

    (A) that the firm carries on in the United Kingdom in compliance with rule 2.01 (business plan) investment business which relates to investments of the same description as the investment the subject of the advertisement, and

    (B) if the advertisement is a relevant publication within the meaning of part 8 of these rules which will or may include recommendations to acquire investments which are not readily realisable, that the firm has reasonable grounds for believing that the issuer will not:

      (I) give or send that publication to any person in the United Kingdom, or

      (II) enter into any arrangement with any person in the United Kingdom or procure any such person to enter into any arrangement under which that person will be regularly given or sent issues of that publication,

    unless that person is a person whom the issuer believes, on the basis of such facts about his financial situation and competence in financial matters as may be expected to be relevent, to be a person for whom investments which are not readily realisable are suitable, and

    (C) that the firm has no reason to believe that the issuer of the advertisement will not treat responders to the advertisement honestly and fairly, and

    (D) that the advertisement contains warnings that rules and regulations made under the Act for the protection of investors do not apply to the issuer of the advertisement and that the Board's compensation scheme will not apply in relation to the investment the subject of the advertisement, and

    (E) except in the case of a tombstone, that the advertisement contains statements that the advertisement has been approved by the firm and that the firm is regulated in the conduct of its business by the Board.

7.04A. Overseas insurers

(1) This rule applies in the case of an advertisement which relates to life policies which is issued at a time when the insurer who is to issue the life policies is not authorised to carry on long term business in the United Kingdom of the class to which the advertisement relates by or under section 3 or 4 of the Insurance Companies Act 1982 and is not otherwise permitted to carry on long term business of that class in the United Kingdom.

(2) A firm shall not issue an advertisement to which this rule applies unless the contents of the advertisement and the manner of its presentation are such that the advertisement would have complied with regulations 65 to 65C of the Insurance Companies Regulations 1981 (Statutory Instruments 1981 No 1654) as amended by the Insurance Companies (Advertisements) (Amendment) (No 2) Regulations 1983 (Statutory Instruments 1983 No 396) as those regulations had effect on 20 September 1990 as if they applied to the advertisement but subject to the amendment that, in regulation 65B there be inserted at the beginning of sub-paragraph (f) of paragraph (3) the following:

except in a case where the insurer is authorised to effect or carry out contracts of insurance to which the advertisement relates in any country or territory which is for the time being designated for the purposes of section 130 of the Financial Services Act 1986 by an order made by the Secretary of State and where any conditions imposed by the order designating the country or territory have been satisfied.

7.05. Prominence of required statements

The significance of any statement or other matter required by these rules to be included in an advertisement shall not be disguised either through lack of prominence in relation to the other matter in the advertisement or by the inclusion of matter calculated to minimise the significance of the statement.

7.06. Approval

(1) A firm which issues an advertisement shall ensure that the advertisement is approved prior to its issue by an individual within the firm, or within a group of which the firm is a member, appointed for the purpose of this rule.

(2) A firm shall not approve the contents of an advertisement in pursuance of rules 7.03 or 7.04 except through the agency of an individual within the firm, or within a group of which the firm is a member, appointed for the purpose of this rule.

Practice Note
In relation to a short form advertisement in the form of a screen price quotation service, the Board considers that an individual empowered by his firm to input its prices to the system might properly also be empowered to approve short form advertisements of that type.

7.07. Advertisements to be clear and not misleading

(1) The content of an advertisement and the manner of its presentation shall be such that the advertisement is not likely to be misunderstood by those to whom it is addressed including, if it be the case, persons who cannot be expected to have any special understanding of the matter in the advertisement.

(2) An advertisement shall not contain any statement, promise or forecast unless the firm issuing or approving the advertisement has taken all reasonable steps to satisfy itself that each such statement, promise or forecast is not misleading in the form or context in which it appears.

(3) An advertisement shall not contain any statement purporting to be a statement of fact which the firm issuing it does not reasonably believe at the time of issue, on the basis of evidence of which it has a record in its possession, to be true.

(4) An advertisement shall not contain any statement of fact which, although true when the advertisement is issued, the firm has reason to believe is likely to become untrue before the advertisement ceases to be current.

(5) An advertisement shall not state that any person is of any particular opinion unless the firm issuing or approving the advertisement has taken all reasonable steps to satisfy itself that the advertiser or other person, as the case may be, is of that opinion when the advertisement is issued.

(6) If the investment or service to which an advertisement relates is available in limited quantities, for a limited period or on special terms for a limited period the advertisement may say so but, if that is not the case, the advertisement shall not contain any statement or matter which implies that it is so.

7.08. Advertisements to be distinguished from other matter

(1) The terms of an advertisement and the manner of its presentation shall be such that it appears to be an advertisement issued with the object of promoting the investment, service or firm to which it relates.

(2) Where the medium in which the advertisement is carried contains or presents other matter the advertisement shall be distinguished from that other matter so that what is an advertisement does not appear to be or to form part of a news item, report, bulletin, entertainment, instruction, story, drama, performance or other such means of communication.

Practice Note
The Board takes the view that an advertisement on a hoarding at a football ground would not contravene this rule but that an advertisement forming part of a dialogue of a televised drama would do so.

7.09. Advertisements to identify the investments or services to which they relate

Except in the case of a short form advertisement or an image advertisement, the nature of the investment or the services to which an advertisement relates shall be clearly described.

7.10. Promotions to be genuine

An advertisement shall not be issued with the intention not of persuading persons who respond to the advertisement to pursue the subject matter of the advertisement but instead of persuading them to enter into an investment agreement, or use financial services, of a description not mentioned in the advertisement.

7.11. Disclosure of advertiser's capacity

An advertisement which invites those to whom it is addressed to enter into an investment agreement with a named person shall:

a   disclose, by statement or by necessary implication, whether it is proposed that the named person will enter into the agreement as a principal on his own account or as an agent for another person, and

b   if the named person is to enter into the agreement as an agent for another person and that person can be identified when the advertisement is issued, state the name of that other person.

7.12. Identity of regulators

(1) An advertisement which is not a short form advertisement or an image advertisement shall state:

a   if the advertisement has been issued by a firm, that the person who has issued it is a person regulated by the Board, or

b   if the advertisement has not been issued by an authorised person but has been approved by a firm, that the advertisement has been approved by a person regulated by the Board.

(2) Where an advertisement offers the product or the services of a person other than the firm which has issued or approved it, the advertisement shall state;

a   whether or not that other person is an authorised person, and

b   if he is an authorised person:

    (i)   the name of the body responsible for regulating his conduct of business, and

    (ii) the fact that the body is so responsible or, if it be the case, that that person is a member of that body, and

    (iii) if it be the case that that body regulates the conduct of that person on an interim basis only that that person has applied to that body:

And any statement in an advertisement that that person has applied to a body responsible for regulating the conduct of that person's business shall be accompanied by the words 'Not covered by The Investors' Compensation Scheme' and may be accompanied by a statement that that person is interim authorised.

(3) An advertisement which is not an advertisement in respect of investment business shall not contain any matter referring to the Board.

7.13. Advertisements not to imply government approval

(1) Subject to paragraphs (2) and (3) an advertisement shall not contain any matter which states or implies that the investment the subject of the advertisement or any matter in the advertisement has the approval of any Government department or of the Board.

(2) This rule does not prohibit the issue of an advertisement which contains or advertises an offer for sale of investments owned by Her Majesty's Government.

(3) Where the investment the subject of an advertisement is recognised by the Inland Revenue for the purpose of qualifying those who acquire the investment for any reliefs from taxation, the advertisement may refer to that recognition.

7.14. Synopses to be fair

An advertisement which states some only of the rights and obligations attaching to an investment or some only of the terms and conditions of an investment agreement shall:

a   state sufficient of them to give a fair view of the nature of the investment or of the investment agreement, of the financial commitment undertaken by an investor in acquiring the investment or in entering into the agreement and of the risks involved, and

b   state how a written statement of all of them can be obtained.

7.15. Commendations

An advertisement may include a quotation from a statement made by any person commending an investment or service if and only if:

a   where that person is an employee or associate of the firm, that fact is disclosed in the advertisement, and

b   the quotation is included with that person's consent, and

c   the statement is relevant to the investment or service which is the subject of the advertisement, and

d   where the whole of the statement is not quoted, what is quoted represents fairly the message contained in the whole of the statement, and

e   the statement has not become inaccurate or misleading through the passage of time since it was made.

7.16. Comparison with other investments

(1) An advertisement shall not compare or contrast:

a   an investment with an alternative application of an investor's funds, or

b   a service or a provider of a service or of an investment with an alternative service or provider,

unless the comparisons and contrasts are fair in relation to what is promoted and to the alternative having regard to what is not stated as well as to what is stated.

Practice Note
The Board considers that it would be a breach of this rule:

a   to omit a feature of possible comparison or contrast so as to exaggerate the significance of what is included, or

b   to misrepresent or unfairly to criticise the alternative or the person who offers it.

(1A) An advertisement of units in a regulated collective investment scheme shall not compare or contrast the performance or the likely performance of an investment in units of the scheme with an investment in a collective investment scheme which is not a regulated collective investment scheme.

(2) Without prejudice to the generality of paragraph (1) if, in the case of an advertisement of units in a collective investment scheme or in a unit linked life policy, comparison is made between the performance of an investment in those units over a period of time with the performance of an alternative application of the investor's funds over the same period of time, the comparison shall be on an offer to bid basis, that is to say, on the basis of what it would have cost to acquire an amount of the investment and the alternative at the beginning of the period and what a disposal of that amount of the investment and the alternative would have realised at the end of the period, and the fact that that is the basis of the comparison shall be stated.

(3) Without prejudice to the generality of paragraph (1) if, in the case of an advertisement of units in a collective investment scheme or in a unit linked life policy, comparison is made between the performance of an investment in those units over a period of time with the performance of an index over the same period of time, the comparison shall be on whatever basis is consistent with the basis on which the

index is constructed, and the fact that that is the basis of the comparison shall be stated.

7.17.   Life policies

(1) The requirements of this Part of these rules apply to an advertisement relating to a life policy in addition to the requirements of rule 5.11 which rule applies in the case of an advertisement as it applies in the case of publications generally.

(2) An advertisement relating to a life policy which gives particulars of any of the benefits payable under the policy shall state:

    a   which of the benefits under the contract (if any) are of fixed amounts and what those amounts are, and

    b   which of them (if any) are not of fixed amounts.

(3) Such an advertisement may describe a benefit of a fixed amount or a minimum amount of a variable benefit as a 'guaranteed' amount but, if it does so and the advertisement refers to the participation of a third party and that third party will not stand as surety for the life office should the life office not meet its obligations, the advertisement shall not contain any matter which implies that the third party will so stand as surety.

Practice Note
An example of a breach of this rule would be the following: an advertisement of a life policy, the benefits under which are linked to the performance of a fund held by a third party as trustee but not as a guarantor, states that certain benefits are 'guaranteed' without also stating that the trustee is not the guarantor of the obligations of the insurance company.

7.18.   Taxation

(1) An advertisement which refers to taxation shall contain a warning that the levels and bases of taxation can change.

(2) An advertisement which contains any matter based on an assumed rate of taxation shall state what that rate is.

(3) An advertisement which refers to reliefs from taxation:

    a   shall state that the reliefs are those which currently apply, and

    b   shall contain a statement that the value of a relief from taxation depends upon the circumstances of the taxpayer.

(4) An advertisement which relates to an investment the income from which:

    a   is payable out of a fund the income of which has already been taxed, and

    b   is not or may not be subject to income tax in the hands of the investor,

shall not describe the investment as one free from liability to income tax unless the fact that the income is payable out of a fund from which income tax has already been paid is stated with equal prominence.

(5) An advertisement which relates to an investment in whose case:

    a   an investor will not be liable to taxation on realised capital gains in the investment, and

b   any realised capital gains of the assets of a fund to which the value of the investments is linked are subject to taxation,

shall not describe the investment as one free from liability to capital gains taxation
unless the fact that the value of the investment is linked to a fund which will be
liable to taxation on realised capital gains in the assets of which it is comprised is
stated with equal prominence.

(6) An advertisement which refers to reliefs from taxation shall distinguish between
reliefs which apply directly to investors and those which apply to the issuer of the
investment or to a fund in which the investor participates.

7.19. Cancellation rights

An advertisement may state (if it be the case) that an investor who enters into an investment
agreement to which the advertisement relates will be given an opportunity to cancel the
agreement but, if it does so, the advertisement shall state:

a   the period during which the investor will have that right and the time when that
period will begin, and

b   (if it be the case) that the right to cancel is conferred by law, and

c   if upon cancellation the investor will not recover his investment in full should the
market have fallen since the investment was acquired:

(i)   that fact, and

(ii) if the advertisement is an advertisement of a higher volatility investment,
notice that the shortfall in what he recovers should the market have fallen
could be very high because of the possibility of sudden and large falls in
the value of the units.

7.20. Past performance

An advertisement shall not contain information about the past performance of investments
of any description unless:

a   it is relevant to the performance of the investment the subject of the advertisement,
and

b   except where the source of the information is the advertiser itself, the source of the
information is stated, and

bb   in the case of an advertisement of a higher volatility investment, information is
given for the period of five years ending with the date on which the advertisement
is approved for issue and beginning five years before that date or, if the fund came
into existence less than five years before that date, beginning when the fund came
into existence, and

c   if the whole of the information is not set out:

(i)   what is included is not unrepresentative, unfair or otherwise misleading,
and

(ii) the exclusion of what is excluded does not have the effect of exaggerating the
success of performance over the period to which the information which is
included relates, and

d if the information is presented in the form of a graph or chart, no part of the information is omitted so as to give a misleading impression of the rate at which variable quantities have changed, and

e in the case of an advertisement of units in a collective investment scheme or in a unit linked life policy, any comparison made between the value of an investment in those units at different times is on an offer to bid basis, that is to say, on the basis of what it would have cost to acquire an amount of the units at the earlier time and what a disposal of that amount of those units would have realised at the later time, and the fact that that is the basis of the comparison is stated, and

f the advertisement contains a warning that the past is not necessarily a guide to the future.

Practice Note
The Board considers that a unit trust manager could commit a breach of this rule if it were to issue an advertisement which:
a advertised all or a number of its funds, and
b either:
  (i) claimed notable successes for some of those funds without indicating that it was some only of those funds which had attained those levels of success, or
  (ii) chose to show only an unrepresentative few months of performance.

7.21. Indications of the scale of business activities

An advertisement shall not contain any statement indicating the scale of the activities or the extent of the resources of a person who carries on investment business, or of any group of which such a person is a member, so as to imply that the resources available to support performance of the firm's obligations are greater than they are.

Practice Note
The Board would regard the following as breaches of this rule:

(1) An advertisement which states the amount of the authorised share capital of a company but does not also state the amount of the issued share capital of that company.

(2) An advertisement which states the amount of a company's issued share capital but does not also state how much of that capital has been paid up.

(3) An advertisement which states the amount of a company's total assets but does not also state the amount of the company's liabilities.

(4) An advertisement which states the amount of a company's income or turnover but does not state the period to which that amount relates.

(5) An advertisement which refers to a subsidiary in a group and which mentions the amount of the capital or of the assets of the group as a whole so as to imply that they are resources on which the subsidiary can draw when that is not the case.

(6) An advertisement which states the amount of funds under a firm's management in such a way as to imply that those funds are assets of the firm.

7.22. Risk warnings

(1) This rule applies to any advertisement which is not:

a   a short form advertisement, or

b   an image advertisement.

(2) An advertisement to which this rule applies shall contain a statement or statements in accordance with this rule warning of the risks involved in acquiring or holding the investment the subject of the advertisement.

(3) Where the advertisement relates to an investment in the case of which deductions for charges and expenses are not made uniformly throughout the life of the investment but are loaded disproportionately onto the early years, the advertisement shall draw attention to that fact and that accordingly, if the investor withdraws from the investment in the early years, he may not get back the amount he has invested.

(4) Where the advertisement relates to an investment which can fluctuate in value in money terms, the statement shall draw attention to that fact and to the fact that the investor may not get back the whole of what he has invested and, where the advertisement is an advertisement of a higher volatility investment, the statement shall draw attention to the possibility of sudden and large falls in the value of the units and to the fact that the investor may lose the whole of his investment.

(5) Where the advertisement offers an investment as likely to yield a high income or as suitable for an investor particularly seeking income from his investment, the statement shall draw attention to the fact that income from the investment may fluctuate in value in money terms.

(6) Where the advertisement relates to an investment denominated in a currency other than that of the country in which the advertisement is issued, the advertisement shall draw attention to the fact that changes in rates of exchange between currencies may cause the value of the investment to diminish or to increase.

(7) Where the advertisement relates to a with profits life policy, that statement shall draw attention to the fact that the return on the investment depends on what profits are made and on what decisions are made by the life office as to their distribution.

(8) Where the advertisement contemplates the customer entering into a transaction the nature of which is such that the customer may not only lose what he pays at the outset but may incur a liability to pay unspecified additional amounts later, the statement shall draw attention to the fact that the investor may or, as the case may be, will have to pay more money later and that accordingly a transaction in that investment can lose the investor more than his first payment.

(9) Where the advertisement relates to a margined transaction which is not a limited liability transaction and which will or may be effected otherwise than on a recognised or designated investment exchange and in a contract of a type traded thereon, the advertisement shall draw attention to the fact that the transaction is only suitable for a person who has experience in transactions of that description:

But this does not apply in the case of an advertisement which advertises the services of an execution-only dealer.

Practice Note
This rule should be read in conjunction with rule 9.11(1)b.(iii) below.

(10) Where the advertisement relates to an investment which is not readily realisable:

a   if the investment is not traded on a recognised or designated investment exchange, the statement shall draw attention to the fact that there is no recognised market for the investment so that it may be difficult for the investor to sell the investment or for him to obtain reliable information about its value or the extent of the risks to which it is exposed, or

b   if the investment is traded on a recognised or designated investment exchange but is dealt in so irregularly or infrequently:

  (i)   that it cannot be certain that a price for that investment will be quoted at all times, or

  (ii)   that it may be difficult to effect transactions at any price which may be quoted, and

the statement shall draw attention to that fact or those facts, as the case may be, and, if there are fewer than three market makers in that investment, the statement shall draw attention to that or to those facts, as the case may be.

Practice Note
(*Deleted by the Financial Services (Conduct of Business) (Amendment) Rules 1997*)

(11) Where the advertisement relates to units:

a   in a property fund, or

b   in a constituent part of an umbrella fund which, if that part were a separate fund, would be a property fund, or

c   in a fund of funds in the case of which one of the schemes to which it is dedicated is a property fund,

the statement shall draw attention:

  (i)   to the fact that land and buildings may at times be difficult to sell so that there may be periods during which the operator will have the right to refuse to repurchase units offered to him for redemption, and

  (ii)   to the fact that a valuation of land and buildings has to be the judgment of an individual valuer.

(12) Where the advertisement is of a life policy and refers to benefits under the policy which are measured by reference to the value of, to fluctuations in the value of or to income from land or any interest in land, the statement shall draw attention:

  (i)   to the fact that the assets to which the benefits under the policy are linked may at times be difficult to sell so that there may be periods during which the life office will be unable to accept surrenders of the policy, and

  (ii)   to the fact that a valuation of land and buildings has to be the judgment of an individual valuer.

(13) Where the advertisement relates to units in a regulated collective investment scheme, and at the time when the advertisement is prepared for issue, the property of the scheme consists, or there is an expectation that the property of the scheme may consist, as to more than 35% thereof in Government and other public securities issued by one issuer, the statement shall include reference to that fact or, as the case may be, to that expectation and shall identify that issuer.

7.22A.   [*Revoked*]

7.23.   General duty of disclosure in 'off-the-page' and 'off-the-screen' advertisements

(i) Subject to paragraph (1A) this rule applies to an advertisement containing:

    a   an offer to enter into an investment agreement with a person who responds to the advertisement, or

    b   an invitation to a person to respond to the advertisement by making an offer to enter into an investment agreement, and

in either case, specifying the manner in which that response is invited to be made.

(1A) This rule does not apply to an advertisement if:

    a   the investment agreement the subject of the advertisement is an agreement for the supply of a publication to which Part 8 of these rules applies, or

    b   the investment agreement the subject of the advertisement is an agreement for the acquisition or disposal of shares, debentures, warrants, options or other securities of a company or of an interest in the securities of a company and the advertisement contains:

        (i)   all such information as investors and their professional advisers would reasonably require, and reasonably expect to find there, for the purpose of making an informed assessment of:

            (A)   the assets and liabilities, financial position, profits and losses, and prospects of the issuer of the securities, and

            (B)   the rights attaching to those securities, and

        (ii) no other matter.

(2) An advertisement to which this rule applies may not be issued if the investment agreement the subject of the advertisement is an agreement for the provision of the services of a portfolio manager or investor broker fund adviser or if it relates to an investment other than:

    a   a life policy, or

    b   units in a regulated collective investment scheme, or

    c   a type A or a type B PEP.

Note. *By rule 17.04 of these rules (as amended by The Financial Services (Conduct of Business) (Amendment No 2) Rules 1994), rule 7.23(2) excludes a fourth category of investment.*

(3) A firm shall not issue an advertisement to which this rule applies if the advertisement contains any matter likely to lead to the supposition that the investment agreement the subject of the advertisement is or is thought to be suitable for a particular individual who is the recipient of the advertisement.

Practice Note
This rule constrains the issuer of personalised circulars to refrain from implying that he knows a recipient sufficiently well to be sure that the investment is suitable. The rule is not intended to constrain the content of letters to individuals whom the firm writing the letter does know.

(4) A firm shall not issue an advertisement to which this rule applies unless the

advertisement is contained in a printed document or is otherwise capable of being examined continuously for a reasonable period of time.

7.24. 'Off-the-page' advertisements for life policies

[A firm shall not issue an advertisement to which rule 7.23 applies which relates to a life policy unless the advertisement contains the information set out in, or required to be included in, a key features document prepared in accordance with the Adopted Lautro Rules as at 20 March 1997.]

(Substituted by the Financial Services (Conduct of Business) (Amendment) Rules 1997)

7.25. ['Off-the-page' advertisements for schemes

A firm shall not issue an advertisement to which rule 7.23 applies in respect of regulated collective investment schemes whether or not held within a PEP, investment trusts where the relevant shares have been or are to be acquired through an investment trust savings scheme or an investment trust where the relevant shares are held with a PEP which promotes one or more specific investment trusts, unless the advertisement contains the information set out in, or required to be included in, a key features document prepared in accordance with the Adopted Lautro Rules as at 20 March 1997.]

(Substituted by the Financial Services (Conduct of Business)(Amendment) Rules 1997)

7.26. 'Off-the-page' advertisements for type B PEPs

(1) A firm shall not issue an advertisement to which rule 7.23 applies which relates to a type B PEP unless the terms of the type B PEP the subject of the advertisement do not give any authority to anyone to make unsolicited calls upon the investor.

(2) The requirements of paragraph (1) are in addition to the requirements of Part 4 of these rules as to the contents of a customer agreement.

7.27. Restrictions on promotion of unregulated collective investment schemes

A firm shall not issue or cause to be issued an advertisement containing any matter which invites any person to become or offer to become a participant in a collective investment scheme which is not a regulated collective investment scheme or contains information calculated to lead directly or indirectly to any person becoming or offering to become a participant in such a scheme unless the issue of the advertisement does not contravene sub-section (1) of section 76 of the Act by virtue of sub-section (2), (3) or (4) of that section.

Practice Note
In relation to an advertisement issued or caused to be issued by a firm, this rule merely restates what is already an obligation under section 76(1) of the Act, but the rule has effect, by virtue of section 58(1)(c) of the Act, in relation to advertisements issued or caused to be issued by a national of a member State other than the United Kingdom in the course of investment business lawfully carried on by him in such a State.

7.28. Advertisements by appointed representatives

(1) A firm which is a collective investment marketing firm shall ensure that an advertisement issued by an appointed representative of the firm (other than an image advertisement or a short form advertisement):

a   does not contain any statement commending the principal or its services or products in such a way as to suggest or imply that the appointed representative was free to exercise independent judgement in deciding to make the commendation, and

b   contains a prominent statement, no less prominent than any other statement describing the relationship between the advertiser and the firm which draws attention to:

(i)   the fact that the advertiser is an appointed representative of the firm, and

(ii)   the fact that the advertiser has entered into arrangements with the firm which preclude the advertiser from selling or recommending any products other than those of the firm, and

c   if the advertisement relates to a product of the firm, is not cast in terms which suggest or imply that the product is that of the appointed representative and not that of the firm.

(2) A firm which is a collective investment marketing firm shall ensure that, in an advertisement issued by an appointed representative of the firm which relates to any activity of the appointed representative which is not investment business as well as to an activity of the appointed representative which is investment business, any claim made to independence in respect of the activity which is not investment business does not appear with such prominence relative to the matter in the advertisement which relates to investment business as to create a likelihood that a person reasonably attentive to the advertisement might suppose that the claim to independence applied to the activity of the appointed representative which is investment business.

(3) A firm which is a collective investment marketing firm shall ensure that an advertisement issued by an appointed representative of the firm which is not an advertisement in respect of investment business does not contain any matter referring to the Board or to the fact that the advertiser is connected with a person who is regulated by the Board.

7.29. Advertisements not to disguise lack of independence

(1) A firm which is not a collective investment marketing firm and which has an associate which is:

a   a collective investment marketing firm, or

b   an appointed representative of a collective investment marketing firm,

shall not issue an advertisement of the products or services of the firm in such manner or containing such matter as is likely to cause a reader of the advertisement in its context to suppose that the associate has the same independence as that of the firm.

(2) A firm which is a collective investment marketing firm and which has an appointed representative which is an associate of a person who is not a collective investment marketing firm shall ensure that no advertisement of the products or services of the firm is issued by the appointed representative in such manner or containing such matter as is likely to cause a reader of the advertisement in its context to suppose that the firm has the same independence as that of the said person who is not a col-

lective investment marketing firm.

(3) A firm which is a collective investment marketing firm and which has an associate which is not a collective investment marketing firm shall not issue an advertisement of the products or services of the firm in such manner or containing such matter as is likely to cause a reader of the advertisement in its context to suppose that the firm has the same independence as that of the associate.

Practice Note

The Board considers the following to be an example of a breach of this rule. The issue of an advertisement of the services of financial adviser X (the appointed representative of life office Y) in a brochure which advertises the services generally of firm Z (an independent financial adviser) without special mention of the status of X and so to give the impression that X has the same independence as Z. This would be particularly so if X and Z, being associates, have similar names.

These rules were reproduced with permission from the Securities and Investments Board (SIB).

SFA CONDUCT OF BUSINESS RULES: CHAPTER 5

Advertising and Marketing

*Issue and approval of advertisements**

5–9 (1) Where a *firm issues* or *approves* an *investment advertisement*, it must –

   (a) apply appropriate expertise; and

   (b) be able to show that it believes on reasonable grounds that the advertisement is fair and not misleading. [rel 13]

   (2) Where a *firm issues* or *approves* a *specific investment advertisement*, it must ensure that the advertisement identifies it as issuer or approver, and also identifies SFA as its regulator. [bn 255]

   Guidance

   In order to comply with (2) above *firms* may need to expand on the statement "regulated by SFA". In particular, *passported institutions* should use the phrase "regulated by SFA for the conduct of investment business in the UK", or similar wording. [bn 284]

   (3) A *firm* must not *approve* a *specific investment advertisement* if it relates to units in an *unregulated collective investment scheme.*** [rel 13]

   (4) In circumstances where a *firm issues* or *approves* an *exempt advertisement*, and states that it is regulated by SFA, it must nevertheless comply with the provisions of (1) above. [rel 16]

   (5) Where a *firm* knows, or ought reasonably to know, that another person intends to *issue* an *investment advertisement*, in the United Kingdom or elsewhere, which advertises directly or indirectly the services of that *firm*, it must take reasonable steps to ensure that the advertisement, or the part of the advertisement referring to that *firm* –

   (a) is fair and not misleading; and

   (b) where applicable, includes the *prescribed disclosure.*

   (6) Where a *firm issues* or *approves* a *specific investment advertisement* (including a *direct offer advertisement*), it must take reasonable steps to ensure that the advertisement contains, where applicable, the information set out in (7), (8) and (9) below, unless the advertisement –

   (a) is *issued* by the *firm*, or *approved* by the *firm* for *issue*, to persons who are not *private customers*;

   (b) clearly states that the *investment* or *investment service* which is the subject of the advertisement is not available to *private customers*;

   (c) is contained in a newspaper, journal, magazine or other periodical publication

---

*For the application of the rules relating to *investment advertisements* see rule 5-1(4)

** *Firms* are reminded that when promoting *unregulated collective investment schemes* the Financial Services (Promotion of Unregulated Schemes) Regulations 1991 will apply. These are set out in **Appendix 7** [rel 15]

published and circulating principally outside the United Kingdom and which is directed to persons outside the United Kingdom; or

(d) is a *short form advertisement*.

General contents requirements

(7) In any *specific investment advertisement* (including a *direct offer advertisement*) *issued* or *approved* by the *firm* in accordance with (6) above, the *firm* must take reasonable steps to ensure that the provisions of the table below are complied with.

Table 5–9(7): Investment advertisements general contents requirements

1	**Clarity of purpose** The purpose of any promotional material included in the advertisement must not be disguised in any way.
2	**Clarity of subject** The nature or type of the *investment* or the *investment service* to which the advertisement relates must be clear.
3	**Statements, promises or forecasts** Any statement, promise or forecast must be fair and not misleading in the form and context in which it appears, and where any promise or forecast is based on assumptions, these must be stated within the advertisement.
4	**No false indications** The advertisements must not provide false indications, in particular as to – (a) the issuer's or approver's independence; (b) the issuer's or approver's scale of activities; (c) the extent of the resources of the issuer; (d) the services the issuer intends to provide; or (e) the scarcity of the *investment* or *investment service* concerned.
5	**Prescribed statements to be clearly visible** Any statements made or risk warnings given in the advertisement in accordance with this rule must not be obscured or disguised in any way by the content, design or format of the advertisement.

Specific contents requirements

(8) In any *specific investment advertisement* (including a *direct offer advertisement*) *issued* or *approved* by the *firm* in accordance with (6) above, the *firm* must take reasonable steps to ensure that, where applicable, the provisions of the table below are complied with.

Table 5–9(8): Investment advertisements specific contents requirements

1	**Guarantees**
	The advertisement must not describe an *investment* as guaranteed unless there is a legally enforceable arrangement with a third party who undertakes to meet in full an investor's claim under the guarantee and gives details about both the guarantor and the guarantee sufficient for an investor to make a fair assessment about the value of the guarantee.
2	**Commendations**
	Any commendations quoted must be –
	(a) complete or a fair representation;
	(b) accurate and not misleading at the time of *issue*; and
	(c) relevant to the investment or *investment service* advertised;
	The author must have given his consent to the commendation and, if he is an *associate* or *employee* of the issuer or approver, the advertisement must state that fact.
3	**Comparisons**
	Comparisons or contrasts must –
	(a) be based either on facts verified by the issuer or approver, or on assumptions stated within the advertisement;
	(b) not mislead;
	(c) be presented in a fair and balanced way; and
	(d) not omit anything material to the comparison.
4	**Material interest**
	Where the *firm* knows that it or its *associate* –
	(a) has or may have a position or holding in the *investment* concerned or in a related *investment*; or
	(b) is providing or has provided within the previous 12 months significant advice or *investment services* in relation to the *investment* concerned or a related *investment*,
	it must include a statement to this effect in the advertisement.
5	**Past performance**
	Any information about the past performance of *investments* or of a *firm* must –
	(a) be relevant to the performance of the *investment* or *firm* advertised;
	(b) be a complete record of, or a fair and not misleading representation of, the past performance of the *investment* or *firm*;
	(c) not be selected so as to exaggerate the success or disguise the lack of success of the *investment* or *firm*;

(d) state the source of the information; and

(e) be based on the actual past performance of the investment or firm, and not based on simulated figures.

Guidance

Past performance figures for derivative funds produced in accordance with CFTC rules (except in relation to simulated figures) will fulfil the requirements of the table above. [bn 147]

6	**Past performance for regulated collective investment schemes**

Any information about the past performance of a *regulated collective investment scheme* must –

(a) include information about the previous five years or, if less, the period from the date of issue of the *investment;*

(b) be made on an "offer to bid" basis, and stated as such, where any actual return is stated or comparison is made with another form of investment;

(c) where a comparison is made with an index or other measure of performance, state the basis on which the comparison is made.

7	**Taxation**

If the advertisement contains any reference to the impact of taxation, it must –

(a) state the assumed rate of taxation on whch any matter is based;

(b) state that tax reliefs are as those currently applying, and state that the value of the tax reliefs referred to in the advertisement apply directly to the investor, to the provider of the *investment* or to the fund in which the investor participates, as appropriate;

(c) state if it is the case, that the matters referred to are only relevant to a particular class or classes of investor with particular tax liabilities, identifying the class or classes and liabilities concerned;

(d) not describe the *investment* as being free from any liability to income tax unless equal prominence is given to a statement, if applicable, that the income is payable from a fund from which income tax has already been paid; and

(e) not describe the *investment* as being free from any liability to capital gains tax unless equal prominence is given to a statement, if applicable, that the value of the *investment* is linked to a fund which is liable to that tax.

8	**A reference to cancellation**

Any advertisement for a *packaged product* must state whether or not any *cancellation right* applies, and contain details of the period within which any *cancellation right* may be exercised.

9	**Government and other public securities funds**

Any advertisement for a *regulated collective investment scheme,* where more than 35% of the assets consist of, or are expected to consist of, *government and public securities* issued by one issuer, must state that fact and the name of the issuer concerned.

Risk warnings

(9) A *firm* which *issues* or *approves* a *specific investment advertisement* (including a *direct offer advertisement*) in accordance with (6) above, must take reasonable steps to ensure that the advertisement adequately explains any unusual risks involved and, where appropriate contains the warnings about the *investment* or *investment service* concerned contained in the table below.

Table 5–9(9): Investment advertisements risk warnings

1 Fluctuations in value
Where the *investment* can fluctuate in price or value, a statement must be made that prices, values or income may fall against the investor's interests or, if applicable, a warning must be made that the investor may get back less than he invested. [bn 131]
1A Suitability
Where the advertisement contains or refers to a recommendation about a specific *investment* or *investment service*, a statement must be made warning that the *investment* or *investment service* may not be suitable for all recipients of the advertisement and a recommendation that, if they have any doubts, they should seek advice from their investment adviser. [bn 131]
2 Higher volatility investments
Where the advertisement relates to a *higher volatility investment*, it must state, if it is the case, that the *investment* may be subject to sudden and large falls in value, and that there could be a large loss on realisation which could equal the amount invested.
3 Investment income
Where the *investment* is described as being likely to yield income, or as being suitable for an investor particularly seeking income from his investment, the investor must be warned, if it is the case, that –
(a) income from the *investment* may fluctuate; and
(b) part of the capital invested may be used to pay that income.
4 Foreign currency denominated investments
Where an *investment* is denominated in a currency other than that of the country in which the advertisement is issued, the investor must be warned that changes in rates of exchange may have an adverse effect on the value, price or income of the *investment*.
5 Past performance
Where the advertisement contains information concerning past performance, it must also contain a warning that the past is not necessarily a guide to future performance.
6 Taxation
Where the advertisement contains any reference to the impact of taxation it must also contain a warning that the levels and bases of taxation can change.

7 Investments which are not readily realisable investments

An advertisement for an *investment* which is not a *readily realisable investment* must state that it may be difficult –

(a) for the investor to sell or realise the *investment*; and

(b) to obtain reliable information about its value or the extent of the risks to which it is exposed.

8 Investments for which the market is restricted

An advertisement for a *security* (except units in a *collective investment scheme*) for which a market is made by only one *market maker* must state that fact and, if it is the case, the fact that the only *market maker* is the issuer of the advertisement or an *associate* of the *issuer* of the advertisement.

9 Investments carrying contingent liability

Where an advertisement relates to an *investment* in which the investor may not only lose all of the amount originally invested or deposited, but may also have to pay more later, the advertisement must warn of this fact.

10 With-profits life policies

An advertisement for a *with-profits policy* must state that the return depends on the profits made by the *regulated life office* and on its decisions about their distribution.

11 Front-end loading

An advertisement for an *investment* subject to *front-end loading* must state that deductions for *charges* and expenses are not made uniformly throughout the life of the *investment*, but are loaded disproportionately onto the early years, and the investor must be warned that, if he withdraws from the *investment* in the early years, he may not get back the amount he has invested.

12 Cancellation

Where *cancellation rights* apply –

(a) the advertisement must state that upon cancellation the investor may not obtain a full refund of the amount invested; and

(b) if the advertisement relates to a *higher volatility investment*, the advertisement must state, if it is the case, that the shortfall in the amount recovereed by the investor on cancellation may be large.

13 Property funds

An advertisement for a *property fund*, or which refers to the fact that a property-linked investment fund may be invested in land or interests in land, must state that –

(a) the land and buildings may be difficult to sell and there may be times when the units cannot be sold; and

(b) the value of property is a matter of a valuer's opinion.

Issue and approval of direct offer advertisements

5–10 (1) A *firm* must take reasonable steps to ensure that it does not *issue* or *approve* a *direct offer advertisement* for the *sale* of *investments* or the provision of *investment services* to a *private customer* unless the advertisement gives information about the *investments* or *investment services*, the terms of the offer, and the risks involved, which is adequate and fair having regard to the (United Kingdom or overseas) regulatory protections which apply and the market to which the advertisement is directed. [rel 13]

(2) A *firm* must not *issue* or *approve* a *direct offer advertisement* for the *sale* of, or the provision of *investment services* in respect of, *derivatives* or *warrants*.

(3) Where a *firm* issues or *approves* a *direct offer advertisement*, it must take reasonable steps to ensure that the advertisement contains sufficient information upon which the investor can base his investment decision and, in the case of an execution-only dealing service, must contain the information required in the table below, or, in the case of a *packaged product*, must contain a key features document, prepared in accordance with the rules of the *SRO* which regulates the relevant *regulated life office* or *operator* or with the relevant PIA rules.* [bn 375][bn 420]

TABLE 5–10(3)A [deleted][bn 375]

TABLE 5–10(3)B [deleted][bn 191]

TABLE 5–10(3)C [deleted][bn 420]

Table 5–10(3)D: Direct offer advertisements for an execution-only dealing service

1	The basis or amount of *charges* payable by the *customer*
2	If it is the case, a clear statement that there may be a delay in the execution of *customers' orders*, including the reason for and maximum extent of any such delay [bn 420]
3	If it is the case, a statement that *customers' orders* may be aggregated and that this may operate to some *customers'* disadvantage on occasions

(4) [deleted][bn 375]

5–11 (1)–(2) [deleted][bn 420]

Issue or approval of advertisements for an overseas person

5–12 A *firm* must not *issue* or *approve* a *specific investment advertisement* which is calculated to lead directly or indirectly to an *overseas person* carrying on *investment business* –

(a) which is not *regulated business*; [rel 15]

(b) with or for a *private customer* who is in the United Kingdom,

unless both the advertisement contains the *prescribed disclosure* and the *firm* has no reason to doubt that the *overseas person* will deal with investors in the United Kingdom in an honest and reliable way. [rel 13]

---

*For details of the PIA's contents requirements for key features documents for non-life packaged products see **Appendix 11** [bn 375]

Overseas business for UK private customers

5–13 (1) A *firm* must not carry on *investment business* –

    (a) which is not *regulated business*; [rel 15]

    (b) with or for a *private customer* who is in the United Kingdom,

unless it has made the *prescribed disclosure* to the customer.

    (2) A *firm* must not give an introduction or advice, or make arrangements, with a view to another person carrying on such business with or for such a customer, unless it has both made the *prescribed disclosure* and has no reason to doubt that the customer will be dealt with in an honest and reliable way. [rel 13]

Business conducted from an overseas place of business with overseas customers

5–14 (1) If, in any oral or written communication made or advertisement *issued* to a *private customer* outside the United Kingdom in connection with *investment business* which is not *regulated business*, a *firm* indicates that it is an *authorised person*, it must also, and with equal prominence, make the *prescribed disclosure*. [rel 13]

    (2) In respect of any oral or written communication, a *firm* need not include the *prescribed disclosure* in accordance with (1) above where it has already made the *prescribed disclosure* in writing to the *private customer* to whom the communication is made. [bn 70]

Fair and clear communications

5–15 (1) A *firm* may make an oral or written communication with another person which is designed to promote the provision of *investment services* only if it can show that it believes on reasonable grounds that the communication is fair and not misleading.

    (2) A *firm* must take reasonable steps to ensure that any written agreement, communication, notification or information which it gives or sends to a *private customer* to whom it provides *investment services* is presented fairly and clearly. [rel 13]

Information about the firm

5–16 A *firm* must take reasonable steps to ensure that a *private customer* to whom it provides *investment services* is given adequate information about its identity and business address, the identity and status with the *firm* of *employees* and other relevant *agents* with whom the *private customer* has contact and the identity of SFA as the *firm's* regulator. [rel 13][rel 15]

Guidance

A *firm* will be regarded as complying with the requirement to give adequate information about the identity of SFA as the *firm's* regulator, if it uses the statement "regulated by SFA" or in the case of a *passported institution*, "regulated by SFA for the conduct of investment business in the UK", or similar wording on relevant documentation. [bn 255][bn 284]

Extracts taken from the SFA Rulebook as at 9 September 1997 and reproduced with permission from the Securities and Futures Authority (SFA).

IMRO CONDUCT OF BUSINESS RULES CHAPTER 11: SECTION 1:
SEEKING CUSTOMERS AND ADVERTISING FOR BUSINESS

Appendix 1.1(1): The Advertising Code

This code describes the standards set by IMRO for judging whether an Investment Advertisement meets the requirements of paragraph (a)(ii) of Rule 1.1(1) and paragraph (a) of Rule 1.3(1).

General Requirements

To follow the code a Firm should [do the following]:

1 **Clarity of purpose:** make it plain that the advertisement contains promotional material and has a promotional purpose and make the advertisement distinct from any other matter contained in the medium which carries it;

2 **Clarity of subject:** describe clearly the nature of the investment or the services to which the advertisement relates;

3 **Avoidance of misleading statements, promises or forecasts:** take all reasonable steps to ensure that any statement, promise or forecast to be included or approved is not misleading in form or context;

4 **Verification of statements of fact:** have formed the reasonable belief (on the basis of evidence of which a record is kept or to which access may be obtained):

   (a) that any statement relevant to the product or services being advertised and purporting to be a statement of fact is true; and

   (b) that any such statement will remain true during the currency of the advertisement;

5 **Statements of opinion:** take all reasonable steps to ensure that the person giving any statement of opinion is of that opinion at the time when the advertisement is issued or approved;

6 **Disclosure of capacity:** if the Firm or an Associate is a Market Maker in any Investment being advertised, state that fact;

7 **Disclosure of Material Interests and conflicts:** if in relation to the Investment or Investment Services which are the subject of the advertisement the Firm has directly or indirectly a Material Interest (except for an interest arising solely from the mere participation of the Firm as agent for the Customer) or a relationship of any description with another party which may involve a conflict with the Firm's duty to the Customer, state that fact and disclose the nature of the interest or relationship.

Note: An example of a Material Interest is where a Firm or an Associate has a Long or Short Position in an Investment which is not a Readily Realisable Investment and the Firm is recommending recipients to buy or, as the case may be, sell that Investment.

General Prohibitions

To follow the code a Firm should not [do the following]:

8 **Promotions not to be disguised:** issue an advertisement with the intention of persuading anyone who responds to it to transact Investment Business of a kind not described in the advertisement;

9 **No false claims of independence:** claim or suggest independence of itself or any of its Associates in giving advice, making recommendations or exercising discretion unless such claim or suggestion may properly be made;

10 **Advertisements not to claim government, etc., approval:** state or imply that the

Investment or services being advertised or any other matter in the advertisement has been approved by IMRO, SIB or any governmental or other public regulatory body unless:

(a) approval has been given in writing; or

(b) the advertisement is issued by or on behalf of Her Majesty's Government;

except that, if an investment has been recognised by the Inland Revenue for the purpose of qualifying investors for relief from taxation, the advertisement may say so;

11 No suppression of required statements: disguise the significance of any statement, warning or other matter required by the Advertising Rules to be included in an advertisement either through relative lack of prominence or by the inclusion of matter likely to detract from it;

12 No false indications about scale of business: include any statement indicating the scale of the activities or the extent of the resources of the advertiser which implies that the resources available to support performance of its obligations are greater than they are;

13 Advertisement not to include inappropriate reference to IMRO: if the advertisement does not relate to Investment Business, include any matter referring to IMRO.

Specific Requirements

If an advertisement contains any of the items [laid out in bold] ... below, to follow the code a Firm should [do the following]:

14 Synopsis or selection: state enough of the relevant features to give a fair view of the Investment or Investment Agreement being advertised, including the financial commitments and risks involved, and state how full details may be obtained;

15 Information about past performance of Investments or of an Investment Manager: include information about past performance only if:

(a) it is relevant to the performance of the Investment or investment management service advertised;

(b) it is complete, or is a fair and not misleading representation of the past performance of the Investment or investment management service;

(c) it has not been selected so as to exaggerate (or disguise) the success (or lack of success) of the Investment or investment management service over the period to which the information relates; and

(d) the source of the information is stated and the advertisement contains a warning that the past is not necessarily a guide to future performance;

16 Invitation to enter into an Investment Agreement with a named person: make it clear, by statement or by necessary implication, whether the person offering any Investment or service is to contract as principal or agent and (if that person is to act as agent) give the name of the principal if the principal can be identified at the time when the advertisement is issued;

17 Information about taxation: if any references are made to taxation:

(a) include a warning that the levels and bases of, and reliefs from, taxation can change;

(b) where a matter is based upon an assumed rate of taxation, state the rate;

(c) (i) state that any tax reliefs referred to are those currently available and that their value depends on the individual circumstances of the investor; and

(ii) make it clear whether any tax reliefs (or freedom from taxation) referred to in the advertisement apply directly to the investor, to the provider of the Investment or to the fund in which the investor participates or, if such is the case, to more than one of them;

(d) state whether the matters referred to are only relevant to a particular class or classes of investor with particular tax liabilities and identify the class or classes and liabilities concerned;

(e) do not describe the Investment as being free from any liability to capital gains tax unless equal prominence is given to a statement, if applicable, that the value of the Investment is linked to a fund which is liable to that tax; and

(f) do not describe the income from the Investment as being free from any liability to income tax unless equal prominence is given to a statement, if applicable, that the income is payable out of a fund which is liable to that tax.

Specific Prohibitions

If an advertisement is of a kind described, or contains any of the items [laid out in bold] . . . below, to follow the code a Firm should not [do the following]:

18 Material stating or implying limited availability: claim or imply limited availability of Investments or services (e.g. limited quantity, limited period of offer, or special terms for a limited period) unless justified;

19 Testimonials: quote from a testimonial or commendation unless the quotation is:

(a) complete, or a fair representation of the whole;

(b) accurate and not misleading at the time when the advertisement is issued; and

(c) relevant to the Investment or service advertised;

and the author has given his consent to the advertisement and, if he is an employee, Officer or Associate of the Firm, the advertisement says so;

20 Comparisons or contrasts: include any comparison or contrast, for example with other Investments, expenditure, assets, services or indices, unless it is fair and the Firm should also not omit factors which are likely to be relevant to an appreciation of such comparison or contrast;

21 Advertisements issued by Appointed Representatives: include any matter referring:

(a) to IMRO except in relation to the Permitted Business of a Firm on whose behalf the Appointed Representative is acting; or

(b) to the fact that the advertiser is connected with a Firm if the advertisement is not in respect of the Permitted Business of that Firm;

or state that the Appointed Representative is an Authorised Person;

22 Guarantees describe any Investment is guaranteed unless there is a legally enforceable arrangement with a third party who undertakes to meet in full an investor's claim under the guarantee.

Risk Warnings

To follow the code a Firm should give the following risk warnings, if applicable:

23 An Investment which can fluctuate in value: for an Investment which can fluctuate in value, a statement should warn that values may fall as well as rise and that the investor may not get back the amount he has invested;

24 High yield Investments: for an Investment described as being likely to yield a high income or as suitable for an investor particularly seeking income from his investment, the investor should be warned, if it is the case, that income from the Investment may fluctuate in value in money terms;

25   Investments involving exposure to a foreign currency: for an Investment involving exposure to a currency other than that in which acquisitions of the Investment are invited, the investor should be warned that changes in rates of exchange may cause the value of the Investment to go up or down;

26 Investments which are not Readily Realisable Investments: for an Investment which is not a Readily Realisable Investment, the advertisement should state that there is no recognised market for the Investment and that it may, therefore, be difficult for the investor to deal in the Investment or for him to obtain reliable information about its value or the extent of the risks to which it is exposed:

27 Investments for which the market is restricted: for an Investment for which a market is made by fewer than three independent Market Makers (that is, persons who are not Associates of each other), the advertisement should state this fact and, if it is the case, the fact that the advertiser is the only Market Maker;

28 Investments which are front-end-loaded or risk significant loss on realisation:

(a) for an Investment where deductions for charges and expenses are not made uniformly throughout the life of the Investment but are loaded disproportionately on to the early years, the advertisement should state this fact;

(b) for a Readily Realisable Investment which in the reasonable opinion of the advertiser may only be readily realisable at a significant loss the advertisement should include a statement to that effect and the reason for it;

29 Investments carrying contingent liability:

(a) for an Investment where the Customer may not only lose all of the amount he originally invested but also may have to pay more money later, the advertisement should warn the investor that he may lose more than the amount of his original investment;

(b) for an Investment of the type described in sub-paragraph (a) above where the advertisement promotes advisory or discretionary services in relation to transactions effected otherwise than on a Recognised or Designated Investment Exchange and in a contract of a type traded on those exchanges, the advertisement should state that such transactions are only suitable for a person who has experience in transactions of that description;

Note: Under Rule 3.13(1) of Chapter 11, a Firm must not effect, arrange or recommend an off-exchange Contingent Liability Transaction to a Private Customer unless it believes on reasonable grounds that the purpose of the transaction is to hedge against currency risk involved in a position which the Customer holds.

30 Warrants: for a Warrant, the advertisement should state that a Warrant often involves a high degree of gearing so that a relatively small movement in the price of the Security to which the Warrant relates may result in a disproportionately large movement, unfavourable as well as favourable, in the price of the Warrant;

31 Advertising of so-called 'High Income' Products: where a Firm issues or approves an Advertisement for an Investment product or service which offers 'high income', it should ensure that:

(a) the use of the term 'income', either in the name of the product or to describe payments to investors, is not misleading in form or context; if 'income' payments to investors constitute a return of capital either in whole or in part, this should be made clear; a Firm should bear in mind what investors are likely to understand by the term; where 'income' payments do not represent a distribution of interest, and/or dividend or other earnings, this should be explained clearly and prominently at an early point in the Advertisement;

(b) the Advertisement makes clear, if it is the case, the extent to which the forecast rate of 'income' will be achieved by foregoing the potential for future capital growth; any claim that the risk of capital depreciation is limited should be balanced by an explanation of any limitation on the potential for capital recovery;

(c) all the risks to an investor's capital, or to maintenance of 'income' payments at the advertised rate are fully explained, having regard to the particular nature of the product;

(d) any comparison of the product the subject of the Advertisement either directly or indirectly with bank and building society deposits or other investment and deposit-based savings vehicles is not made unless its distinguishing features and attendant risks are adequately explained.

(e) the use, size and prominence afforded to the description of the 'income' payments, together with any associated graphics or figures are not such as to distract from the salient features of the product and the nature of the risks involved; in particular, the advertised rate of income should not be presented in such a way as to imply that it is 'guaranteed' or 'certain' where this is not the case; and if the relevant risk factors are not placed alongside or immediately after the advertised rate of 'income', prominent signposting should be provided indicating where they may be found, and all the risk factors should appear with sufficient prominence relative to other text to ensure that the significance of the risks is not disguised;

32 Higher Volatility Funds: that, in the case of a Higher Volatility Fund, the loss on realisation [or cancellation] may be very high (including total loss of the investment), as the value of such an investment may fall suddenly and substantially;

33 Real Property: that, where the underlying investments of a fund consist wholly or substantially of real property, it may be difficult or impossible to realise an investment because the real property concerned may not be readily saleable, and that the value of the real property concerned is generally a matter of a valuer's opinion;

34 Government and Other Public Securities: that more than 35% of the property of a Regulated Collective Investment Scheme (at the time when the advertisement is prepared for issue) consists, or is likely to consist, of Government and other public, securities issued by one issuer, together with the identity of that issuer;

35 Charges deducted from capital: in relation to units in a Regulated Collective Investment Scheme, a statement:

(a) explaining that the objective of the scheme is to maximise distributable income, or to place an equal emphasis on the generation of income and on capital growth, and to this end all or part of the Manager's periodic charge will be taken out of capital. The likely effect of this should also be explained, in particular how capital may be eroded or future growth constrained; and

(b) where a gross distribution yield is quoted showing the level, or maximum level, of the Manager's periodic charge which may be charged to capital, explaining that the distributable income is increased by that amount and that the capital will therefore be reduced by a similar amount. Reference should also be made to the fact that when compared with a fund which charges expenses to income, and unless units are held within a PEP, the increase in income will result in some increased income tax liability for unitholders and, where applicable, a reduction in liability for capital gains tax.

Other Provisions Relating to Packaged Products

If an advertisement relates to a Packaged Product which is not a Life Policy, to follow the code a Firm should [do the following]:

36 Forecasts or illustrations: not include a forecast or illustration of the realisable value of an investment in units in a Regulated Collective Investment Scheme except in accordance with the requirements of rule 6.2(4);

37 Comparisons with Unregulated Collective Investment Schemes: not include any comparison or contrast of the performance or the likely performance of an investment in units in a Regulated Collective Investment Scheme with an investment in an Unregulated Collective Investment Scheme;

38 Past performance: not include any information about past performance of such a Packaged Product unless the advertisement includes information relating to the performance of the investment during the period of five years, or if it has been in existence for less than five years, for the period during which it has been in existence, ending with the date on which the advertisement is approved for issue; and

(a) if reference is made to an actual return to an investor, or a comparison of performance is made with other forms of investment, the reference or comparison is made on an 'offer to bid' basis, and the basis is stated or otherwise apparent;

(b) if a comparison is made of performance with an index or with movements in the price of units, the basis on which the comparison is made (for example, 'offer to offer' or 'offer to bid') is stated or otherwise apparent;

and any such comparison is fair;

39 Cancellation state: the period within which any right to cancel may be exercised and whether that right is granted by the Cancellation Rules or given voluntarily, and should state:

(a) if it is the case, that upon cancellation the investor will not recover his investment in full should the market have fallen since the investment was acquired; and

(b) in relation to a Higher Volatility Fund, that the shortfall in what he recovers should the market have fallen could be very high because of the possibility of sudden and large falls in the value of the units.

These rules were reproduced with permission from the Investment Management Regulatory Organisation (IMRO).

PIA RULES ON ADVERTISING AND PROMOTING YOUR BUSINESS

PIA: Part 18

TABLE 18A: WARNINGS

Type of investment	Warning to the investor
An investment designed to be retained over a long period	This investment is intended as a long-term investment.
An investment that is *front-end-loaded*	If you withdraw from this investment in the early years, you may not get back the full amount invested.
An investment that may fluctuate in monetary value (including high yield investments); and	Because this investment may go down in value as well as up, you may not get back the full amount invested.
(where the advertisement refers to cancellation rights) falls	If you have cancellation rights and exercise them you will not receive a full refund if the value of the investment before the cancellation notice is received by the product provider; the reduction in the refund will be equal to the fall in the price of the investment
An investment denominated in a foreign currency	Changes in rates of exchange may have an adverse effect on the value or price of the investment in sterling terms.
An investment which is **not** *readily realisable*	It may be difficult to: (a) sell or realise the investment and (b) obtain reliable information about its value or the extent of the risks to which it is exposed.
An investment carrying a *contingent liability*	If the value of this investment falls, you may not only lose all of the amount you originally invested or deposited, but may also have to pay more money later.
An investment about which *the member does not intend to give advice*	This investment is not suitable for everyone. If you have any doubt whether it is suitable for you, you should obtain expert advice.
A *security* for which the market is made by only one *market maker*	It may be difficult to sell or realise the investment.

TABLE **18B**: DISCLOSURE REQUIREMENTS

If the advertisement includes:	
a **quotation** from any statement praising or recommending the investment or service advertised	you must ensure that the quotation is: (a) complete, or a fair representation of the whole; (b) accurate and not misleading at the time when the advertisement is *issued*; **and** (c) relevant to the investment or service advertised; you must not use the quotation unless the author or publisher has given his consent to the advertisement and, if he is a *connected person* of yours, the advertisement must say so;
a **forecast** of a specific growth rate or rate of return	the advertisement must clearly indicate: (a) the basis upon which the forecast is made; (b) whether reinvestment of income is assumed; (c) whether account has been taken of taxes (and if so, the rate of tax); **and** (d) whether the forecast will be subject to any deductions upon premature realisation or otherwise;
information about past performance of an investment or business	(a) the information must be relevant to the performance of the investment or business advertised; (b) the information must be a complete record of, or a fair and not misleading representation of, the past performance of the investment or business, and must relate to as recent a period as is practicable; (c) the information must not be selected so as to exaggerate the success or disguise the lack of success of the investment or business; (d) (i) if reference is made to an actual return to an investor, or a comparison of performance is made with other forms of investment, the reference or comparison must be made on an 'offer to bid' basis, and the basis must be stated or otherwise apparent;

	(ii) if a comparison is made of performance with an index or with movements in the price of units, the comparison must be made on an 'offer to offer' basis, and the basis must be stated or otherwise apparent;
	(e) the advertisement must specify whether or not the past performance was based on income reinvestment; the advertisement must state the source of the information, identify the time period to which it relates and contain the following statement: 'The past is not necessarily a guide to future performance';
a **guarantee**	the advertisement must clearly identify the elements of the investment that are guaranteed and those that are not;
	it must include the following statement:
	'If the performance of this investment does not match the guarantee given you will not, for that reason alone, be entitled to compensation under the Investors' Compensation Scheme';
a reference to the impact of **taxation**	the advertisement must:
	(a) contain the following warning: 'Levels and bases of, and reliefs from, taxation are subject to change';
	(b) where a matter is based upon an assumed rate of taxation, state the rate;
	(c) state that any tax reliefs referred to are those currently applying and that their value depends on the individual circumstances of the investor;
	(d) make it clear whether any tax reliefs referred to in the advertisement apply directly to the investor, to the provider of the investment or to the fund in which the investor participates;
	(e) state whether the matters referred to are only relevant to a particular class or classes of investor with particular tax liabilities and identify the class or classes and liabilities concerned;
	(f) not describe the investment as being free from any liability to capital gains

	tax unless equal prominence is given to a statement, if applicable, that the value of the investment is linked to a fund which is liable to that tax; **and**
	(g) not describe the income from the investment as being free from any liability to income tax unless equal prominence is given to a statement, if applicable, that the income is payable out of a fund which is liable to tax;
a **comparison** or **contrast**	the comparison or contrast must be based on facts verified by the issuer or approver, must be presented in a fair and balanced way, and must not be misleading or omit anything material.

TABLE 18C: REQUIREMENTS RELATING TO OVERSEAS BUSINESS AND OVERSEAS CLIENTS

(1) If

  (a) you issue an **advertisement** to *private clients* who are **outside the United Kingdom** in connection with investment business which is not *regulated business*,

and

  (b) the advertisement indicates that you are an *authorised person* (by referring to your FIMBRA membership or in any other way)

you must, with equal prominence, make the Prescribed Disclosure set out below.

(2) If you *issue* or *approve* a *specific investment advertisement* which is likely to lead to an *overseas person* conducting investment business

  (a) which is not regulated business

  (b) with or for a client who is in the United Kingdom

you must

    (i) have no reason to doubt that the overseas person will deal with investors in the United Kingdom in an honest and reliable way, **and**

    (ii) ensure that the advertisement contains the Prescribed Disclosure set out overleaf.

THE PRESCRIBED DISCLOSURE

A written statement making clear

(1) that[all] [most] of the rules, regulations and arrangements made under the *Act* for the protection of investors do not apply;

(2) that (where relevant) the client will not have the following rights under the United Kingdom regulatory system:

   (a) the right to refer a complaint against you to arbitration under the Consumer Arbitration Scheme for FIMBRA;

   (b) the right to have money which you hold on his behalf protected under the *Client Money Regulations*;

   (c) the right to be informed in advance about any commission you will receive and any fees you will or may charge, and for those fees not to be excessive;

   (d) the right to receive recommendations which are suitable to him and his circumstances;

   (e) the right to an explanation of the risks involved in any transaction;

   (f) the right to have a transaction executed at the best price available in the relevant market at the time ('best execution');

(3) if the business in question is outside the territorial limits on the Investors' Compensation Scheme (because, for example, the client is overseas and the business will not be done directly with your base in the United Kingdom, or for any other reason), that compensation under the Investors' Compensation Scheme will not be available.

(You may include in the statement a reference to any protection or compensation available under another system of regulation.)

APPENDIX 2B: ADDITIONAL REQUIREMENTS FOR SPECIFIC INVESTMENT ADVERTISEMENTS
(including Direct Offer Advertisements)

*The requirements in this Appendix 2B are **in addition to** any relevant requirements set out in Table 18A or 18B (see Rules 18.9 and 18.10).*

NOTE 1

LIFE POLICY OR PENSION CONTRACTS

A   Specific Investment Advertisements

Contents

No additional requirements.

Warnings

If with-profits
'The return on this investment depends on the profits made by the life office and on its policy as to their distribution (whether on early encashment or in adverse market conditions or other circumstances).'
If linked to a *higher volatility fund*, as in Appendix 2B Note 3A.
If linked to a *property fund* or a *life office* investment fund comprising land or interests in land, as in Appendix 2B Note 4A.

Disclosure

Whether any benefits are fixed and the amounts of such benefits, and which benefits are not fixed amounts.
Details of the period within which any right to cancel under The Financial Services (Cancellation) Rules may be exercised.
If linked to a *higher volatility fund*, as in Appendix 2B Note 3A.
If linked to a *property fund* or a life office investment fund comprising land or interests in land, as in Appendix 2B Note 4A.

B   Direct Offer Advertisements

Contents

(1) If the advertisement is directed at a particular client, or at any person whose circumstances or investment objectives you know, you must comply with Rule 29.8.2(1) as if the advertisement were a recommendation.

(2) If the policy advertised is unit-linked, you must include in the advertisement

   (a) how details about the prices and yields of the units may be obtained;

   (b) the most recent difference between the *bid* and *offer prices* for the units, expressed as a percentage of the maximum offer price;

(c)   the maximum difference permitted or, if there is no maximum, the discretion available to the life office to vary the difference;

(d)   the basis on which units will be allocated on payment of premiums, including allocation rates, the timing of the allocation and any charges that may be payable.

Warnings

No additional requirements.

Disclosure

No additional requirements.

NOTE 2

Regulated collective investment schemes

A Specific Investment Advertisements

Contents

No additional requirements.

Warnings

No additional requirements.

Disclosure

Details of the period within which any right to cancel under The Financial Services (Cancellation) Rules may be exercised.

If more than 35 per cent of the property of the scheme consists, or may consist, of Government and other public securities issued by one issuer, a statement to that effect and the identity of the issuer.

B Direct Offer Advertisements

Contents

(1) a description of the investment objectives of the scheme and of any policies that the scheme operator proposes to adopt in selecting the investments in which the funds of the scheme will be invested;

(2) the most recent difference between the *bid* and *offer prices* of the units in the scheme, expressed as a percentage of the maximum offer price;

(3) the maximum permitted difference or, if there is no maximum, the discretion available to the scheme operator to vary the difference;

(4) the price at which the units will be issued or, if the price is not fixed at the time the advertisement is issued, the basis for determining the price;

(5) the nature and amount (or rate) of the charges payable by the investor (including charges included in the price at which units are to be issued) and what discretion the scheme operator has to vary them;

(6) what the annual gross yield is expected to be on the basis of the most recent price at which units are to be issued;

(7) how information about current prices of units and the most recent yield or the anticipated yield may be obtained;

(8) whether (and, if so, how) an investor may authorise the income due to him to be reinvested in the scheme;

(9)   the name and address of any trustee or custodian, or both;

(10) when certificates will be sent to the investor;

(11) the frequency with which the property of the scheme is valued for the purposes of determining the issue and redemption prices of units;

(12) when the scheme operator will be available and willing to deal in the units;

(13) how units may be redeemed;

(14) when payments on redemption will be made;

(15) the address from which scheme particulars can be obtained.

Warnings

No additional requirements.

Disclosure

A key features document complying with Rule 29.8.2(2)(d), or all the information such a document is required to contain including a statement about any commission receivable by you or any of your *associates*.

*(If the scheme is also a Higher Volatility Fund or a Property Fund,
or linked to such a fund, see Note 3 or 4 below.)*

NOTE 3

HIGHER VOLATILITY FUNDS

(INCLUDING LIFE POLICIES, PENSION CONTRACTS AND REGULATED COLLECTIVE INVESTMENT SCHEMES LINKED TO SUCH FUNDS)

A Specific Investment Advertisements

Contents

As for *regulated collective investment schemes* (see Appendix 2B, Note 2A).
Forecasts or illustrations of benefit, performance or realisable value are **not permitted**.

Warnings

'Because of the volatile nature of the investment, a fall in its value could result in your recovering nothing at all.'

Disclosure

Details of the period within which any **right to cancel** under The Financial Services (Cancellation) Rules may be exercised.

If any figures are given for past performance, they must be either for the 5-year period immediately preceding the issue of the advertisement, **or** (if the fund has not been in existence for 5 years) for the whole period since the fund began

The advertisement **must not compare or contrast the performance** (or likely performance) of the investment with that **of an unregulated** *collective investment scheme.*

B Direct Offer Advertisements

Contents

Not additional requirements.

Warnings

No additional requirements.

Disclosure

No additional requirements.

NOTE 4

PROPERTY FUNDS

(INCLUDING LIFE POLICIES, PENSION CONTRACTS AND REGULATED COLLECTIVE INVESTMENT SCHEMES LINKED TO SUCH FUNDS)

A   Specific Investment Advertisements

Contents

As for *regulated collective investment schemes* (see Appendix 2B, Note 2A).

Warnings

(Where the advertisement refers to the fact that the fund may be invested in land or interests in land).

'The value of land and buildings is generally a matter of a valuer's opinion rather than fact.

You may not be able to encash your investment whenever you choose because the land and buildings in the fund may not always be easy to sell and, during periods when they are not readily saleable, [the fund manager may refuse to repurchase your units] [the *life office* may refuse to accept a surrender of your policy].'

Disclosure

Details of the period within which any **right to cancel** under The Financial Services (Cancellation) Rules may be exercised.

The advertisement **must not compare or contrast the performance** (or likely performance) of the investment with that **of an unregulated collective investment scheme.**

B   Direct Offer Advertisements

Contents

No additional requirements.

Warnings

No additional requirements.

Disclosure

No additional requirements.

NOTE 5

BUSINESS EXPANSION SCHEMES

A *BES specific investment advertisement* is not permitted unless it is for

(1) *BES shares* by means of a prospectus or private offer;

(2) a *BES fund* the terms of which permit no more than 27.5 per cent. of the subscriptions to be invested in any one company;

(3) a *BES managed portfolio.*

A Specific Investment Advertisements

Contents

Forecasts or illustrations of performance or realisable value are **not permitted**.

You **must not use the term** '**guaranteed**', or any other term signifying certainty, in relation to the security or performance of a BES investment unless there is an arrangement with a third party, legally enforceable against it by the client, under which that party undertakes to meet the client's claim if the performance of the investment fails to match the guarantee given or representation made in respect of it.

Warnings

'Because this investment may go down in value as well as up, you may not get back the full amount invested.'

'It may be difficult to:

(a) sell or realise the investment

and

(b) obtain reliable information about its value or the extent of the risks to which it is exposed.'

'Levels and bases of, and reliefs from, taxation are subject to change.'

(If the advertisement is for a *BES scheme*)

'You should not subscribe to this scheme until you

(a) have read and understood the terms and conditions of the scheme particulars, and

(b) are aware of the risks involved in BES shares and BES schemes.'

Disclosure

A statement that

(a) any tax reliefs referred to are those currently applying;

(b) their value depends on the individual circumstances of the investor, and

(c) they are only relevant to a particular class or classes of investor with particular tax liabilities (identifying the class or classes and liabilities concerned).

B   Direct Offer Advertisements

Contents

1   *(BES shares)*

A statement of all such information as the addressee of the advertisement and his professional advisers would reasonably require and reasonably expect to find in the advertisement for the purpose of making an informed assessment of the assets and liabilities, financial position, profits and losses and prospects of the company in question and the rights attaching to those shares (a 'statement of prescribed information').

2   *(BES Schemes)*

(1) A copy of the prospectus or (if none) a statement of prescribed information relating to each company in which at the time the advertisement is issued the *scheme manager*

(a) has to his knowledge a *material interest*, and

(b) intends to acquire interests on behalf of the scheme; and

(2) a prominent statement that applications may only be made and accepted subject to the terms and conditions of the scheme particulars; and

(3) the scheme particulars, as follows:

Scheme Particulars

Required Contents

1   The following statements with particular prominence:

(a) a statement that investment in unquoted shares carries higher risks than investment in quoted shares, and

(b) a statement to the effect that investments in unquoted shares may be difficult to realise, that there can be no certainty that market makers will be prepared to deal in them and, where the investment objectives of the scheme include investment in private companies, that restrictions may apply to the transfer of shares in such companies, and

(c) a statement that proper information for determining the current value of investments may not be available, and

(d) a statement to the effect that the recipient should before proceeding seek expert advice, and

(e) a statement that the scheme manager is regulated in the conduct of his investment business by FIMBRA.

2   The following statement:

'The [member][fund manager][scheme manager][and its directors][has][have] taken all reasonable care to ensure that all facts stated in this document are true and accurate in all material respects and there are no other material facts the omission of which would make misleading any statement herein whether of fact or opinion.

The [member] [fund manager] [scheme manager] [and its directors] accepts(s) responsibility accordingly.'

3 The name and business address of:

(a) the scheme manager, and

(b) the promoter of the scheme (if any), and

(c) every person acting in a professional capacity in relation to the scheme, and

(d) every person likely to take part in any decision or recommendation relating to investment of money subscribed to the scheme.

4 The opening and closing dates for receipt of subscriptions.

5 The maximum and minimum sizes, if any, proposed for the scheme.

6 The maximum and minimum permitted individual subscription to the scheme.

7 A statement of the arrangements for the holding of subscription money pending investment.

8 The arrangements for the return of subscription money should the scheme be over-subscribed or the money not accepted for other reasons.

9 The arrangements for the return of subscription money remaining uninvested at the time when the final investment of the scheme has been made or the final date for investment has passed.

10 Any arrangements by virtue of which any preferential treatment will or may be given in relation to subscription to the scheme to particular persons or classes of person subscribing to the scheme.

11 The circumstances in which persons or particular classes of person are excluded from participation in the scheme or in any particular investment of scheme money.

12 The manner in which shares in companies in which money is to be invested are to be held on behalf of participants in the scheme and the manner in which, according to their subscriptions, interest in such shares is to be allocated to each participant.

13 Any arrangement for registering shares in the names of participants in the scheme at or after the end of the period during which shares must be held in order to obtain tax relief.

14 Any arrangements for the payment of dividends, if any, to participants in the scheme.

15 The circumstances in which a person's participation in the scheme may be terminated.

16 Any arrangements for dealing with scheme money which becomes available as a result of a sale of scheme investments by the scheme manager.

17 The scheme manager's powers and discretions in relation to the scheme, including, for example, the exercise of voting rights, the selection and the disposal of investments and syndication of the scheme with other sources of investment.

18 The following information concerning charges and costs to be stated together in a part of the document dealing solely with that information:

(a) the amount or rate of the scheme manager's remuneration currently charged, whether that may be varied in any way in the future and, if so, the maximum to which it may be increased, and

(b) the same information as under sub-paragraph 18(a) but in relation to any other charges or costs made or arising in connection with the scheme.

19　The commission rate payable to any intermediary in return for his introducing participants to the scheme.

20　Whether the scheme manager remains free to subscribe for shares, or to hold options to do so, in companies in which the scheme is invested and, if so, an indication of the price or the formula by which a price is determined at which he may subscribe and the maximum proportion of the ordinary share capital of those companies for which he may subscribe or which may be the subject of options in his favour.

21　Whether the scheme manager proposes to establish another BES scheme, and, if so, whether or not arrangements exist to ensure that the scheme manager does not discriminate between one BES scheme and another and, if such arrangements exist, what they are.

22　A summary of the fiscal provisions concerning the Business Expansion Scheme.

23　A description of any arrangements there may be:

(a) for securing that any person who knowingly has a material interest in any decision or recommendation concerning the investment of subscriptions which is not subject to independent approval is excluded from participation in the making of that decision or recommendation, and

(b) for securing independent approval of decisions and recommendations concerning the investment of subscriptions which may be made by persons who have a material interest in them,

or, if no arrangements exist relating to any of the above matters, a statement to that effect.

24　If the arrangements described in accordance with paragraph 23 do not cover any of the following interests:

(a) an interest of the scheme manager or of an associate of his arising by way of remuneration in connection with the management or operation of the scheme or any other BES scheme,

(b) an interest arising from investment of subscriptions of the scheme or of any other BES scheme of which the scheme manager of the scheme in question or his associate is also the scheme manager,

(c) an interest of an authorised institution within the meaning of the Banking Act 1987 resulting from a loan made by such an institution,

(d) an interest arising from the formation by the scheme manager or his associate of a company with a view to interests in that company being acquired on behalf of BES schemes of which he or his associate is the scheme manager,

the fact that they do not cover that interest need not be disclosed if there be disclosed the fact that investment may be made despite the existence of such an interest and, in the case of (c), details of any arrangements made to avoid conflicts of interest or, if there be no such arrangements, that fact.

25 If the scheme manager has any interest (whether direct or indirect) or duty the nature of which may place him in conflict with the interests of participants in the scheme or his duty to those participants, particulars of that interest or duty.

26 A statement at the head of any summary contained in the scheme particulars that the summary must be read subject to the full terms and conditions of the scheme as set out in the scheme particulars.

27 A statement of any arrangements to enable participants in the scheme to notify the scheme manager of companies with which they are connected within the meaning of section 291 of the Income and Corporation Taxes Act 1988.

28 A statement of the investment policies and objectives of the scheme including, for example, details of the status, nature, location and types of business activities of the companies in which it is intended the scheme should be invested.

29 A statement of what periodic reports will be made to participants and how frequently those reports will be made in compliance with the requirements of these Rules.

Warnings

No additional requirements.

Disclosure

No additional requirements.

NOTE 6

INVESTMENT TRUST SAVINGS SCHEMES

A   Specific Investment Advertisements

Contents

No additional requirements

Warnings

No additional requirements.

Disclosure

No additional requirements.

B   Direct Offer Advertisements

Contents

No additional requirements.

Warnings

No additional requirements.

Disclosure

A key features document complying with Rule 29.8.2(2)(d), or all the information such a document is required to contain including a statement about any commission receivable by you or any of your *associates*.

NOTE 7

PERSONAL EQUITY PLANS

A Specific Investment Advertisements

Contents

No additional requirements

Warnings

No additional requirements.

Disclosure

(If the Plan invests only in *regulated collective investment schemes*)
details of the period during which any right to cancel under The Financial Services
(Cancellation) Rules may be exercised.

B Direct Offer Advertisements

Contents

(If the Plan invests to any extent in regulated collective investment schemes) as set out in
Appendix 2B Note 2B.

Warnings

No additional requirements.

Disclosure

No additional requirements.

NOTE 8

PROPERTY ENTERPRISE TRUSTS
AND
ENTERPRISE ZONE PROPERTY UNIT TRUSTS

A   Specific Investment Advertisements

Contents

No additional requirements

Warnings

(The following warning must be included in any advertisement for these investments. Where the advertisement is issued to a *private client*, the risk warning must be signed by the client and returned to you before you arrange or carry out for him any transaction to which it relates.)

Investments in [Property Enterprise Trusts] [Enterprise Zone Property Unit Trusts]

This warning notice draws your attention to the risks associated with investments in [Property Enterprise Trusts (PETs)] [Enterprise Zone Property Unit Trusts (EZPUTs)].

As with property in general, the value of the property in these schemes can go down as well as up. Enterprise Zone property is subject to an initial price distortion as a result of the tax allowances and other benefits available; it may often be necessary to pay a higher price for such property than for property which does not carry similar benefits.

[PETs] [EZPUTs] are established to be held as an investment for a very long period (normally 25 years). Although mechanisms may be available to enable the underlying property to be realised during this period, you may have difficulty in selling your investment before realisation of the underlying property and you should not invest in [a PET] [an EZPUT] if you may need to sell your investment prematurely.

There is no established market in [PETs] [EZPUTs]. You may have difficulty in selling your investment or in obtaining reliable information about its value.

Accordingly **you should carefully consider whether such investments are suitable for you in the light of your personal circumstances and the financial resources available to you.**

I have received the risk warning notice set out above.

....
(Signature of client)

....
(Date)

Disclosure

No additional requirements.

B   Direct Offer Advertisements

Contents

No additional requirements.

Warnings

No additional requirements

Disclosure

No additional requirements.

NOTE 9

OPTIONS, WARRANTS AND MARGINED TRANSACTIONS

A   Specific Investment Advertisements

Contents

No additional requirements

Warnings

(The following warning must be included in any advertisement for these investments. Where the advertisement is issued to a *private client*, the risk warning must be signed by the client and returned to you before you arrange or carry out for him any transaction to which it relates.)

Options, warrants, margined transactions

Introduction

This Warning Notice draws your attention to some of the risks associated with options, warrants and margined transactions.

The risks attaching to instruments and transactions of this kind are usually different from, and can be much greater than, those attached to securities such as shares, loan stock and bonds, such transactions often having the characteristics of speculation as opposed to investment.

Gearing

Warrants and **options** may involve a high degree of 'gearing' or 'leverage'. This means that a small movement in the price of the underlying asset may have a disproportionately dramatic effect on your investment. A relatively small adverse movement in the price of the underlying asset can result in the loss of the whole of your original investment. Moreover, because of the limited life of warrants and options, they may expire worthless.

Warrants

A warrant is a right to subscribe for shares, debentures, loan stock or government securities, usually exercisable against the original issuer of the securities. Because of the high degree of gearing which they may involve, the prices of warrants can be volatile. Accordingly, **you should not buy warrants with money you cannot afford to lose**.

Options

There are many different types of option with different characteristics and subject to different conditions.

Index options are investments in which the profit or loss is defined by reference to fluctuations in an index; this includes options on the FT-SE index and the Euro FT-SE index.

You should ensure that you have all the relevant details before committing yourself.

Buying Options — If you buy an option you acquire the right to buy, or sell, the underlying asset at a fixed price at a point in the future.

A 'call option gives the holder the right (but not the obligation) to **buy** the underlying asset at a specified price on or before a specified date.

A 'put' option gives the right (but not the obligation) to **sell** the underlying asset at a specified price on or before a specified date.

Buying options normally involves a limited risk because, if the price of the underlying asset moves against you, you can simply allow the option to lapse, but **you should not buy an option unless you are prepared to sustain a total loss of the premium** plus any commission or other transaction charges.

Selling Options (sometimes called '**writing**' or '**granting**' options) — is much more risky than buying options. If you sell (or 'write') an option, you accept a legal obligation to buy, or sell, the underlying asset if the option is exercised against you, however far the market price has moved away from the exercise price.

If you are selling 'covered call options' (ie if you already own the underlying asset which you have contracted to sell) the risk is less — only that of losing the opportunity to enjoy a greater profit from the underlying asset if the option is exercised against you and the price then rises above the exercise price; but if you are selling 'uncovered' or 'naked' options (ie if you do not already own the underlying asset), the risk is very great. If you have granted an option that may require you to sell an asset you do not own, and that option is exercised, you will have to go to the market place to buy the asset at the prevailing price in order to fulfil your contract. The risk is therefore potentially unlimited.

Only experienced persons should contemplate selling uncovered options, and then only after securing full details of the applicable conditions and potential risk exposure.

Margin

Options may be traded on **margin**. Instead of paying the whole purchase price immediately, you may be asked to make a payment against the purchase price.

The writer of an option is required to pay margin as security for the performance of his obligations.

The way in which margin will be treated will vary widely according to the type of instrument and where it is traded.

Different markets calculate the amounts of margin to be paid on different bases, and may require margin to be paid in particular forms. Before entering into a transaction you should check how your collateral will be dealt with, whether it will retain its identity as your property, and under what circumstances you may be called upon for additional collateral or other payments. Even if your dealings should ultimately prove profitable, you may have to accept payment in cash and not get back the actual assets which you lodged.

When you trade on margin you can be required at short notice to pay additional margin to maintain your position. If you fail to do so your position may be closed out and you will be liable for any resulting loss.

Margined transactions are not suitable for many members of the public and you should think carefully about them before you commit funds to them. It is essential that you fully understand the nature of the instrument and the transaction you are entering into, and the true extent of your exposure to risk.

As with other investments they may also have tax consequences and on this you should consult your tax adviser.

I have received the risk warning notice set out above.

....
(Signature of client)

....
(Date)

Disclosure

No additional requirements.

B   Direct Offer Advertisements

Contents

No additional requirements.

Warnings

No additional requirements.

Disclosure

No additional requirements.

NOTE 10

PENNY SHARES

A Specific Investment Advertisements

Contents

In addition to the requirements for advertising such *investments* in Part 18, if you include an indication of the price of a particular *penny share* in the *investment advertisement*, you must also include the *bid-offer spread*, which, for this purpose only, must be based on the best price available in the relevant market at the time for transactions of the largest quoted size for that share.

Warnings

(The following warning must be included in any advertisement for these investments. Where the advertisements is issued to a *private client*, the risk warning must be signed by the client and returned to you before you arrange or carry out for him any transaction to which it relates.)

RISK WARNING

You run an extra risk of losing money when you buy shares in certain smaller companies including 'penny shares'.

There is a big difference between the buying price and the selling price of these shares. If you have to sell them immediately, you may get back much less than you paid for them.

The price may change quickly and it may go down as well as up.

Disclosure

If you are a Category 1 Member, you must not deal as *principal* with a private client in penny shares or procure an *associate* to do so unless you have disclosed to the client

(a) if practicable, your or your associate's *mark-up* or *mark-down*, or,

(b) if not, the basis of calculation of the price,

in time for the client to reach an informed decision whether to deal with you.

B Direct Offer Advertisements

Contents

No additional requirements.

Warnings

No additional requirements.

Disclosure

No additional requirements.

These rules were reproduced with permission from the Personal Investment Authority (PIA).

Appendix 3

The Advertising Standards Authority: Selected Rulings from ASA Monthly Reports

(relating to the period December 1996 to June 1997)

THE ROYAL BANK OF SCOTLAND PLC,

31 St Andrew's Square, Edinburgh EH2 2YG

National press

Industry complaint from: *London*

Complaint: National Westminster Bank plc objected to a national press advertisement for The Royal Bank of Scotland Gold Visa that was headlined '24 CARAT Gold . . . ONLY 14.5 per cent APR' and claimed 'If you're making do with a standard credit card why not move up to a Royal Bank of Scotland Gold Card? For a start it could save you money. Just look at the table opposite . . .' The advertisement showed a table that compared the advertisers' interest rate with those for other credit cards with higher rates, including that of the complainants' standard credit card. The complainants believed the advertisement misled by comparing the advertisers' interest rate selectively.

Adjudication: Complaint not upheld.
The advertisers said the advertisement was intended to encourage readers to trade up from their standard credit card. They pointed out that the standard credit cards named in the comparison were labelled as 'standard'. The Authority considered the advertisers were entitled to show how their Gold Card's interest rate compared with those of other types of card. It considered readers would not assume that the table was a comprehensive list of cards that might have lower interest rates. The Authority concluded that the comparisons were clear and fair.

PRIVATE PATIENTS PLAN LTD T/A PPP,

PPP House, Vale Road, Tunbridge Wells, Kent TN1 1BJ

Direct mail

Industry complaint from: *Somerset*

Complaint: Western Provident Association Ltd objected to a direct mailing for corporate health insurance that claimed: 'The best customer care service levels in the business'. The complainants challenged the claim.

Adjudication: Complaint upheld.
The advertisers believed they were the only UK healthcare organisation to offer every customer a dedicated Personal Advisory team who could be contacted even outside office hours on a freephone number. They said they offered a unique, 24 hour Health Information Line and had won the Teleperformance Customer Care award four years in a row. The Authority considered the claim would be seen to mean that the advertisers had undertaken comparative customer care research that showed they offered a service that was better than that of any of their competitors. Because the advertisers did not hold evidence about their competitors' standard of service, the Authority concluded that they had not substantiated the claim. It therefore asked the advertisers not to repeat the claim.

BANK OF IRELAND HOME MORTGAGES LTD,

Plaza West, Bridge Street, Reading RG1 2LZ

National press

Complaints from: *London & Middlesex*

Complaint: Objections to a national press advertisement, for mortgages, that claimed 'all we ask is that you transfer your household insurance to our competitive terms'. The complainants, who believed there was a cancellation fee if the mortgage was redeemed within five years, objected that the advertisement was misleading because it did not make this clear.

Adjudication: Complaints not upheld.
The advertisers acknowledged that a redemption fee was charged if a customer repaid their mortgage within five years but pointed out that this was made clear in their follow-up leaflet along with the full terms and conditions. The Authority noted that the advertisement invited enquiries and the mortgage was not sold off-the-page. It concluded that reference in the advertisement to the early cancellation fee was not necessary.

SCANLAN INSURANCE SERVICES,

4 Market Court, Bedale, North Yorkshire DL8 1YA

Direct mail

Industry complaint from: *North Yorkshire*

Complaint: Angus Thompson & Co objected to a direct mailing for an insurance intermediary. The complainants challenged the claim '. . . our ability to offer you Independent Insurance advice on any Insurances you may require' because the advertisers were not authorised to give advice on all types of insurance.

Adjudication: Complaint upheld.
The advertisers said the mailing was designed to promote a specific insurance policy. They acknowledged that they were not authorised to give advice on insurance products covered by the Financial Services Act but pointed out that the mailing did not mention these. They said, if a client wanted advice on a regulated product, they introduced him to an Independent Financial Adviser. They believed the wording of the advertisement implied only that they made advice available, not that they always gave it themselves. The Authority considered readers were likely to infer from the mailing that the advertisers were authorised to give advice on all insurance products. Because that was not true, it asked the advertisers to rephrase future advertisements to avoid this impression.

NATIONAL WESTMINSTER BANK PLC T/A NATIONAL WESTMINSTER HOME LOANS LTD,

Level 12, Drapers Garden, 12 Throgmorton Avenue, London EC2N 2DL

Poster

Industry complaints from: *London & Cheshire*

Complaint: Bradford and Bingley Building Society, their agency Leo Burnett and the Cheshire Building Society objected to a poster that was headlined 'Which Building Society was voted Best Overall Lender?' and featured a confused-looking old woman and a young boy giggling behind his hand. The footnote stated 'The "Best Overall Lender" Award was issued by "Your Mortgage" magazine and was judged by an independent panel of 100 mortgage brokers'. The complainants objected that the headline was misleading because the advertisers were a bank and not a building society.

Adjudication: Complaints not upheld.
The advertisers said the advertisement was meant to communicate that it was not a building society that had won the award, as would normally be expected with a 'Lender' award, but NatWest Bank. Their objective was to make people aware that NatWest, despite being a bank, arranged mortgages. The Authority considered that consumers would know that NatWest was a bank, not a building society, and therefore accepted that the advertisement would not mislead.

KURTIS ESTATES & PROPERTY SERVICES,

600 Green Lane, Goodmayes, Ilford, Essex IG3 9SR

Leaflet

Industry complaint from: *Essex*

Complaint: Hambro Countrywide objected on behalf of Abbotts Estate Agents to a canvassing leaflet that:

1   claimed 'we will pay to sell your house' because they believed a fee was payable by vendors and that the scheme involved vendor cashback and was therefore misleading; and

2   showed photographs of properties the complainants believed were not on the market with the advertisers. They objected that the photographs were misleading.

Adjudication: Complaints upheld.

1   The advertisers said the claim 'we will pay to sell your house' referred to their offer to reduce their fee after a pre-arranged period if they were unsuccessful in selling their customers' properties. The Authority considered the claim was misleading and asked the advertisers not to use it in future advertising.

2   The advertisers said the photographs were selected from a range of properties that had either been available with them or that had been available at one time or another. They said they had chosen them to illustrate the areas they covered. The Authority considered the mailing implied that the illustrated properties were currently on the market with the advertisers. Because this was not so, it asked the advertisers not to use them again.

INSURED WINDOW GUARANTEES LTD,

Kirkgate Business Centre, Chantry Bridge, Wakefield, West Yorkshire WF1 5DL

Magazine

Industry complaint from: *London*

Complaint: The Glass and Glazing Federation objected to a specialist magazine avertisement, for an insurance-backed double glazing guarantee, that claimed 'Meets all Department of Trade and Industry requirements YOUR Customer is the Insured'. The follow-up material featured the terms and conditions, which included 'The insured is Insured Window Guarantees Ltd as trustees on behalf of its members' customers'. The complainant objected that:

1   the company acted as trustees for the guarantee scheme on behalf of the companies selling it and customers would not therefore be personally guaranteed as claimed; and

2   the claim to meet Department of Trade and Industry (DTI) requirements was misleading because the insurance was with an off-shore company.

Adjudication:
1   Complaint not upheld.
The advertisers said they acted as trustees so that, if they or a double glazing company that sold the guarantee went out of business, the customer would still be covered. They also said customers would be personally insured although no written contract existed between the insurance company and a double glazing company. The Authority considered the advertisement acceptable in this respect.
2   Complaint upheld
The Advertisers said the insurance was with an off-shore company that offered insurance in the UK. They asserted that the DTI had confirmed that they did not fail to comply with their requirements. The DTI said the Insurance Companies Regulations 1994 required those advertising insurance provided by an off-shore insurer to include in their advertisements a statement drawing attention to the absence of protection under the Policyholders Protection Act 1975 if the insurer should be unable to meet its liabilities. The advertisements in question contained no such statement but only the courts could decide if the company had broken the law. The Authority considered that readers would infer from the advertisement that the scheme had DTI approval and complied with the law. The Authority asked the advertisers to change the claim to avoid giving that impression and to remove references to DTI requirements.

WOOLWICH LIFE,

Regent House, 1–3 Queensway, Redhill, Surrey RH1 1NH

Direct mail

Complaint from: *Shropshire*

Complaint: Objection to a mailing for life assurance. The envelope stated 'Policyholder: Insurance Document Enclosed'. The letter inside claimed 'Dear Policyholder, A short time ago you were provided with documents recommending increased financial protection against accidents. You may recall that this additional protection—available to you and your spouse—is very economical and easy to activate. If you have not returned your AUTHOR-ISATION form, please note that the 15 October 1996 close date is only a matter of days away . . . Since a large number of insureds have already recognised the value of strengthening their existing financial security arrangements with this cover, we are enclosing duplicate documents for your use'. Another document in the mailing claimed 'Woolwich Life recommends that you and your spouse supplement the benefit payable under your life policy in the event of accidental death—by activating the accompanying Policy Document, evidencing £26,479 accidental death protection for each of you. Thus total benefits for accidental death will be the death benefit of your Woolwich Life policy at the time of death plus £26,479 per person'. The complainant objected that the mailing was misleading, because it implied that her existing policy would not provide enough money in the event of her death or that of her husband.

Adjudication: Complaint upheld.
The advertisers argued that they intended the mailing only to offer recipients a chance of increasing their accidental death cover through this Plan and had not meant to imply that their present insurance cover was inadequate. The Authority considered that recipients were likely to infer from the words 'recommendation' and '1996 Cover Review' in the mailing that the advertisers had reviewed their personal circumstances and had concluded that the present cover was inadequate. It asked the advertisers not to use the approach again.

MIDLAND BANK PLC T/A FIRST DIRECT,

Millshaw Park Lane, Leeds LS98 1BX

National press

Complaint from: *Flintshire*

Complaint: Objection to a national press advertisement, for First Direct, that claimed 'By telephone, 24 hours a day. We provide the ultimate in convenience. You can bank with us at any time, 365 days (and nights) of the year, from wherever there's a telephone'. The complainant telephoned after 4pm to transfer money between his accounts. He was told that the money would not be available until the end of business the next day. He considered the claim misleading.

Adjudication: Complaint not upheld.
The advertisers said the claim was meant to highlight that their customers could call at any time to arrange their banking and they did not claim that transactions would be carried out

on the same day. The Authority considered that readers would infer only that they could arrange transactions 24 hours a day and would not expect those transactions necessarily to be processed outside normal working hours. It therefore concluded that the claim was acceptable.

CARRINGTON THE ESTATE AGENT,

138 Shenley Road, Borehamwood, Hertfordshire WD6 1EF

Regional press

Industry complaint from: *Herts*

Complaint: Barry Allsuch & Co objected to two local press property advertisements. The first advertisement claimed 'Since we opened our doors, our business has gone from strength to strength. There's hardly a street, road, walk or path in Borehamwood or Elstree where we haven't sold a property'. The second advertisement claimed '8 sales in one week'. The complainants:

1   Objected that the claims in the first advertisement were misleading because they gave the impression the advertisers were long-established, whereas they believed they had been in business for eight weeks in Borehamwood; and

2   questioned whether the sales claim was true.

Adjudication:
1   Complaint upheld.
The advertisers said the claims referred to the two partners having both worked as estate agents in the Borehamwood area for over five years and argued that the claims sought to emphasise their experience of selling properties in the area. The Authority understood the company had been trading for a few months. It was concerned that, when the advertisement was read as a whole, readers would infer that the claims related to the estate agency, not to the individuals, and that therefore the advertisers were a long-established company. Because that was not true, the Authority asked them to amend the claim and to take copy advice.
2   Complaint not upheld.
The advertisers submitted a copy of their sales ledger, which confirmed that eight sales had been recently agreed in one week. The Authority accepted the claim.

BARCLAYS BANK PLC T/A BARCLAYCARD,

Barclaycard House, Marefair, Northampton, Northamptonshire NN1 1SG

Direct mail & insert

Complaints from: *Gloucestershire, Hampshire (2) & Cornwall*

Complaint: Objections to a booklet, for Barclaycard, that was sent out as part of a direct mailing and another one that was inserted loose in the national press, that claimed on the front 'give you up to £150' and, inside, 'Switch to a Barclaycard and we'll give you up to £150'. The complainants objected that the claims were misleading, because the condition 'we reserve the right to require repayment of the refund in full if in the next 12 months the sum of the annual account fee plus the interest charges paid on your account are less than the amount of the refund' was stated only in very small print inside the booklet.

Adjudication: Complaints upheld.
The advertisers argued that the claims were accurate and were not misleading because they had stated the condition prominently enough in the booklet to draw it to readers' attention and had asked recipients in a letter in the mailing, to read the booklet carefully. The Authority concluded that the condition made the offer so much less attractive than it first seemed that it should be stated no later than the inside front-cover of the booklet and in easily legible print.

ABBEY NATIONAL PLC,

Abbey House, 201 Grafton Gate East, Milton Keynes, Buckinghamshire MK9 1AN

National press

Complaints from: *Lancashire, West Yorkshire & Kent*

Complaint: Objections to a national press advertisement headed 'UP TO 140% GUAR-ANTEED PLUS, FOR EARLY INVESTORS, A PREMIUM RATE OF 8% GROSS P.A. UNTIL 1.2.97'. Customers were asked to invest £10,000 over a three or five year period. The complainants challenged the claims because they understood that the rate included the original investment: £14,000 was the return after five years, not £24,000 as implied.

Adjudication: Complaints upheld.
The advertisers said they did not believe the advertisement was misleading and the full terms of the offer were stated in a legally required footnote. The Authority considered that the advertisement was misleading because the headline claim could be interpreted as the rate of gross interest and it was concerned that the nature of the offer was not immediately apparent to readers. The advertisers were asked to ensure that future advertisements explained in the body copy instead of a footnote, that the 140 per cent was the total return, including the original investment.

ABBEY NATIONAL PLC,

Abbey House, Baker Street, London NW1 6XL

National press

Public & industry complaints from: *Oxfordshire & Norfolk*

Complaint: Objections to a national press advertisement that was headlined 'TESSA WORKS HARDER AT THE STOCKMARKET. POTENTIALLY 198% RETURN' and claimed 'Imagine it, the tax free benefits of a TESSA, the guaranteed return of your capital, plus the potential of stockmarket-linked high returns—that's the beauty of Abbey National's new stockmarket TESSA' and 'returns are linked to the performance of the UK and US stockmarkets—for every month in which both indices rise, no matter by how little, interest is added to your account at a rate of 1.15% gross. Should this happen every month over the 5 year period this would equate to a return, over and above your original capital investment of 98%—tax free'. The complainant objected that the advertisement gave a misleading impression of the probability of getting the maximum return.

Adjudication: Complaints upheld.
The advertisers believed the maximum return was possible but admitted it was unlikely and

had not occurred since 1984, when both indices were first calculated. They argued that the advertisement made this clear and pointed out that no one could invest in the TESSA without getting more information. The Authority considered that the advertisement was misleading because it implied that the maximum return, or close to it, was likely to be achieved. Because the advertisers had not substantiated this, the Authority asked the advertisers to reword the advertisement after getting copy advice.
Previous complaints upheld in the last 12 reports: 1

BIRMINGHAM MIDSHIRES BUILDING SOCIETY,

Pendeford Business Park, Wobaston Road, Pendeford, Wolverhampton, West Midlands WV9 5HZ

Leaflet

Complaint from: *Hertfordshire*

Complaint: Objection to a leaflet, available in Birmingham Midshires Building Society branches, for the Quantum Instant Access Account, that claimed 'A better rate of interest and instant access'. The complainant challenged the claim because he found he could obtain a better interest rate on comparable accounts from other companies.

Adjudication: Complaint upheld.
The advertisers submitted a list of interest rate figures for other instant access accounts; it showed that some of the accounts were not directly comparable and, of those that were, most offered a higher interest rate than the Quantum Account. The Authority considered that readers would infer that the advertisers offered a higher interest rate than all their competitors. Because the advertisers could not support this, the Authority asked them to delete the claim from their advertising.

Index